The Urbana Free Library

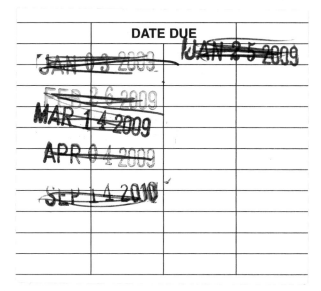

12-08Amazon 11-

CLOCKWORK PHOENIX
Tales of Beauty and Strangeness

Edited by Mike Allen

All Rights Reserved.

Cover Painting:
"Head of a Tudor Girl" by Eleanor Fortescue-Brickdale (1871-1945)

Cover Design Copyright © 2008 by Vera Nazarian
(with Bob Snare and Mike Allen)

ISBN-13: 978-1-934169-98-8
ISBN-10: 1-934169-98-6

FIRST EDITION
Trade Paperback Edition

July 1, 2008

A Publication of
Norilana Books
P. O. Box 2188
Winnetka, CA 91396
www.norilana.com

Printed in the United States of America

CREDITS

Also by Mike Allen

Poetry
Defacing the Moon
Petting the Time Shark
Disturbing Muses
Strange Wisdoms of the Dead
The Journey to Kailash

Fiction
Follow the Wounded One

As editor:

New Dominions:
Fantasy Stories by Virginia Writers

The Alchemy of Stars:
Rhysling Award Winners Showcase
(with Roger Dutcher)

Mythic

Mythic 2

Clockwork Phoenix
tales of beauty and strangeness

Norilana Books
Fantasy

www.norilana.com

CLOCKWORK
PHOENIX

tales of beauty and strangeness

Edited by

Mike Allen

ACKNOWLEDGMENTS

This volume could never have risen from the ashes of concept and dream without the labor and support of many others besides myself. My wife Anita, who helped me choose the sequence of links in this surreal chain; Catherine Reniere, my assistant editor, who vigorously tackled the daunting task of sorting submissions; Vera Nazarian, without whom, let's face it, there would be no book. Wise advice and heartfelt encouragement from the likes of Kathy Sedia, Sonya Taaffe, Jessica Wick, Amal El-Mohtar, Charlie Saplak and Mike Jones proved invaluable during the long march to publication. Thanks to all, and to any deserving individual whose name has slipped through my porous memory.

CONTENTS

12 CONTENTS

INTRODUCTION

by Mike Allen

We begin with fire.
        A furnace that burns so hot it seems not even time could survive its temperatures, but yet inside this crucible something is wrestling time backward, condensing matter into a molten pool still too bright to look at as it gathers itself up and white hot parts within start to move.

Ticks and clicks. Springs and gears. Sprockets and chains. Wheels and crowns. Pinions are the small gears in a drive train. Pinions are the outermost feathers on a bird's great wing. A rack and pinion convert circular motion to linear motion, like a wheel squealing on a train track.

The raptor stretches its wings until the razor sharp edges of its pinions score and scar the furnace walls. The curved knife of its beak flashes as it tilts its head, as it returns our gaze; hour and minute hands move within its iron-black eyes.

It draws up the needles of its talons and rises from the burnings coals, floats for a moment in the fire. Then it throws itself against the firebox hatch, once, twice, thrice, with thunderous force. A fourth time, and the hatch flies off, and the great bird is birthed from the furnace—

Into the cabin of a roaring locomotive. Where is it bound, and where is its Engineer? The cabin is empty, and outside the windows shadows flicker in a greater darkness. The door to the next car is open, and through it a watery trickle of voices underscores the boiler's screams. The phoenix clacks its wings once and glides across the gap.

Borne on its wings, we see what it sees as it soars through the oddly long chamber, a space opulent despite the way it narrows, like the inside of an elegant throat.

The car is paneled in ivory and white marble, every squared frame carved with pale faces, some sleeping, some blind; some appear to roll their gilded eyes to follow our flight. Window slats stabbed into the walls reveal more darkness outside, but openings that iris in the ceiling breathe in merciless light, drawn in from some unseen source or unreal place.

Three pillars at the car's far end reveal themselves as we approach to be three identical men, each wearing three-piece suits tailored in midnight black, each with the same shirts pleated harsh white, the same blood red bow ties clasped with a grinning death's head, their bearded faces sculpted into circus masks. The only differences between these pundits are their words.

One says: Form need not be the end. Function need not be the end. Take my breath away both with the tale and how it's told. The beautiful must slave for a purpose. The purpose must serve to feed the beautiful.

One says: To admit boundaries is to admit defeat. To admit boundaries is to admit defeat. To admit boundaries is to admit defeat. To admit boundaries is to admit defeat.

One says: The law is mad. The law is madness, but madness is not the predicate of law. There is no madness in absence of the law. Before its opposition to the law became flesh, madness could never be conceived.

The raptor's gaze reads noon. *Let us not suffer these fools to live.*

Wings stretched to full length fan feathers sharp as razor blades. Their blood is ink, this long shaft of carved white a blank page.

When the pundits have succumbed, the phoenix shakes its wetted feathers and plummets on, through the next car, and the next, and the next. They are all linked, but not in a row; some cars connect through hoops of time; some nestle beside each other, sharing membranes of possibility; some are intertwined like clusters of hearts filled by the same arteries; some are stitched together like quilts, or grafts.

And what of the chambers we rush past within this train's strange body, our wings beating against the air in hopes we won't be ash before the end? What marvels do we see as we leap from gear to spinning gear, hustling daredevil to the precarious edge just for the views? Shadows growing across wallpaper ripples as other forms rustle within the walls; upholstery grown in future times, where arms stretch from the floor and lifeblood warms the ceiling; a train at least as mad as the bird that bears us.

To say nothing of its freight; or its passengers; or its stowaways; or the crazed hobos beneath that ride the rails.

THE CITY OF BLIND DELIGHT

by Catherynne M. Valente

There is a train which passes through every possible city. It folds the world like an accordioned map, and speeds through the folds like a long white cry, piercing black dots and capital-stars and vast blue bays. Its tracks bind the firmament like bones: wet, humming iron with wriggling runnels of quicksilver slowly replacing the old ash wood planks, and the occasional golden bar to mark a historic intersection, so long past the plaque has weathered to blank. These tracks bear up under the hurtling train, the locomotive serpent circumnavigating the globe like a beloved egg. Though they would not admit it and indeed hardly remember at all, New York and Paris and Tokyo, London and Mombasa and Buenos Aires, Los Angeles and Seattle and Christchurch and Beijing: nothing more than intricate, over-swarmed stations on the Line, festooned and decorated beyond all recognition.

Of necessity, this train passes through the City of Blind Delight, which lies somewhat to the rear of Ulan Bator, and also somewhat diagonally from Greenland, beneath a thin veneer of Iowa City, lying below it as a the bone of a ring-finger may lie beneath both flesh and glove, unseen, gnarled and jointed ivory hidden by mute skin, dumb leather. The Line is its sole access point. Yet in Chicago, a woman in black glasses stands with a bag full of celery and lemons and ice in her arms. She watches trains silver past while the cream and gold of Union Station arches behind her and does not know if this one, or this, or even that ghostly express gasping by is a car of the Line, does not know which, if any of these graffiti-barnacled leviathans would take her to a station carved from baobab-roots and papaya rinds, or one of mirrors angled to make the habitual strain of passengers to glimpse the incoming rattlers impossible, so that the train appears with its headlight blazing as if out of thin air, or to Blind Delight itself, where the station arches and vestibules are formed by acrobatic dancers, their bodies locked together with laced fingers and toes, stretching in shifts over the glistening track, their faces impassive as angels. It is almost painful to imagine, how close she has come how many times to catching the right one, but each day she misses it without realizing that she has missed anything at all, and the dancers of Blind Station writhe without her.

She will miss it today, too. But he will catch it. He will even brush her elbow as he passes her, hurrying through doors which open and shut like arms, and it is not impossible that he will remember the astringent smell of cold lemons long afterward. She has no reason to follow him—this train has the wrong letter on its side, and he is running too fast even to look at the letter, so certain is he that he is late. But she longs to, anyway, for no reason at all. She watches the tails of his blue coat slip past the inexorable doors.

The car this man, whose name is Gris, enters is empty even at five o'clock. An advertisement looms near the city map, a blank and empty image of skin spreading across the entire frame, seen at terrible closeness, pores and hair and lines beaming bright. It is brown, healthy. There is no text, and he cannot think what it is meant to sell: lotion? Soap? Perfume? He extends a hand to touch the paper, and it recoils, shudders. The hairs bristle translucent; goosebumps prickle. Gris blinks and sits down abruptly, folding his hands tightly around his briefcase. The train rocks slowly from side to side.

He does not worry about a ticket-taker: you use your ticket to enter the station these days, not the train. Once within the dark, warm station, which is not unlike a cathedral, all trains are open to the postulant. He is a postulant, though he does not think in those terms. He once took an art history course in college—there was a girl, of course, he had wanted to impress, with a red braid and an obscure love of Crivelli. The professor had put up a slide of Raphael's self-portrait, and he remembers his shock on seeing that face, with the projector-light shining through it, that face which had seemed to him disturbingly blank, vapid, even idiotic. He is like me, Gris had thought, that is my face. Not the man who was a painter, but the man who was affectless, a fool, the man who was thinner than the professor's rough mechanical light. I am like that, he thought then, he thinks now. Blank and empty, like a child, like skin.

He falls asleep and does not hear the station call. But the Line is patient. The doors wait, open into the dark, a soft, sucking wind blowing out of the tunnels and across the platform. The Line has determined the trajectory of its passenger. He stirs when the skin-advertisement shivers above him, and bleary-limbed, steps off of the silver car, into the station-shadows.

The sun filters in a pink wash through the lattice of bodies. Gris thinks of Crivelli's angels, how sharp and dour they were on the walls of the girl with the red braid's bedroom. These people are like that, the top-most ones staring down at him, their hair making strangely-colored banners, fluttering with the train-generated winds. He is grateful the floor is plain tile, that he does not have to walk on stomachs and thigh-bones. He gapes—

do not all tourists gape? He gapes and his chin tilts up to the banners of hair, ignoring the rush of those for whom the human ceiling is no more unusual than one of glass and iron. They swarm around him; he does not notice.

Across the gleaming floor, a calf clicks its hooves. Gris shifts his gaze numbly, the smell of the calf beguiling—for it is roasted, brown and glistening, its ears basted in brown sugar, its skin crisp and hot. There is a long knife in its side, and with clear, imploring eyes, the calf looks up at him, turning its pierced flank invitingly. It swishes its broiled tail. A girl runs up in a blue smock, knocking Gris's briefcase down, and pulls the knife out, cutting a pink slice of veal and chewing it noisily. She thrusts the blade back in towards the calf's rump, a tidy child. He feels his mouth dry, and though he has found his way to the City of Blind Delight in place of the woman with the black glasses and the lemons, he is lost as she would not have been.

Near the apex of the ceiling, a woman with long red hair like sheeting hensblood and black eyes detaches herself from the throng, smoothly replaced by a young man with hardly any hair at all on his legs. She climbs down the wall as nimble as a spider dropping thread, and in no time at all slaps her bare heels on the clean floor, retrieving a green dress and golden belt from a darkened booth and covering her skin, chilled from the heights. Barefoot, she strides towards the conspicuous tourist as the calf wanders off, holding her hand out in a nearly normal gesture of the world to which Gris is accustomed. This woman is called Otthild, and she was born here, in Blind Station. Her mother was a ticket-taker, a token-changer. She kept her hair bobbed and curled like a silent movie gamine, her uniform crisp and red, even when it was stretched by her belly and the buttons uttered brassy cries of protest. When the time came, she shrugged off her blazer and trousers, hung her hat on a silver peg, and climbed up the wall of limbs, helped along by a crooked knee here and an elbow there, until she reached a rafter of long, thick torsos clasped together leg by arm, and on this she lay, and gave birth to her child in mid-air, a daughter caught by the banisters and neatly deposited at the gleaming turnstile by an obliging windowsill with a yellow beard. Otthild was thus the darling of the Station. She had never taken the Line out of the City of Blind Delight, nor desired to.

There are many words for what Otthild does. They have little meaning in the City, but she collects them like seashells from the tourists. Of all, she prefers *fallen woman*, since this describes her birth perfectly. Most of her customers are tourists—she prefers them to locals, and the pay is better. She shakes the stranger's hand, and he is absurdly grateful. She guides him to the door of the station, a gorgeously executed arch of four women, standing on each other's red shoulders—the topmost pair held their children outstretched, and the youths clasped hands in a graceful peak. She instructs her bewildered charge to purchase a return ticket from the coiffed man in a glass booth before they leave, and again he is grateful for her. The arch winks as Otthild passes beneath them, her polished hair shining against her dress.

Outside the Station, the City of Blind Delight opens up in a long valley. No road in its heart connects to any road which might lead into a long avenue or highway by which, traveling quickly, a man might reach the smallest town on any map he knows. The Line is entrance and exit, mother and father. There are lights down there, in the vale, as there are lights in any city. But here the light comes from strange lamp-posts, faceted diamonds, each face as large as a hand, and more like bowls than lamps, full of clearest water. Within, black fish circle, their luminous lures dangling green and glowing from thin whisker-stalks. Otthild ticks the glass of one near her with her fingernails, and the light swells up, washing her cheeks.

"Come down," she says, "come into the city, down to the river."

Gris goes. He does not know why, though he suspects it has something to do with her hair, and his blankness. She leads and he follows and he wants to be surprised that he is not hanging his clothes up in a half-empty closet and drinking scotch until he falls asleep in his computer chair, but she is walking before him down a long road to a long river, and the late sun is on her scalp like Crivelli's annunciation.

The river that flows through the City of Blind Delight is filled with a rich brandy, and all folk take their sustenance there. It has no name, it is simply "the river." Other cities have a need for names. It floods its banks regularly—there is a festival, but then, there are festivals for everything here. The river inundates its shores and fields of grapevines sprout in the swampy mud without the need of vintners to tend them. In the fall, the purple fruit drops off and rolls back into the water, and the current is so sweet on that day. But now it is summer, and the vines loop and whorl, and some few lime trees bend over the water, their branches heavy with green tarts.

There are women by the river when Gris and Otthild arrive, knee-deep, but they are not washer-women—the profession is unheard of here. They splash playfully in the red-gold surf with long ladles the size of croquet mallets, scooping up the redolent water and serving it to each other. Otthild takes a ladle from the grassy park which leads into the current, one with a red and gold flecked handle, and dips it deep, offering it to him.

"My name is Gris," he says. She tilts her head.

"Grey? How odd. I found a man in the station once called Vermillion. He was shaking and hiding his eyes in the vestibule—he wouldn't even come out of the train. He looked up at me from the steel floor like a calf, imploring, uncomprehending. He said he came from the north, from the City of Quaint Despairing, and he could not bear to look outside the doors of the carriage. His mother had been an agoraphobe in pearl earrings, his father a claustrophobe in iron cufflinks, and between them he could hardly move for terror. His brothers had dragged him to the train, but he could do no more than huddle and quiver and hide from the light. I kissed him so many times! I let my hair fall over him, so that he was neither exposed nor shut away, and against the rocking walls of that little vestibule I wrapped my legs around his waist. He paid me in his mother's earrings."

Gris starts. "Are you a whore, then?"

She smiles. "What profession could remain in a city where the river makes one drunk and the trees bear cream and crust? Even still, I am not anyone's for the taking, I am not a calf. I am not a lime or a grape. But here we are impatient with all that is not readily available, and so in the province of ease, all things are simplified. There are two occupations in the City of Blind Delight—the Station dancers and the prostitutes. I am both."

Gris rubs his forehead and drinks from the proffered ladle. It tastes harsh and he coughs a cough of burnt grapes. "Why am I here?" His voice is so small. He cannot even now remember what sort of scotch he has at home, or how far it is from Union Station to his apartment.

"The Line must have wanted you. It has its own reasons. Like anything that lives in the earth it dreams and becomes restless, curious, even morbidly so. What would happen if this substance were added to that one, even though it says expressly not to on the label? There is a Conductor, I have heard that. Perhaps she has brass buttons on her uniform like my mother. Perhaps she has circuits on her eyelids. Perhaps she saw your blue coat and your briefcase and thought: 'Otthild is lonely.' Perhaps she was hungry for lime tarts and you stumbled onto her train because you could not be bothered to check the track number. You can go and wait for the evening train if you like. It makes no difference to me."

He looks at her, and it is a look she knows. No one is hungry in the City of Blind Delight, except those who look at Otthild that way.

"I used to know a girl who looked like you." He mumbles, looks at the girls splashing each other in the murky river. "She had your hair. She loved this old painter that no one has ever heard of, a painter obsessed with perspective who could never get it quite right, but he painted these cities, these cities like cut jewels, terrible and crisp and clear, with a woman in the corner, sometimes, full of the light of God like an afterthought."

"Most men knew a woman who looked like me." Otthild laughs.

"What would I have to pay, in a city without want?"

She frowns, looks at him seriously, her dark eyes fixing him to the riverbed. She opens the top three buttons of her emerald dress and takes his hand, gently, guiding it to her breast. She feels like the advertisement. "We are not without want." She whispers. "No one is without want."

Her house is made of brown cakes. It reminds him of the house in the fairy tale, but there are no red candies glinting in its cornices. Bricks of solid cake and barley sugar mortared in cream-icing the color of an old woman's hair stack sedately into a small cottage, at the end of a prosperous street—but all streets are prosperous here. Her street is paved in bread. There are no doors or locks. Fat citizens lie about in the road, telling jokes about the size of their bellies. She leads him to a bed which is mercifully of the linen-and-wood variety, and lies down on her back, toes pointed downward. All around the bed are intricate boxes of gold and silver and ivory—he does not ask. She indicates the buttons on her dress, black jet with tiny engravings of peasants carrying water, and wood, and tilling fields decorating each one. Gris undoes each one carefully—her dress is a simple thing, with buttons from collar to hem. Beneath it she is as naked as the ceiling of the Station, and he thinks of the annunciation, the slender golden light penetrating the grey belly of Mary. But she is not grey, he thinks, he is, he is grey and blank, he is the Raphael of idiot features. The Line was not looking for him, how could it look for him? Perhaps it wanted the woman with the black glasses, and he only slipped by because she was burdened with her fruit and her ice.

He leans in to kiss her, but Otthild stops him, and indicates her sternum. He sees there as he had not seen before, when she was a rafter swaying high above his head, four knobs of bone. She smiles encouragingly, and he slips each one loose like buttons. Her skin opens, soft as cloth, and her bones, and her lungs, peeling back like gift-box tissue. Beneath all this is her heart, and it is golden, gleaming, bright at the bottom of her body. A good part of her blood is gold, too, flowing out from the metallic ventricles. She is terrible, and crisp, and clear, a Jacobean diagram of womanhood, her heart burning, burning, burning golden as God. Gris begins to weep, and his tears splash on its hard, glittering surface.

"I told you," she chuckles. She does not move to fasten her chest. "There was a man a long time ago, when the City was new, and the Line had only just come through—the tracks just unfurled here, like a wet fern, and where there are tracks there eventually is a city. The edges of the railroad curl out into the valley, and drag up a town from the earth, whatever town the Conductor dreams of that day, whatever city the tracks long to see. And so there is a river of brandy, and the lime-tart trees, and roads of bread. The Line brought folk, and they stayed. There was a man with a hand of gold, being the son of a jeweler and having lost the flesh one in a factory which pounded out ice by the thousand cube load. When he left the Station and saw the river winding thick along the vale, and the roads with their brown crust, he wept, for nothing here freezes, and resolving never to leave pounded his hand into a railroad tie to honor the Line. Now the train comes to rest precisely on the golden tie, and that man, long dead, holds the City to the Line.

"My mother grew up working in the Station beside her mother and her grandmother, and she saw the tie glitter at the bottom of the tracks every day. She thought it the most beautiful of all the things in the City of Blind Delight, chiefly because it was so often hidden, down in the dark of the tunnel. She thought often of the ice-pounder whose fingers lay thus across the track, and came to love this thing in her mind which was less than a memory, and more than a dream. One night, after the train had sped down the tunnel, she crept across the platform and scrambled down to the gleaming tie. She lay down upon it, and felt it warm against her cheek. She wept for the dead man, and for a thing called ice which she had never seen. When I was born, she said I was so heavy, because of the gold, because of my father, and she polished my heart every night for me before bed."

Otthild touches Gris's face, his smooth, blank cheeks. "You see? We are not without want. But we are peculiar and refined in our ways of wanting, since vulgar food necessity is satisfied."

Gris cannot bear to look at her heart with its slow, clanking beating. He closes up her chest with shaking hands and sits on the edge of her bed.

"Would it help," Otthild says, "if I had a knife in my side?"

She draws his face down to hers, and he feels the hard bone buttons beneath him. He looks at her red hair coiled on the pillow as he presses into her, and thinks of the girl with the braid whom he had only loved once, who had, afterwards, stared at her stucco ceiling and told him that Crivelli sometimes used chalk rendered in glue made from rabbit-fat to make the tears of his Pieta. It dried hard and clear, so that if you could touch one of his paintings, you would feel the tears falling beneath your hands, falling like tiny stones of grief, like little buttons of bone.

It is properly always dark after sex. Gris wants to feel guilty, but he feels nothing. After all, a businessman and a prostitute are as near a thing to an archetype as he can think of these days. *A salaryman and whore walk into a bar—stop me if you've heard this one.* He stops. He looks over his naked shoulder at her, at her four small buttons. Her hair falls over one heavy breast. She pulls a strip of drywall-pastry and chews it thoughtfully.

"What can I pay you?" he sighs. "What do you want?"

She rolls onto her stomach and smiles softly, her lips without paint, pink and thin. "Most of us in the City are collectors," she says. "Some are monomaniacal, like my mother. But when the sun is always warm and your house is made of food, desire curls in on itself and finds other objects. I know a woman by the butter-pits who collects calf's tails. She has a whole coat of them. I collect tickets."

Gris's mouth opens slightly. He pulls his creased return ticket out of his discarded coat's pocket.

"But if I give it to you, I can get another, for the morning train, can't I?"

Otthild shrugs. "You buy a ticket to enter the station these days, not the train. But the glass booth is well within the arch. Maybe they would sell you a new one. Maybe they would let you inside. Maybe not. We are often perverse. Maybe the Station is full of Midwesterners trying to buy a ticket home with everything they own, even flesh, even bone. Perhaps that long-dead man did not lose his hand in an ice factory, but to buy a ticket here, or a ticket back. All of that is your business, curious histories, and I do not collect those."

She kneels beside the bed and clicks open the jeweled boxes, one by one. Gold, silver, ivory. Opal, onyx, lacquer.

Inside them all are countless tickets, old and new, with magnetic strips, without. Some have the City of Blind Delight as a destination, others are simpler: New York to St John's, Odessa to Moscow, Edinburgh to Glasgow. But there are carefully inked and stamped tickets from the City of Envious Virgins to the City Without Roses, from the City of Variable Skylines to the City of Mendicant Crows. There is one, almost dust, from Venice to the City of False Perspective. She opens a box for him, of polished steel, tableware melted into a cubical shape.

Gris reaches out and strokes her sternum, his eyes sliding closed. He feels her fastened chest, the buttons like hardened tears. He lets his ticket fall into the box. Shadows drift over the neat printing: *The City of Blind Delight to Chicago, Midnight Express.*

There is a train which passes through every possible city. It folds the world like an accordioned map, and speeds through the folds like a long white cry. Of necessity, this train passes through Chicago, the City of Winds, a city which was once a lake-bed, and even now, if you were to dig far enough beneath the railroad tracks, you would find the thin, translucent skeletons of monstrous fish with fins like scythes.

A woman in black glasses stands with a bag full of strawberries and wheat-flour and frozen trout in her arms. She watches trains silver past while the cream and gold of Union Station arches behind her, as she has done every day since she moved here from California. A long, pale car screeches into the platform before her; she does not look at the track number, or the arcane code of the letters blazing on the side. With only a small hesitation, as she shifts the weight of her groceries from one hip to another, she steps through the doors that open and close like arms. Light shines through the glass ceiling and illuminates the spot where she stood just a moment before, like an afterthought.

OLD FOSS IS THE NAME OF HIS CAT

by David Sandner

He has many friends, laymen and clerical;
Old Foss is the name of his cat;
His body is perfectly spherical,
He weareth a runcible hat.

"How Pleasant to Know Mr. Lear" —Edward Lear

Old Foss watched the Old Man out barefoot in his nightshirt ranting in the rain; at least the rain had chased away the boys throwing mud and rocks. The Old Man had black stains along his back and a welt on his forehead, not that he noticed. But as night pushed over the town, growing from shadows leaning along the ramshackle red tile roofs, darkness spreading like ink across a tabletop, Old Foss knew there were worse things than rain or boys with rocks. Soon, the Jumblies would rise from the water's edge to bring the Old Man to sea in a sieve. And anyone who goes to sea in a sieve, of course, never returns. They sink and they drown.

The rain wept against the glass as Old Foss watched

impassively behind the window. The Old Man ran back and forth across the cobbled street, his long white nightshirt soaked and clinging to his ungainly frame, his paunched belly and skinny pale legs. His long bedraggled beard leaked, sloughing off water when he shook his head and bellowed: "Where is my Jumbly Girl?" The Old Man knocked on every door he came to, but no one answered for they knew the old Englishman too well.

At first, when the fugues came on, the locals had only shaken their heads at him, then argued with him in broken English or too fluent Italian, especially when the rain came up fast. They pushed him towards the villa he and Old Foss rented; but when the confusion came upon him he would only look at them uncomprehendingly, or look at their doors long after they had shut them with the oddest expression of thwarted desire, then he would wander away again and knock on another wrong door. For no one could see the Jumblies but him and Old Foss. None could know of his time with his Jumbly Girl but Old Foss and himself. Old Foss and he is how it should be for the Jumbly girl would bring him only death for all her promises. Why couldn't he see that, Old Foss thought crossly, twitching his tail, and was it really so much as all that to love a Jumbly Girl?

The sun reflected blindingly on the sand and burst across the blue water in shimmers and rolling spots of light, like crystal broken on tile, like sparks shooting and spinning into the air from a roaring fire, like nothing the Old Man could capture on his canvas.

"It's like nothing, Old Foss, why can't the poets ever say that? It's like nothing we can see or say, like something more than we can know, like less than I can rhyme and more than I can show."

The Old Man dabbed at the canvas anyway with his paintbrushes, trying to somehow put a glimmer of white behind, between, before smears of blue. He swayed his pear-shaped body, shoved into a too-tight brown suit, frayed white cuffs showing at the wrists, coat open to display a mismatched plaid vest missing every other button; he moved from side to side considering the canvas from different angles, cocking his head with deliberation. How to capture the certain slant of light, the moment out of joint, when time pulsed below the threshold of meaning before it can be said? He took the painting off its easel, still rickety in the soft sand, and flung it end over end into the sea.

"Old Foss, what shall we do instead? What is it this moment deserves?"

Old Foss, striped orange and black, fat and with a wide full tail, lay on a red-checked picnic blanket in a way no human would ever know—stretched out backwards almost in upon himself again, only his tail's end moving when a wind ruffled his fur, only his ears listening; he hadn't moved for an hour. It was what Old Foss considered giving the moment its due already. When Old Foss opened his eyes suddenly it was not to answer the Old Man, but to look out to sea after the canvas. He made one mew.

"What's that?" The Old Man turned to look, and his rotund body seemed to deflate and go limp, his mouth slack, opening in a kind of dumb wonder. The Jumblies sailed out of nothing—or from the edge of things, but too fast, sailing out of his discarded canvas, glancing off blinding light to land on the white sand beach, singing sea chanteys, and laughing too loud like prisoners before a gallows or dreamers awakened too soon from perfect dreams.

The Jumblies sailed in a sieve of glinting polished silver with holes and holes and holes that spouted water as they ran before the wind with a mast made of an upright coat-rack and a sail of fine, aged Swiss cheese stitched with red and gold thread.

"This can't be good," Old Foss said.

The Old Man blinked and without taking his eyes from

the Jumblies said, "why can I only sometimes understand you? Sometimes you are just a cat and other times a voice, a friend. Why is that Old Foss?"

"I am always your friend," Old Foss said, "only you are sometimes deaf. I don't know why."

The Jumblies tumbled out and came galumphing up the shore all together, kicking up sand with their bootheels, until they seemed to arrive in a heap before the Old Man and Old Foss, their green gangly arms stuck out at odd angles, eyes peering from the most unlikely spaces, under elbows and over shoulders, and who was who and which was which and how many were there and how did they move all together like that were questions that could not be asked or answered so the Old Man didn't bother. They were pea green except when they smiled, then they shifted to a kind of off blue. They smiled at the Old Man just then, bluely.

"Will you come with us," they asked, "to the sea in our shining sieve?" They smiled in a beguiling manner with teeth half-sharpened but blindingly white, and shuffled about together in a way that made the Old Man ache with longing to belong to something as they belonged—it was a dream of empathy, that heap of blue inhumanity smiling up at him, of being so close to others that one speaks as another speaks and each knows what is meant, not something else but just that and every word, at last— finally!—meaning what it means and not so many other things, not a tragic failing off to loneliness, to war, to hunger, to darkness, to death.

"We will see such sights as never have been seen by you or any of yours. We will trade baubles with the Keepers of the sixty winds in their caverns beyond the edge of things; we will live where the Bong-Tree grows in the endless summer of the islands of the sun; we will sail beyond the stars, lifted by Phoenix birds into the sky on silver ropes held in their fiery beaks and we will tread the inky darkness until we reach the river of night and dream along its banks of unknown things. What do you say?" There was a pause. "You must say."

"What do I say, Old Foss?" said the Old Man, never turning his eyes from them.

"They are like what should be over the horizon," Old Foss said, "or a poem dreamed but left unfinished; they are desire and loss. Say no. Say no now and turn and run and do not look back."

"Why not go?" the Old Man said. "I wish to, with all my art, my heart, my feet, to go with them."

"Ah," Old Foss said, "but a sieve will only sink and bring you certainly to a place you cannot know now, but death has been visited by others before and will be again and is common enough that we can wait until it finds us without looking for it. I think there are no dreams there."

And the Old Man turned his head to look at Old Foss, then, and it was enough that first time to save him. For Old Foss yawned and was just a cat again. And the Jumblies were just the wind piling sand and unpiling it again back into the sea, a whisper that did not ask, will you come with us?

But when they came again only she came, the Jumbly Girl, in the night when he dreams, where Old Foss could not protect him.

Old Foss paused to wrinkle his nose for the rain he would have to endure. But he loved the Old Man, and the Old Man loved him; the Old Man had found him long ago when he was a lost kitten, and picked him up and took him in and fed him. Some debts, Old Foss reflected, are always still to be paid, no matter what we do.

He dropped to the floor and hurried to see if the front or back door has been left ajar, but no. The windows were all shut up tight for the storm. So it would have to be the hard way, to slip through a crack between here and there, to unravel the world for a moment as only cats know how to do.

I am too old for such things, Old Foss thought; too fat, he reflected, too comfortable, too tired, too selfish, too peevish, too everything.

Out of the world and back into the world again, but outside. No mean feat, Old Foss thought, even for a cat. He ran around the room, reaching out to catch at the frayed threads of the world where he could find them, pouncing, missing them as they seemed to curl around the corners of things into nothing; faster, he thought. He became wild-eyed with the pursuit, chasing the shadows of elsewhere across the hearth, up the wall, around turns that weren't there. Soon, he was tearing as fast as he could around the room, panting with the exertion, until he disappeared.

Then he was there, like being under a rug, in a dark corridor with light poking through the frayed edges to show him where to go. He pushed through, his ears back, mewing with the work of it, until he felt, through one thin patch, the rain. It would have to do; he tore out, nearly running into a wall, running up it instead and stopping only when he reached the top—a red tile roof, wet and slick. He scrabbled for footing indecorously, caught himself, pulled himself upright and looked about, his eyes big, his heart pumping, the rain cold against his fur and already bringing forth a musty smell. He mewed forlornly with self pity.

But Old Foss from his vantage saw the Old Man receding in the distance like a wave going out at low tide. No, Old Foss thought, no, he's headed to sea.

Old Foss began to run, clattering over rooftops after the Old Man stepping so briskly to meet only death who waited, Old Foss knew, so patient and still below the unceasing heaving of the water.

Once before the Old Man had gone to sea in a sieve with his Jumbly Girl and her eyes of jade to match her skin and her smiles like sweet heartache in blue. Her touch against his cheek was a heart stopped, her voice in his ear a thought to fill immensity. They went indeed to visit with the sixty contending winds, who traded them wine for their baubles brought out of the world, giving a manna sweet drink called Ring-Bo-Ree for little rings from the noses of pigs or unfinished paintings thrown discarded into the sea, or perhaps for the occasional runcible spoon. They sailed into the shifting thickness beyond the edge of things and were drawn into the sky by fiery birds and dreamed beside the islands of the sun and the night river. And—who knew?—sieves sink more slowly then one might suppose. At least sometimes, when the wind is right to hold them up, perhaps, or, perhaps when one moves too fast to notice one is sinking.

Old Foss had come after him, hiding in the rigging, or under the bundles to trade, watching and waiting.

And one day when the water of night came in too high and no one was left to bail it out and it was too late by far, Old Foss whispered in the Old Man's ear as he dreamed: "Time to come home, for the water's rising. Time to wake up, now or never. Time to dream a little less and live a little more, old friend," and a partial payment on a debt never to be repaid was made.

"Thank you," the Old Man said, when awake and in his bed again, "for surely I would have drowned."

And yet, something was taken from the Old Man too, something taken that can never be returned—what the Jumbly Girl meant to him—and for that there was a new debt, never to be repaid.

"Why did you bother me," the Old Man would say at other times, when the confusion came to him, "why didn't you leave me to drown in peace, in bliss of other things, with my

Jumbly Girl?"

For they had tried to keep him:

"Stay," they had told him, despite the rising water, the leaking of the sieve. "Stay and dream with us."

"Come with me," he had said to his Jumbly Girl, "come with me and be my love; we will think of things to do to pass the time, though it will not be this—we will paint unfinished pictures by the shore and hold hands inside the rain. I will write you poems and you will tell bad jokes. It's not this but isn't it something?"

And she agreed to come with him, to meet him in the morning, by the shore of everything, below the sun, beside the night, where the sky birds came to draw them home by silver cords in their fiery beaks, on a raft made of fronds from the Twangum Tree; he and Old Foss waited for her to come from the sieve as it sank in the river of night, but she did not appear.

Somehow, it seemed, in stepping from the sieve to the shore to the raft, he had misplaced her; when he had turned back to hold out his hand and help her out, she was gone.

She never reappeared. And the Jumblies disappeared from the sieve with the morning light, like fog retreating into the sea, but with an ache like when you remember what you thought the world was going to be like when you were young and foolish.

"Come on, Old Man," Old Foss had said, "the sieve is sinking fast."

"Will I ever see her again?"

There is no answer to such questions and he offered none, but the Old Man asked it again, asked it so many times over the years that Old Foss finally said, "I'm sorry, Old Man."

"Oh, I know, it's all right, Old Foss."

But it wasn't.

Old Foss leapt from roof to roof like a young cat with nothing to lose, not a fat old cat with everything at stake. The rain had depressed him, then frustrated him, then made him ironic and bitterly elated. He sang: "How many lives, how many lives, how many more lives for the cat? At least one more, at least one more, and another one after that!" as he leapt across an alleyway and scrabbled onto the roof on the other side. When he reached the edge of town he climbed quickly, nosily, awkwardly down a drainpipe full with leaking water rushing. Leaping off the pipe, he landed badly, quickly looking around, licking his shoulder uselessly in the rain, and walking with what dignity he could muster toward the shore, his orange and black fur matted to his bulging body where it wasn't sticking out ridiculously.

Then he saw the Old Man curled into a ball on the hill, halfway down to the beach, a white blur among the grey of water falling; Old Foss ran to him.

Old Foss whispered in his ear, "Come, Old Man. Time to come in, the water is falling fast and your nightshirt is thin."

"She came to me in my dreams," the Old Man shouted suddenly, his eyes opening wide and wild, "she came to me in my dreams. They've come again in the sieve to take me to sea."

"This would be the last time," Old Foss said. "Wait a little while longer and we will find ways to pass the time—painting unfinished pictures by the shore, or you can pet me by the fire when it rains, or. . . ."

He didn't know what to say. Could he do this to the Old Man again, take him from his Jumbly Girl?

For the Jumblies were by the shore, and the Jumbly Girl was with them. As the rain lessened they came into sight. She was leaving them and wandering up the hill, a ghost in green, her voice on the wind:

"Come with us, come to stay, and we will sail under the sea, and we will never leave but we will never want to. . . ."

Old Foss turned away from looking at her.

I suppose you should go, Old Foss thought, I suppose you could go and I should stay for I only wanted you for myself, an old debt I will never be able to repay. He didn't say it because it hurt too much to say it.

But the Old Man did not turn his head to look at his Jumbly Girl.

She came closer, calling again, "Come, come, come to sea, to the sieve that sinks below the waves until we drown, to the lost worlds below the sun."

But the Old Man did not turn his head.

The Jumbly Girl stopped. "Can't you hear me, love?"

Old Foss dared not turn to look at her again. The Old Man did not hear. He could not see. Old Foss would not give away her presence.

The Jumbly Girl stood, her body heaving, crying, Old Foss supposed, but the rain made that indeterminate. That at least was what he tried to tell himself.

The Old Man cried, too, and that he could see despite the rain, for the Old Man beat his breast and tore at his thinning hair, and pulled hard on his frumpy old beard until he pulled the hair out in uneven patches.

"I want to die," the Old Man said, as the Jumbly Girl reached out for him with arms of green embrace, with love forever and ever for him, to death, yes certainly to death but perhaps beyond as well.

"I'm sorry I made a mistake, so long ago," Old Foss said, "that time by the river of night, I should have let you drown. Or maybe you have with me."

But the Old Man didn't hear, or couldn't listen.

Old Foss mewed piteously, wet through.

"Oh, Old Foss," the Old Man said, "look at you, oh, you're wet through."

Old Foss shivered and looked to him like he had looked to him once long ago as a kitten lost in the rain.

"Come on, Old Foss, let's go home," the Old Man said, rising, pulling Old Foss against him, heading back up the hill. "They're not coming after all." He choked on the words. "They're not here."

The Old Man leaned over Old Foss, and Old Foss peered over the Old Man's shoulder to see the Jumblies come in a heap to the Jumbly Girl crying on the hill. They covered her in their love, with their arms at all angles and their boots kicking out, and their eyes green compassion. They smiled a blue benediction.

"I'm sorry," they said to the Jumbly Girl, and turning they all walked, or rolled, or shambled downhill. "I'm sorry," they said together and held her in their arms until they vanished in rain.

"Home again soon," the Old Man said, soothing, but tired like a drunk man sobered by sorrow on his way home again from a lost night on the town, or like a storm-tossed sailor thrown on the shore, wobbling inland to safety.

"It's all right, it's all right, it's all right, Old Foss."

"I'm sorry," Old Foss said.

"There, there," the Old Man said, though he couldn't hear. "It's all right. It's all right."

But it wasn't.

ALL THE LITTLE GODS WE ARE

by John Grant

It is an easy enough mistake to make—the most natural mistake in the world.

It's late on a Thursday afternoon and, although the air is cool in the library, the day is hot enough outside that even just the sunlight roaring in through the windows is enough to put thoughts in mind of darkened bars and long cold beers, condensation silvering the outside of the glass . . . You know the kind of day, surely. The kind of day on which, when there's just over an hour before you'll be free to go home or at least away from here, you think it'd be a good idea to phone up one of your unmarried friends and suggest getting together after work to sink a few.

In my case the friend in question is called Bill, and that's exactly what I do.

Bill lives only a few blocks away from where I live, in a similarly solitary apartment. His bachelorhood expresses itself in what I would describe as a near-obsessive neatness and a near-compulsive shedding of unnecessary possessions, so that his apartment is always full of space, shining surfaces, emptiness.

My own bachelorhood manifests instead in the form of clutter: top-heavy heaps of books on the shelves and floor, CDs scattered everywhere, ashtrays and waste baskets and kitchen sink brimming with all my claims to a productive life. But his wide open spaces and my lack of them are both symptomatic of the same thing: while neither of us is short of friends and acquaintances, neither of our lives is very long co-tenanted by another. His life has occasional lodgers, if you will, who stay a night or three and leave a smell of eau de cologne in the rooms until Bill manages to scrub the air molecules clean of it. My own is shared by myself alone, not so much by deliberate choice as through a lack of inclination to have it otherwise.

Because his apartment isn't far from mine, our telephone numbers have the same local code, and indeed the same first five digits, differing only in the last two.

The day has been long and hot, the borrowers have been unusually annoying in their demands ("Are you sure that's the *right* version of *Pride and Prejudice*? The one my friend's been reading has a grey cover, not a blue one"), a teacher from the local junior school brought in a bunch of the kids to show them how to use the Dewey Decimal System, and so on, and so on. Just to add to my irritation is the thought that Bill, as a freelance copywriter, is able to work at home and avoid all this; probably the reason he chose that profession, in fact, so that he wouldn't be troubled by the clutter of *other people*.

No wonder, then, that, as I turn my head away from Mrs. Baldeen at the lending counter in case she thinks I'm calling a friend to suggest going out for a beer, the number I stab out on the pad in front of me isn't Bill's, but my own.

I realize my error almost as soon as I've made it. If I were in a call-box I'd hang up, but I'm aware of the vigilant eye of Mrs. Baldeen so I stay on the line, thinking I'll leave some jokey message on my answerphone when it cuts in after the fourth ring, and then I'll dial again.

Except that my call never gets as far as the fourth ring, because on the second ring someone picks up.

"Hello," says a man's voice.

For a moment I assume that not only have I dialed the wrong person's number—my own rather than Bill's—but I've managed to dial the number wrong as well.

"I'm sorry," I start. "I seem to have . . ."

The voice—the, now I think about it, very *familiar* voice—overrides my words. "John Sudmore here."

Which of course stalls whatever it was I was going to say, because *I'm* John Sudmore.

Psychologists have a term I can never remember for the type of unconscious censorship our brains practice. When confronted by something we "know" to be "impossible", we either refuse to perceive it at all or we instantly conjure up some byzantine explanation for it that, no matter how implausibly complicated, seems somehow more commonsensical. It's the latter that happens to me in this instance.

"What a strange coincidence," I say as soon as my tongue and lips start working again. "My name's John Sudmore, too. I didn't realize there were two of us here in Lampitt."

I chuckle with self-conscious naturalism.

"Is this some kind of telemarketing stunt?" says the other John Sudmore. He sounds suspicious, but more interested than displeased.

"No, it's not," I assure him. "I've dialed the wrong number. I was meaning to call a friend of mine and I made a mistake. Silly of me." I know I'm beginning to burble. I don't have to look at Mrs. Baldeen to know that I've kindled her attention. "I must have dialed Bill's number a thousand times, but . . . or maybe it's a foulup in the network, not my fault at all."

It's not enough to assuage the other John Sudmore's suspicions. "You're not trying to sell me anything?"

I'm just about to answer this when down the line I hear an infant wail in the background. Then there's that distinctive sound of someone moving the telephone receiver away from their face to couch it on their shoulder.

"Hey, Jus!" calls the other John Sudmore. "Can you get Maggie to cool it? I'm trying to speak on the phone here. Some fruitcake, I think, but . . ."

There's a response from the distance. I'm not able to make out many of the words the woman says, but I gather the unseen child Maggie has bumped her knee on the table-leg. This is not what makes my body tense up, however.

And now the crazy theory my mind desperately constructed to explain how there could be another John Sudmore living in Lampitt—even though I knew there wasn't, because in a town this size we'd already have been aware of each other—and how his voice could, by coincidence, be so like my own, and how our telephone numbers might be almost the same, and how . . . This house of cards I've built out of steadily more improbable coincidences comes tumbling down.

What shocks me out of that fool's dream is that I recognize the *woman's* voice, too.

And her name.

Jus.

Short for Justine.

Justine Parland.

I could credit the existence of another John Sudmore, even if it meant twisting my mind around to believe something I knew to be untrue, but I cannot accept that he might have married Jus Parland.

I throw my mind back twenty years—no, let me see, it must be twenty-one.

I was fifteen when a new girl arrived in the school. Her family had just moved the thirty miles out of Manhattan to live in Lampitt. Her dad, Mr. Parland, would still commute into town every weekday to where he worked as a stockbroker or something infinitely tedious like that, but Justine and her mom and her quite *maddening* kid brother David would enjoy the benefits of living in semi-rural Jersey while, incidentally, Mr. Parland would pay about half the mortgage for a sprawling five-bedroomed house in four acres that he'd been paying for a cramped apartment on 48th Street.

I discovered all of this and quite a lot more because Jus—she soon told me she preferred the contraction to her full name—because Jus and I were seated next to each other in her first class, which happened to be math, and I made a point of welcoming her to the school as we packed up our books to move on to literature. I was very shy back then—still am, although meeting so many of the public every day in the library has gone some way towards curing my timidity—and in the normal course my reticence would probably have won out, but I conquered it and spoke to her, smiled even, because during the math class I'd been taking occasional peeks at her face as she leaned forward, earnestly taking notes, and during those glances I'd grown up a little.

Before the start of that class, if you'd sat me in front of an easel and given me a brush and asked me to paint my ideal of womanhood—and assuming I could actually draw or paint, which I couldn't and can't—I'd have put on the canvas some anatomically impossible creature composed of masses of tumbling blonde hair, breasts that strained at a skimpily revealing garment and that demanded to be called not "breasts" but "tits", lips that pouted like a baseball mitt, pants that seemed to have been sprayed on and whose zipper was beginning slowly to unpeel its two halves, and eyes of purest blue that, with stark animal lust and yet a virginal romantic eloquence, spoke the plain and simple message: "John Sudmore, you paragon among superstuds, there is nothing in the world that I desire more than to get hot and heavy with you in the back of a Merc." I had never in fact met a girl who even remotely resembled my paradigm, but I knew that somewhere she must exist. She was probably called Elektra, although Tabitha would do, or . . . To be honest, I wasn't much concerned about the name so long as she was someone all the other guys would be insanely jealous about.

Studying Justine rather than quadratic equations, however, I realized I never *would* meet Elektra or Tabitha. More than this: I didn't *want* to any more. It wasn't that my fifteen-year-old self was instantly enamoured of my new classmate— not at all, I don't think—but that for the first time I began to understand there was more to the attractiveness of girls than physical stereotypes and availability, more than sex or the apparent promise of it.

Justine's hair wasn't a froth of gold. It was straight, quite long, and its colour was either mousy or bronze depending on how the sunlight caught it. She used her left hand, always her left, to push back her hair behind her prettily shaped ears whenever it fell forward—something it did often—over her cheek, which had the faintest down of transparent, cobweb-fine hairs on it. Her fingers were slender, the nails raggedly chewed. Her nose was quite thin, and a little too long. Her eyes were brown, and when she glanced up at me to catch me hastily looking away I could see they were lit by intelligence—a quality whose possibility had never even entered my head during my secret masturbatory sessions with the specter of Elektra or Tabitha. Her mouth was small, her lips thin. So fascinated was I by the discovery that, even though she was so far from my template, she nevertheless drew me, that I didn't notice how far her breasts pushed out the front of her blouse, although I was well aware they were *there*.

And she was easy to smile at, and to talk to, as we gathered up our books.

When the lunch break arrived she cut through the crowds

of other kids to stick out her hand.

"Hi," she said. "I'm Jus. If you're not eating your sandwiches with anyone else . . . ?"

"John," I said, moving over on the low wall even though there was no one else for yards around. We knew each other's names, of course, from when Mr. Dorrigan had introduced Jus around the class, but it seemed necessary to exchange them personally.

And so we sat and we talked for half an hour or so in the sunshine as we ate, and this time I confess I did check out the size of her breasts (small but definitely in attendance, so far as I could make out through the blouse and the bra, my perceptions heightened to X-ray status by the fact that I was fifteen, male and omniscient) even though they didn't seem especially significant by comparison with the sound of her voice, the animation of her face, the laughter in her eyes, her unassumed articulacy.

We were born to be friends. We both knew it. The Australian Aborigines have the traditional belief that a complete human being comprises two parts that are split before birth, that we spend our lives seeking the other part to make ourselves whole again, and that only the lucky succeed in doing so. Jus and I recognized, only a minute or two into that half-hour, that we were among the lucky.

The curious thing is that I can't now remember much of what we talked about during this most important half-hour of my life beyond the mere data of our existences: our names, our family members, our potted histories. I know we covered our hopes and dreams as well, but the details of what we said then are lost to me. It was as if neither of us had to make a conscious effort to remember them because we knew them all already. This wasn't an exploratory conversation: it was just a passage of reminder, a reassurance that nothing had changed since the last time.

We were, of course, inseparable after that, we two halves of the same person: all through school and beyond. Yet what we'd probably both assumed from the outset would be the route-map of our future wasn't followed by the reality. I know that I expected after that first lunch together that we'd travel along the familiar pathways: sweethearts, lovers, marriage. This wasn't the way it went, though, over the years. Oh, sure, there was so much physical rightness between the two of us you almost felt it was a bubble around us you could tap your fingers on; and we could hardly go out on so many dates together, or be visiting so often in each other's homes, or go on so many long hikes just the two of us, without there having been some reasonably steamy sessions—kissing, hugging, touching. Her breasts proved indeed to be small, two delicious little apples, so much *prettier* than any I ever saw in skin mags—which I never in fact got much into, although there were always plenty around at school—or at the movies. But somehow all our love and our passion never developed into full-scale sex; the occasional voyages of discovery we made together were just that—two dear friends helping each other out by sharing what they didn't have in common so they'd both know what to expect when it was some stranger's body they were doing the actual sex thing with.

It was one of the few matters—perhaps the only one, now that I think on it—about which we disagreed. I was as if I'd been born with the knowledge that we'd be lifelong lovers; Jus was as if we'd certainly be together all our lives long, yes, but that what we had between us, the unity, transcended and perhaps even obviated our being lovers at all. "I can't make love to you, John," she said more than once. "It'd be like having sex with my brother, or—no, I got that wrong: with *myself.*"

I agreed with her that the thought of making love with her brother David was pretty horrendous—whiny, stupid, probably liked pulling the wings off flies; not really surprising he was so successful in later life. But that didn't stop me from pressing my case. We were made for each other. It was inevitable. Why waste time on others, or even just waiting in celibacy? Why not cut straight to the chase? Accept this glorious gift we'd been given, and rejoice in it?

None of my arguments ever prevailed. In a way it didn't matter; in a way it did. Our love for each other was unaffected. We were still Jus and John, Jusandjohn, Jusnjohn, Jusjohn, the one person with the two different names, the two independently mobile halves of a single organism.

I thought one of the real problems, the real reasons for her resistance, was that her parents approved of me.

And approve of me they certainly did. They were nice people. David Sr. was no conversationalist, having little interest outside stocks and sports, the former for the weekdays and the latter for the weekends and public holidays, all carefully compartmentalized; but he had a geniality that made his tediousness easy to tolerate. Ellen-Anne, her mother—Ellie, as I was soon taught to call her—was quite different. Mercurial, very lovely in a minxy way, sometimes waspish, always curious for new knowledge, always alert for anything of interest, she was one of the most attractive women I've ever known. I once in a moment of stark idiocy confessed to Jus that several times, when her mother had casually brushed against me, I'd found myself with an incipient hard-on—an awful thing to admit about somebody's *mother*, for chrissake. Jus only laughed; her mother, she said, had that effect on men.

I'm giving the impression that thoughts of sex were near the forefront of our minds all through those years, but that wasn't the truth of it. Yes, those thoughts were always there; but they were only a sort of darkened backdrop at the rear of the brightly lit stage that was the life we shared together. Often, as we went through high school, I'd get teased by the other guys about it—not so much teased as incredulously interrogated. In the height of summer Jus, like all the other girls, would be wandering around wearing not very much—a brief halter and ultra-short pants that did little to hide the fact that she was young, and female, and lithe. How could I stand it, the boys would earnestly ask me, being near to such unconquered but surely conquerable tracts of exquisite femininity and yet never so much as succumbing to the temptation to indulge in a seemingly accidental grope? I didn't tell them, of course, that Jus and I were relatively familiar with each other's bodies, that sometimes we'd lounge around naked together if that was more comfortable, that physical exposure and nudity in themselves don't *matter* because it's the baring of *selves* to each other that's what lovemaking's all about. They were disbelieving enough already; that mental censor I spoke of earlier would have distorted the information so that what they'd have perceived was that Jus and I spent our time alone mindlessly fucking.

I can hear it now: "Well, you know, guys, sometimes we lie around without any clothes on and talk about string theory."

Yeah. Right. You a faggot?

String theory wasn't the only thing we discussed. Cosmology was just one of our passionate interests. Pinball was another. Classic mystery novels. Photography. Existentialist philosophy, until in the end we concluded that Sartre had his head in the clouds just as much as anyone else. Music—rock, classical, jazz, exotic. The Surrealist school—art in general, in fact, although we decided ninety per cent of the Abstractionists were just clones producing sub-Pollocks in a factory line somewhere. Microbiology. Menstruation—both in terms of its being one of life's great tedia and in terms of its relation to the lunar cycle ... and so we rambled on into biorhythms. Cryogenics. Black-and-white movies, preferably with Edward G. Robinson or Veronica Lake in them. Sunsets. Fantasy fiction, most of which we detested as being Harlequin Romance set in Tolkien Country but some of which we adored. Politics and the corruptibility of the human soul, those two topics being natural bedfellows. The situation in whichever part of the world the situation was in at the time. Sex and, in a world-weary way, its follies. Crossword puzzles. Quantum theory. The history of stupidity. Religion—we were rationalist, and abhorred the efforts of the bigots to impose their nonsense on not just the rest of us but their own children. Love, in all its forms. Tennis—we played, badly, but spectated avidly. How ghastly just about everything was that was shown on MTV, and how little we wanted to be rich and famous . . . although we both knew with an absolute certitude that one day we would be.

Rich and famous *together*, as Jusjohn.

As it is, John's on his own and he's a Deputy Chief Librarian in a small-town library.

Of course, we both went to the same college. Our families, who by this time were really just one large family, always assumed it, as did we. There was no question of being able to afford one of the major institutions, but Rembrandt University, while undistinguished, had a highly respectable reputation. It was actually a very good university with a top-notch literature faculty—we'd decided on literature rather than the sciences. The campus was large and in a superb setting; the nearby town of Ilchester was just the right size to accept but not overwhelm us college kids. We both joined a bad campus rock band called The Flaming Ghoulies that reformed every week or two until finally, after a full three months, to the silent but intense relief of everybody it split permanently amid a deluge of accusations and counteraccusations over who'd purloined the lead guitarist's private half-gallon of rye. (In fact, the rest of us had shared it one hilarious night, but the details got confused.) Jus and I studied together; after the first semester we took an apartment together and our parents acted extremely cool about the whole thing because of course we were Jusjohn and would soon enough be married. They'd have been less cool if they'd known we weren't sleeping with each other—at least, never in the usual euphemistic sense of the term.

Midway through that first semester I lost my virginity to a girl called, strangely enough, Tabitha; I can't remember much about her except that her breasts were too big and the wrong shape, not being Jus's, and that she knew more about Sean Connery than anyone else I've ever known, discussing his movie career with greater and greater intensity and louder and louder up to and through orgasm—a detail that had Jus, when first told about it, pummelling the floor in gleeful laughter. Over the space of a couple of months I must have slept with Tabitha a dozen times or more, because I could, until I discovered that she was extending the same privilege to several of the other guys, including a chemistry professor, and I began to worry about disease. Jus followed the liaison—it could hardly be called an affair—with fascination; it was the Jusjohn organism's first experience of physically "going the whole way", and thus obviously of potent interest to both of us. The Jusjohn organism might not have been so emotionally equable about it all if Tabitha had been more than an educational aid and receptacle, of course.

As I learned when Jus started dating and eventually sleeping with Martin.

This wasn't a matter of double standards—the "it's OK for the guy to screw around, but heaven help the girl who does the same" principle. Jus seriously *liked* Martin. She didn't talk about their lovemaking when she came back to the apartment, to me, didn't tell me everything they'd done. The two of them spent a lot more time talking or going around together—all the activities that I regarded as my prerogative, in other words— than they did grappling. And, worse, I could quite understand why she liked him. As I sat at home alone in our apartment nursing a bottle of whatever was on special offer that week at the liquor store I tried to find something—*anything*—about Martin that I could legitimately detest, and I always failed. I mean, *I* liked the guy as well.

Despite being liked by both parts of the Jusjohn being— "in their different ways", as I fastidiously put it to Jus one time—Martin was a casualty of our first long vacation from Rembrandt. I spent much of that vacation reconciling myself to the notion that, although Jus was the other half of me, we didn't own each other exclusively, that what she did with her body was irrelevant to the fact that we two were one, indivisible, our essences united, that even if she *married* this guy Martin he would always be an irrelevance in the light of . . . you can fill in all the other rationalizations yourself. Sometimes I voiced them to Jus; sometimes she agreed; sometimes she kept quiet.

It was almost an anticlimax to get back to college and discover that, during his weeks away from Jus, Martin had found "somebody else", which "somebody else" he was going to marry.

When I first heard about it, Jus had to restrain me from stomping round to his place to bawl him out for his treachery.

She got over it quicker than I did, because Richard came along. He lasted nearly six months, until he suggested it could be more fun if he invited a friend to join in. (Jus wasn't against the idea in principle, as she explained to me, but she was deeply offended by the presumption.) I had a nostalgic weekend with Tabitha—to hell with worries about infection—and then, later on, another; her field of expertise had shifted to Keanu Reeves, and I couldn't help feeling she was on a potentially fatal slide. Who next? Adam Sandler?

After Richard came Derek. Then another Martin. I didn't like Nigel very much—he didn't last long—but Nick and Peter were both excellent choices, I felt.

For my part there was Annette, in whom I was quite

absorbed for a full semester; where Tabitha had taught me a lot about fucking, Annette patiently and with considerable skill and versatility taught me virtually everything I know about lovemaking. She was also a very dear friend; Jus had to put a lot of effort into consoling me when Annette and I broke up.

And then there was Jennifer. I adored Jennifer and probably we could have spent the rest of our lives together, a perfect match; but *she wasn't the other half of me*. I told Jus this one night, and over the next few weeks we combined our ingenuities to let Jennifer down as lightly as was possible, so that in the end she thought it was *her* idea for us to go our separate ways after graduation.

Because graduation was where Jus and I had got to in our shared academic career.

My relationship with Jennifer—more specifically, the realization by both Jus and myself that it would be wrong of us ever to expect anyone else to substitute for, to approximate for, the other halves of the Jusjohn organism—brought about in both of us what used to be called a paradigm shift.

We talked the last of it through one afternoon after we'd got home to Lampitt from college for the final time. Neither of us had jobs in prospect, and our parents were contentedly permitting us to be lethargic for a few months about chasing opportunities—my dad might have thought differently, but he'd died during our previous semester at Rembrandt. We were sitting by the edge of the Greenemill River, watching butterflies—this was in the days before the river got so polluted by the Sharplet Chemicals plant, which had just started construction a few months earlier.

Jus slowly twirled a pale blue flower between the fingers of her two hands, hoping a butterfly would be attracted to it.

"You know something, darling?" she said.

"Know what?"

I could see on her face that she was taking her thought to

completion before speaking it. I almost knew what the thought was.

"We're virgins," she said at last.

"Yes," I said.

In strict dictionary terms, of course, neither of us was—Tabitha and Martin and Jennifer and the others, even Nigel, could have told you that (and Nigel probably *would*, in great detail for the full length of a bar-propping evening)—but in truth that's what we were.

We were virgins to one another.

The two parts of the Jusjohn creature had experimented both physically and emotionally, but they'd done so *separately*—independently.

I lay back flat on the cool, slightly damp grass, my hands behind my head, and gazed at a couple of small white clouds and a dissipating jet-trail that ran alongside them.

"We should maybe someday do something about that," she continued.

"Someday," I agreed.

It wasn't really so important, after all. Because in *another* way we weren't virgins to each other at all. No two people, it seemed, had ever been so closely and steadfastly entwined; even that was understating it, because we weren't two people, just one.

She waited a few moments before speaking again.

"John, we're going to spend the rest of our lives together. I thought maybe we could do that without physically living together, especially when I was with Peter, but then . . ."

"It was the same as with me and Jennifer," I said.

"Yes."

"Could have been a marriage made in heaven. Really it'd have been the wrongest thing you and I ever did, if we'd let me marry her."

"Yes," said Jus again.

A green butterfly meandered briefly above my nose and then sailed on breezes only its wings could detect towards Jus. I raised my head and followed its indecisive flight. It pirouetted around the blue flower, which she was now holding determinedly still, and then landed on it.

"Look," she breathed.

"We're making love," I said, just as softly.

In a minute or less the butterfly tired of the bloom—at least, that was the way someone else might have seen it. In reality, it had pulled us back into the unity of the Jusjohn, it had made our love for us; the fine and delicate task done, it was free to grace other flowers, other lovers.

Neither of us spoke for a long while, then:

"There are practicalities," she said. "If we're going to get married, I mean. Parents to tell, that sort of thing."

I chuckled. "It's hardly going to be a surprise to them. They think we've been living together—I mean 'living together'—these past three years."

"Yes, but they'll still want the formalities to be observed. And they'll want to be able to think they helped us fix the date, and gave their blessing, and—oh, all the usual shit."

She stood up and brushed with one hand at the back of her jeans. With the other she threw the blue flower down onto the slowly moving water of the Greenemill. It floated a few yards downstream, and then was taken by the eddy formed around a moss-covered rock that broke the surface. As we watched, the abandoned bloom bobbed once, bobbed twice, and then was pulled under.

"Take my hand," she said, "as we walk back to tell the others. I want your hand in mine."

And, still, "Jus" is the name this stranger has just used to the woman behind him in the room, the woman who seems clearly to be the mother of his child.

The child whose father is called John Sudmore and has my voice.

He's speaking to me again, but I can't hear his words through the cacophony of my memories. And then the memories in turn are superseded by the rush of my thoughts.

I can believe in many things, but one of these is not that there is a creator god—still less one who, not satisfied with having brought his universe into being, continues to tamper with its course of events. Nor can I accept the idea espoused by some of the quantum scientists that each and every moment of our universe sparks off a myriad other universes, each defined by a single one of all the different outcomes of all the different events a moment can contain. Yes, I can conceive that this might happen, that the passage of every instant of time is characterized by near infinite creation; but surely all those other possible universes that are generated are like pairs of virtual particles— springing spontaneously into existence but then instantaneously returning to the base level, the nothingness, as they annihilate each other. In the case of universes, the base level is the universe we know, can see, can test, can probe. The almost infinitude of individual alternative possible existences persist for barely a quantum of time before they all converge back upon the base level. In short, I can no more believe that the universe creates and re-creates itself than I can believe in the creator god.

So the idea that I might have somehow dialed into an alternative reality, where there's an alternative John Sudmore who married an alternative Justine Parland, does not even enter my mind as a possibility; well, as a possibility, perhaps, but one to be instantly dismissed.

Yet I do believe in creations, and I do believe in gods.

I believe in all the little gods we are.

I believe in the power each one of us has to create a future so forcefully that it imprints itself irrevocably upon the fabric of spacetime, or whatever it is that forms the substrate of reality.

And I believe that my younger self did that, creating for himself a future that, while it was not *my* future, was nevertheless so vital that it has played itself out . . . somewhere *else*.

Somewhere that I've just accidentally phoned.

None of this can I even attempt to explain to the man who's now back on the line speaking to me. He's inquisitive as to who I might be in relation to himself; his suspicions assuaged, now he's trying to work out if maybe we could have had a common ancestor. Do I have a great-aunt who was called Julie Petersen before she married and became Julie Halstread? Was my father's name Clive?

Of course, the answer to both questions is "yes", but I'm not going to tell him that.

Instead I babble: "Look, I'm terribly sorry to have disturbed you. I got a wrong number and then . . . well, I don't know what came over me, claiming I had the same name as you, and all that stuff. Must be the heat. Heat and boredom—the twin curses of telemarketers. Make us do funny things sometimes."

And so on. I'm hoping Mrs. Baldeen isn't picking up too much of this.

He says nothing for a moment, and to fill the silence I speak again, unable to stop myself.

"Give my love to Jus."

I put the phone down as quickly as I can, even though he's talking once more, his curiosity now fully aroused.

I swivel my chair and stare straight into Mrs. Baldeen's eyes, which are cold and gray. They remind me of the way I see the world. I could never explain to those eyes why it is I can believe in the little gods—the little creator gods who are *us*.

And now I'm back walking home across the fields with Jus's hand in mine, birdsong in the air, long grass and occasional tough wildflowers swishing at our ankles.

We didn't speak much as we ambled together, just once or twice an "I love you" or a warning to steer around a cowflop. I don't think I've ever been as *aware* of existence as I was then; it seemed as if Jus's presence was a lens that focused onto me messages from every atom of the world. I was as one with everything, though most of all, of course, with the warmly glowing sun alongside me.

And then it all began to change. The first I noticed of this was when the knowledge arrived in my mind that things had been changing for some little while. The day wasn't as welcoming; the breeze didn't caress my face with the same tender attentiveness; the wildflowers had paler, dirtier colors.

And the grip of Jus's hand, so firm in mine just a few moments ago, was subtly fading.

I glanced up at her. She was still there, of course, but the face which had been so emphatically full of life, so very *present*, was now a texture of floating shadows, a pattern of light and dark that seemed to have been serendipitously thrown together to take the form of a face. Through her smile I could see a cloud that hugged the horizon.

I came to a halt.

"Jus!" I said desperately.

A gust of the breeze ran through the unkempt grass, the rustling of the blades drowning any reply she might have made.

We turned and walked on together—there was still enough of her in the air beside me for that. It was as if I was being accompanied by strains of an orchestral piece so faint that I couldn't quite make out what music was being played. The touch of her fingers against mine was a grace note so elusive that you barely notice it, yet would notice it were it not there.

I suppose I should have been feeling some sort of grief, but what was going through me was too profound for that, was *beyond* grief. Loss—yes, there was an aching sense of loss that seemed to make heavy every part of my body, slowing the pulse of my blood and the sparking of my synapses, chilling my skin. Pain, too—the ghost pain felt in an amputated limb. But more than anything else what I felt was *acceptance*.

Jus and I had shared our sandwiches and our selves sitting on the low wall outside the school. Once or twice our hands had brushed, the touch as light and insubstantial as the feel of her hand in mine now was. In her eyes I had seen my future; I had read it in its entirety, page by page, word by word, and I'd joyously accepted it. All the afternoon, through classes that were mere blurs, I'd pored over its pages, reading and re-reading, living, a story in which I was one of the main protagonists—*part* of one of the main protagonists, part of the Jusjohn organism.

At the end of the school day I'd danced home, cheeks radiant with excitement, with life. For once I'd been communicative over the dinner table with Mom and Dad, telling them that there was, you know, this girl I'd met, and maybe they would like to meet her too, could she come to dinner on Friday, perhaps? She was really nice, they'd like her a lot. I saw my parents exchanging glances, glances that said something like, "He's always been too shy to tell us about girls before. Maybe this one really *is* a cut above the others. It's about time. Remember when we were like this?" And I didn't care that there was something a little patronizing in all this.

That night, although I'd expected to lie awake for hours thinking of her, expected when at last I did fall asleep that I'd dream of her, in fact I dropped right off and dreamed of pirate ships and cabbages and kings, and I didn't wake until the alarm clock shrilled at me. I'd have eaten no breakfast at all if my mother hadn't stood over me.

Even though I reached school twenty minutes early—an unheard-of over-punctuality in my life to that date—I was far from the first to get there. Already there were little huddles in the corridors, many earnest faces, some of the girls in tears. "The new girl, the new girl, the new girl," the echoes whispered along the walls.

The new girl had been waiting for her dad to pick her up in his car after school the evening before when a truck had swerved because old Fatso Berringer had been drunk at the wheel *again* and it had plucked her from the sidewalk as neatly as the clawed hand in one of those fairground machines might pluck up a trinket and it had carried her on its hood for fifty yards or more before crushing her, and the life out of her, against the wall of the hardware store, blood falling onto the splayed pages of the books that spilled out of her satchel so that it was unlikely even the thrift store would now accept them for resale.

I lost a month of my life after that.

It was all a dreadful mistake, you see. I had already read the story of the future and, in it, the character called Justine, or Jus, was very much alive. If she'd been killed by a drunkard's truck, that story would be negated before it had even started. Yet the story was the *truth*; I knew it was. The falsehood was what people were telling me. Those kindly people, the new friends who suddenly appeared, Mom and Dad, the doctors—however well they were intentioned, they were lying to me.

Or, if they were not, I would make it so.

And I did.

I insisted to reality that the story would be told, that if reality itself would not tell the story of its own accord then I would do so for it.

And I had done that, too. I had lived the future that I knew to be the truth, and Jus had lived it alongside me.

Yet now she was fading from alongside me. Now, after nearly a decade, the conviction that had made me mold reality to suit my wishes was ebbing. And the sign of this ebbing was that Justine ebbed.

What was it that scattered my concentration? Was it the prospect of finally announcing to our parents—my Mom, Mr.

and Mrs. Parland—that the fusion of the Jusjohn organism, so long established, was now to be formalized? Was it that my mind couldn't embrace the clash between the two realities? Was it, and I've hardly ever dared admit this to myself, that I didn't, at the core of me, really *want* our unity to be recognized by the world? Could it even be that my emotions rebelled against the thought of finally making physical love to Jus, that I was repelled by the notion?

I don't know. I still don't know.

But I know that as Jus and I strolled slowly home across the fields she trickled out of my existence as fine dry sand might trickle away through my fingers, until by the time I got home all traces of her had vanished. And I was entirely at ease with this—on one level.

"Did you have a good time down by the river?" asked Mom as I kicked the mud off my boots. And: "Isn't it about time you got yourself a steady girlfriend to go on these walks with you, John?" And: "I've made a meat loaf for supper. Dad should be home any minute. I've already opened him a beer. Would you like one too?"

Yet on another level I wasn't accepting of the new non-Jus future at all. The Jusjohn being was still there. There could never be a Pollyjohn, or a Veronicajohn, or a Katiejohn, or . . .

I say that I live alone in my apartment. But that's not quite true. Sometimes Jus is there also. I have never seen her or heard her, but there are times I walk from the cramped kitchen into the cramped living room and I'm aware that the sound of her laughter has been there just a moment before.

None of this could I have said on the telephone. None of this can I ever hope to explain to Mrs. Baldeen's hard gray eyes.

I stare at the phone. Will I be able to pick it up again and call Bill, as I originally intended?

I've been living a wrong existence, I now know, since that afternoon when we walked home from the river.

Parts of the truth I got right, parts I got wrong.

As I was washing my hands and going back downstairs for the beer Mom had poured for me I assumed, as I've been assuming ever since, that the future I'd created was somehow the *lesser* reality, the subsidiary one—that the primary reality had reasserted itself, compelled my version of creation to converge back towards the mainstream of time's flow. It had chipped my conviction, then stood aside to watch it crumble.

But now I know, having spoken to the other John Sudmore, having heard the voice of Jus, how mistaken I've been.

The effect of my conviction crumbling was not that Jus faded away into a rejected subsidiary reality.

It was that *I* did.

I shrug my shoulders, as if I could discard the weight of infinity from them.

I reach out to pick up the receiver. I'm going to call Bill and arrange to meet him for a drink at the Tobermory Inn or O'Riley's or Duncan's Place, and we're going to talk about old baseball games and new movies and I'm going to submerge my knowledge of the reality I've lost. Of the reality that lost me.

But the receiver is only halfway to my ear when I change my mind and return it to its rest.

Tonight . . .

Tonight is a night for drinking alone.

THE DEW DROP COFFEE LOUNGE

by Cat Rambo

The minute the woman walked in, Sasha sensed it. Her head went up, that characteristic Sasha motion, like a blind bear sniffing the breeze. The well-dressed suburbanite glanced over the surroundings as she entered the coffee shop. Her hair glimmered with red dye and was cut in a Veronica Lake bang that obscured one eye. I couldn't see more from where I sat.

Sliding her notebook back into her bag, Sasha leaned forward, her gaze intent on the arrival, who looked back, first sidelong, then openly. As though pulled by that stare, she moved through a clutter of tables towards Sasha.

Her interrogatory murmur was inaudible except for its tone. Sasha nodded, gesturing to the seat across from her.

First there was coffee to be ordered, and the obligatory would-you-like-something, no-nothing-thank-you while Sasha cleared an old mug and several napkins away from the shared surface.

Then just as the redhead was pulling her chair back, Sasha's voice, pitched loud and clear. "I only agreed to meet with you to say I can't do this anymore. My husband is in Iraq, stationed in Basra."

The other woman stopped, looking as though she had been socked in the gut, halfway between heart torn out and tight-lipped anger. Sasha studied the table, tracing a finger across the constellations of blue stars. She looked as though she were worrying over a grocery list rather than declaring an end to a romance.

In the other woman's blank face, her eyes were a shuttered, washed-out blue. The Universe watched as the painful moment played itself out, watched with a grim and inexorable regard that I was glad was fixed on Sasha and the stranger rather than on me.

When the redhead had vanished onto the street without a backwards glance and the door had jangled shut behind her, Sasha claimed the untouched latte and croissant.

"Pig," I said from my seat.

"Don't you have some gathering of finger-snapping beatniks to get to?"

"I'm writing a poem about you right now. I'm calling it 'Sweet Goddess of the Dew Drop Coffee Lounge'."

The name of the shop was originally the Dew Drop Inn, back when it was a bar. As it had passed through the successive hands of owners who had not understood the original name's charm, it had become The Dew Drop Restaurant, The Dew Drop Donut Shop, The Dew Drop Take and Bake Pizza and most recently, the Dew Drop Coffee Lounge.

In this incarnation, the owner, Mike, had decorated the walls in neo-mystic. Posters showed translucent, anatomically-correct figures with chakra points set like jewels along their forms, backed by Tibetan mandalas. Sunlight slanted in through the crystals dangling from monofilament line in front of the French doors, and sent wavering rainbows across the glass cases by the counter, trembling on the scones and dry-edged doughnuts. Painted stars and moons covered the Frisbee-sized tables.

At first I hadn't liked the hearts of space music Mike insisted on, but after hours, days, weeks, now months of it, the aural paint of synthesizers and whale song had crept into my thoughts until mall Muzak now seemed strange and outré to me.

Sasha went back to her reading. I got up and started opening the doors to take advantage of the spring weather. The breeze ruffled the foam heart atop Sasha's latte and tugged at her newspaper. A skinny man in a red baseball cap came in, looking around, and she caught his eye, gestured him over, preparing her next brush off.

"Everything's alchemical," Mike had told me the week before. We were cleaning out the coffee machines with boiling vinegar and hot water. Wraiths of steam rose up around his form, listening as he spoke.

Whenever we were working together at night, he would deliver soliloquies that explained the secret inner workings of the world. While much of it was dubious and involved magnetism, UFOs, and a mysterious underground post office, it was a world that I found more appealing than my own. More interesting, at any rate.

It was a decent job, all in all, and it paid fair money in an economy that was so tanked that my already useless English degree was worth even less. So I tidied up the coffee shop, carried ten gallon bottles of water in, swept, and refolded newspapers after customers had scattered them like ink-smeared autumn leaves. It did mean the occasional late night labor, but Mike was a good sort and helped with the scutwork.

"Yes," I said noncommittally. I had learned that the best thing to do with Mike was not to stand in the way of the current rant.

"The thing is this. You know Tarot cards?"

"Like fortune tellers use?"

"Yeah, sorta kinda. See, Tarot cards have pentacles and swords and cups and rods, and that's diamonds and spades and hearts and clubs. With me so far, yeah?"

"Yeah."

"There's twenty two cards beyond that. The Major Arcana, they call them."

"Aren't there Minor Arcana too?"

"Yeah, those are the pentacles and stuff. Anyhow, each Major Arcana shows a step in our life journey."

"Which is how you use them for fortune telling," I said.

"No, well, kinda sorta. But they're steps that everyone goes through, the stages of life."

"All right," I said. I tipped the jug into a tank and drained it, frothing with heat. I sniffed the steam. Was that a last trace of vinegar?

"You should write about it," Mike said. "A lot of great literature is based on alchemy."

"Yeah, that's certainly a thought," I said. "Is that one done?"

He sniffed at the tap. "Another pass, maybe. Then let's mop the floor, as long as we have the hot water. Call it a night after that."

"The thing is this," he said after a long and reflective silence in which I'd forgotten what we were discussing. "There's these Avatars that walk around. They're foci for the Universe's attention, moments that get repeated over and over again, like in the Tarot cards. Sasha's one, for example."

"Sasha?"

"That skinny blonde who comes in around ten, reads and drinks coffee for a couple of hours, turns up in the late afternoons sometimes."

"She's a what?"

"An Avatar. It's the shop. It's a Locus."

"I thought you said it was a *foci*."

"No, people are the foci. The Avatars. The shop now, it's a *Locus*, a place where foci converge. Like Stonehenge, where all the ley lines meet."

"The Dew Drop is like Stonehenge?"

He laughed. "Yeah, crazy, isn't it? I don't understand why, either." He pulled a bottle of whiskey out from behind a blocky pyramid of stacked coffee bags. "But we'll drink to it all the same."

The next day, I watched Sasha.

It was a little before ten, a slack hour with only a couple of customers. I appreciated the lull, since I was hungover and queasy from last night's drinking.

A kid came in, maybe fourteen or fifteen. He had long brown hair tied back with a red bandana, bell bottoms, the kind of teenage body that looks like one long stick. He slouched in the doorway until she gestured him over and said something.

His jaw dropped.

I'd always thought that was a figure of speech until I saw him go literally slack-jawed with surprise at her words. And I would have said something, done something, but I felt it. The weight of the Universe's attention, just for a moment, not on me, but so close that you'd think space and time had collapsed at the point where Sasha sat, looking up at the kid.

He turned and pushed past me to the door. The back of his jacket had a picture of a chimpanzee with the legend "Got Monkey?" under it.

I gave her a little wtf? look and she shrugged at me and went back to the paperback she was reading, *The Biggest Secret*. But fifteen minutes later, another person came in, an elderly woman carrying a yellow flower in her hand.

She was taken aback by Sasha's wave, and made her way over to the table like someone advancing to feed a stray dog that they don't trust. Sasha stood and held the chair out for her, but the woman shook her head, laying her daffodil down.

"He's not coming," Sasha said. "He's happily married, and he asked me to break it to you. He gave me a little money to buy you a coffee, a pastry perhaps." She fumbled with her wallet.

"No," the woman said. She wore a lavender pants suit and was carefully made up, her colorless hair freshly combed and set. "No, that will be all right."

With chilly dignity, she left.

"That was awful!" I let Mike take the register and sat down across from Sasha, indignation pulling at my vocal cords. "What the hell was that all about?"

"It's my role in life, sunshine," she said.

"You pretended to be someone else! You're interfering in those people's lives!"

"It's not as evil as all that, Clay." She pointed at the front entrance. "It's something about this place. Maybe it's the dumping ground of the Universe. I noticed it when I first started coming here to get coffee and read. People come here all the time to meet blind dates that never show up. I've never seen anyone actually meet here, but I've seen plenty lingering in the doorway, looking around, trying to catch your eye to see if you, you're the one."

She leaned forward. "So I started leaping into the breach. I give them a reason to run, to have a story they can tell at dinner parties for the next few years, the Blind Date from Hell, who seemed so nice in e-mail, then turned out to be . . ." She twisted her hand. ". . . a little cuckoo."

"You're not just a little cuckoo, you're insane," I said. "There ought to be a law about people pulling crap like that. How many dates have you thwarted?"

"You're not listening. I don't thwart them. They only show up here if the other person isn't arriving."

"Bullshit."

"Watch." She pointed at a small ginger-haired man as he stepped in. "I can spot them a mile off. I can hear it in the cadence of their steps coming along the sidewalk and read it in their faces when they open the door. But I won't catch this one, and you'll see what I mean. He'll linger and wait."

I rose and took his order, a double espresso. He wore horn-rimmed glasses and a robin's egg blue cashmere sweater. He looked around as I prepared the coffee, glance falling on Sasha. She didn't look up, just kept on reading.

He took the drink with a thanks and sat down by the door, checking his watch. Each time someone came in, he looked them over. After forty minutes and a dozen people, he drained the coffee and exited, shoulders a tight line of anger.

I went back over to Sasha, not sure what to think.

"See?" she said.

"How can you field all of them?"

She gestured at herself. "Online I could be anyone."

"So you stand in for the men too?"

"Sure." She licked crumbs from her fingertips.

"How do you make them think you're the same person they've been talking to?"

"They come pre-fooled," she said. "Ready to drop into the seat and talk to the one heart in all of the universe that knows them."

"You disillusion them."

"I teach them what the world is all about. What doesn't kill you makes you stronger, and what you can laugh at, you can live with."

"Is this tied in with that crap Mike was spouting last night? You're an Avatar?"

"A whatty-tar?"

"An Avatar. Mike said something about Avatars and Tarot cards and focuses."

"Mike says all sorts of crap and only ten percent of it actually makes sense. You should know better than to pay attention."

"Like any of this makes sense? Sasha, it's just weird and awful that you do this."

"Fuck you, emo-boy," she said.

I guess I wouldn't have minded so much if I hadn't been having shitty luck with blind dates myself. I'd set up match.com and yahoo.com and OKCupid and FriendFinder and all the rest.

I got replies from women who wanted me to send them money so they could come visit, one hard-core rock chick in Alaska who said flat-out that she didn't do in person but was fine with "long distance commitments", and a Chicago woman who said she'd seen me at a poetry slam when visiting Seattle. She wouldn't post a picture of herself, leaving me to believe that she was actually a fourteen year old boy.

But at least I was getting a trace of hope every night. I'd log on to the computer and check my messages, send a couple of Woo!'s or raves or whatever the flavor of the flirt was. And here was Sasha, skinny unappealing Sasha, dirtying the taste of it. Making it meaningless.

"You're a sadist," I said. "A goddamn sadist."

"Do you think I really like it?" she said.

"Yeah, I think you do. You get off on it, the power of crushing people's dreams," I spat out.

"So I can sit here and watch them die, or I can give them a little closure."

"Seriously, it's screwed up," I said. I stood and went in back to rinse filters.

Mike caught me there later.

"Hey, did you and Sasha have some kind of fight?" he said worriedly.

"I told her she's a twisted fruitcake," I said. "I know you're a friend of hers, but the blind date crap . . . Jesus, it's wrong!"

He held up a hand, forestalling me. "Yeah, well. It's a long story." He looked unhappy in his long-nosed, spaniel-eyed way. "Look, you know how she started coming here?"

I guessed. "Did she work here at some point?"

"No. See, I'd answered this ad in *The Stranger* personals, couple years ago, you see?"

"I don't know what you're trying to say."

"I stood her up," he said. "I told her to meet me here at 10:30 on a Thursday morning, and I was so ready, but then there she was and I chickened out and just served her coffee and watched her wait. She waited half an hour, ate a warmed butter croissant and drank a hot chocolate and left. The next day she showed up at the same time and brought a book with her, something by Camus. Ever since then, she shows up three, four times a week, sometimes more."

"Why didn't you ever say anything?"

"She's an Avatar," he said, his voice dropping in awed intensity. "You felt it too, didn't you? Larger than life. It's what's so frightening, so appealing about her." He stopped, looking at me as though the thought had just occurred to him. "You're attracted to her, too, aren't you? Is that why you're so pissed at her?"

"I'm pissed at her because she's acting out some sort of outrageous psycho-drama that you're enabling and messing with people's lives in the process," I said. "Does she know you're the one she was supposed to meet?"

"Don't you get it?" he said. "It's a genuine supernatural occurrence that happened. I brought her here and she became an Avatar. I don't know how."

My head throbbed. "I need to go home," I said. "I'm going to throw up."

"Go, go." He flapped a hand at me. "But come back when you feel better and don't fight with Sasha anymore."

I didn't show up for work for four days. I went out with old college friends every night to a hip bar in a former barbershop. Vintage hair dryers had been lined up like studded alien helmets along the wall and baggies stuffed with peroxide curls were thumb-tacked to the ceiling. Band after band sang each night's anagrammatic lyrics in smoke-hoarsened voices. When I came back, I was still tipsy. Mike didn't say anything, just eyed me and served up a jumbo mug of the coffee of the day, a Tanzanian roast, before I swept the floors and used clothespins to clip the day's newspapers to the rope racks on the north wall.

Sasha came in a little before noon, pausing when she saw me. She laid her book—some Charles Williams title—down on the table in front of her while sorting through her pockets for bills.

"Clay," she said, carefully unfolding the crumpled ones. "Clay, man, I wanted to say, with the blind dates, I don't mean they can't work. I'm sure they can, I'm sure they do."

The words tumbled through her lips like pebbles, like diamonds, like some fairy tale princess speaking truths.

"The ones that end up here, those are the only doomed ones, you know what I mean? I'm not dissing the love thing. You're a nice guy, and I don't mean to be saying anything about that at all."

The sun gleamed through the window and fell on her straw-like hair, as yellow as the daffodil. I said something reassuring and offered to buy her next coffee, and realized somewhere in the middle of that transaction that one thing Mike had said was true. I was attracted to her, an attraction as mysterious and unexpected as though I'd found an impossible door, opened a closet to find Narnia waiting instead of coats.

What could I do? I lapsed into silence. From then on, Mike and I exchanged glances whenever she came in, both of us acknowledging that lodestone pull, so elemental and so deep within our bodies that we couldn't imagine wanting anyone else.

And I wondered about the Avatars. Was Sasha right, did she fill some cosmic gap? Were there others? Did I know them, had I seen them walking down the street or taking a double hot chocolate, no whip, from my hand?

When he appeared, when the magnet that governed our movements jolted in galvanic response to his presence, Mike and I both knew it instantly. It was something in the way Sasha's breath caught, something in the way her shoulders shifted, the way she set down her cup and lifted her head.

He was clean-jawed as some young Galahad, and there was an aquiline elegance to the planes of his nose, to the curls that clustered on his scalp in Greco-Roman order.

His stare went to Sasha and for once she didn't smile or beckon. She just sat there staring wordlessly at him, her eyes as wide as windows. He came over to her table in three graceful strides and stooped to say something.

"Yes," she said, giving him her hand. "That's me." He drew her hand to his lips and kissed the palm, a gesture as startlingly intimate as though he'd taken off his shirt.

Was he an Avatar as well? Was his job to console selfless women? To pick up people in coffee shops? To piss off unrequited lovers? What role did he fill?

Mike and I stood side by side, watching, ignoring the customer trying to get a refill on her mocha. We stared while Sasha gathered up her things and the young man helped her into her jacket, tucking his arm around her hand.

For a moment she looked back, and it would have been the time to say something then, but Mike's heel ground into my foot. I yelped and she half-laughed, and waved at Mike, and left.

"Give the poor girl a little happiness," Mike said. "Breathing room."

"Will she be back tomorrow?"

He shrugged, finally looking to the counter and the empty mocha cup sitting there. "Maybe. I don't know. Maybe she won't be an Avatar any more."

The customer gathered her drink after he refilled it and looked around, meeting my eyes. She took a step towards me.

I felt an ethereal weight, as though someone were watching me from just past her shoulder.

"Excuse me," she said. "I'm supposed to meet someone here at two fifteen . . ."

The bell over the door jingled as another customer entered: plaid jacket, crew-cut, elderly, his gaze scanning the shop.

I squared my shoulders.

"First off," I said, leaning forward to touch her sleeve. "Everything I told you in my e-mail was a lie."

BELL, BOOK, AND CANDLE

by Leah Bobet

Bell, Book, and Candle met for the five thousand and fifty first time on a rainy November night.

Bell hung her cloche on Cafe Mariposa's gnarled hatstand and left her gloves on. She worked in a fancy dress shop on the other end of town and was wary of needles and pins. Book had got them a table. He hunched over it, tweed and brown, his hair thinning monklike at his spiraling centre part. A rough-shouldered gambling man slipped him a twenty, and he smiled sharks-teeth and made a notation in his brown leather notebook.

"Book," she said in greeting, and ordered a cardamom coffee; her voice plucked violin counterpoint to a glam-fusion-rockabilly band. She hummed a few bars with them, but her singing voice came down rough, stuck on the gears between the march of the wooden soldiers and Jack getting ready for the chorus.

Bell blushed. Book patted her hand. He smelled like binding glue and the sweat of fine horses.

Candle was late.

He arrived on the arm of a Duchess, and bright sea-green ribbons twined through his trouser laces. He hung his hat on the tree that grew through the floor of the Cafe Mariposa, and it sparkled with forest-dark velvet, gold trim, a feather that bowed down in passing to waiters and witches and kings.

"Darlings," he said, bright-flushed and drunken, and perched on his seat like a fairy. His shirt was trimmed with lace. Bell wanted to touch it with her naked hand.

Book pursed his lips. "You're late."

Candle laughed and heads turned. Candle waved and a drink was brought. He tossed it back, and the Cafe Mariposa watched the duck and swell of his long golden throat. "So tell me," he said, his voice striding through shattered conversations and dancing on the shoulders of the stereo music. "What word?"

"No word," Book grunted. Bell's shoulders sagged. No word.

"Of course there's no word." He waved his hand expansively. It glittered with jewels; they refracted light over the tables around. Hands reached out for a million reflected rubies and closed fingers around air. "There's never word."

"Wick," she said, and took his right hand. He pulled it away. "We've just got to be patient."

He shot her a dark look—even his darkest look was dazzling. Hearts trembled, thighs warmed under the edges of his scorn. She put her hands between her knees to keep them prim and straight. "If we were to be called for, they'd have called for us already."

He was likely right. It had been centuries. But Bell always felt like that when he was in the room. "We just have to be patient," she repeated, and because she was the voice he subsided and drank his liquor, a fizzing bright-coloured thing that was not as bright as he.

"One day I won't come when you call me," he said, and kissed her on the cheek with a nip that drew blood.

He left on the arm of a Baron, and the lustre of the moss between the world-tree's bark faded when the door slammed shut behind him.

"Want him?" Book asked, and Bell blushed high and hot, sunburned with desire.

"Everyone does," she said, and put on her hat to go.

The snow fell. The fairy lights were strung and restrung over shopfronts and around trees: the electricity strangled dryads and kept the brownies away. Bell, Book, and Candle gathered at the Cafe Mariposa, where the speakers threw Bing Crosby at crumbling stucco murals of Puerto Rico and false butterflies glimmered in the ceiling foliage.

The leaves had fallen off the hatstand tree. They crunched underfoot on the flagstones as the waiters danced between wrought-iron tables, bearing sugar-plum tea on silver trays. It smelled like winter and cinnamon inside.

Bell ordered hot cider spiced with rum; it warmed her hands through the black kidskin gloves. Book waited in muffler and fedora, his thick suit pilling at the lapels, his breath redolent with sixteen-year-old highland whiskey. "There's word," he said, and scratched another notation onto a curling crimson page.

Bell almost spilled her drink. "For when?"

"Tonight." Book's hands shook. The gamblers stayed well away, threading through the corners of the room and fingering bills in their pockets. Book's hands frayed and fretted at his old quill pen's feathers.

Bell rubbed at the absence on her shoulder blades until they were sore. And asked for more rum in her cider.

Candle swept in like the Puerto Rico summer, wrapped in a red velvet gown that flared and dragged behind him heedless of the dirty churned snow. Holly and mistletoe girdled his waist; the admirers he pressed close gasped as it pricked their bellies and then stared after him, dabbing the blood away. He took off his curled honey-coloured wig and doffed it to Bell elaborately, and there was a chorus of laughter and sighs.

"There's word," Bell told him. Flat and unmusical.

Candle clenched a fist. The chandeliers in the Cafe Mariposa trembled, hissing with electricity, and every bulb blew in a shower of sparks.

Bell, Book, and Candle walked single file down Dry Street South in the snow, picking their way around puddles: Bell's patent-leather boots and Candle's stiletto heels clacked one-two against the concrete. Book consulted notes taken in his own arcane hand, scribblings and arrows and dashes and dots, and they stopped at the Grand Cathedral at the centre of the city. It twisted with sculpture and screaming mouths and rubble: it was long-ago ruined. Bell tightened her hat.

The doors of the broken cathedral were open. The ironbound wood hung slick with rot: a night insect crawled out of one hole and into another. Bell kept her hands clasped behind her back and squinted into cobwebbed darkness.

"Book," she whispered. "What do you see?"

Book took her elbow, eased her carefully aside. "An altar with the gems dug out," he said. "Tapers rusted into their chandeliers. Rats in the nave. Bats in the belfry. The ringer's rope, frayed, and the vestments in dust." He paused. "Light."

They followed the light.

It glowed soft down halls with niches of marble, stripped of their statues and gilt. It glowed brighter along the curving stairs to the crypts, the sea-kissed crypts where coffins floated and the dead screamed to be saved from drowning whenever it rained all night. Bell lifted her skirts and followed Book down into a chapel cleared and dusted, ringed with men in coats of brushed, severe black wool. They wore inquisitorial masks. Bell's skirts hissed and tangled from her trembling.

"We've come," Bell said, and the room echoed with ringing like a cathedral mass. "We didn't think you'd call again."

"We are still here." A voice, bitter as strong coffee. "We'll always be here."

"We . . . we serve," Bell said, hesitant. It had been so long since they'd been asked for. She'd forgotten all the words.

Candle took her hand and squeezed it so it hurt.

"Who is brought before us?" asked the man with the voice like coffee, and the gathered rumbled a reply, a name magnified into nothing by the stones of the falling crypt. Men moved up to surround them, cloaked and hooded, marked with cross and censer and axe.

"We separate him, together with his accomplices and abettors, from the precious body and blood of the Lord," he began, and Bell's back straightened with the anxiety of ritual, the reflexes of performance. Someone whimpered beyond the light, mashed flat by cloth and rope. Words blurred in her ears. Voice built in her throat, hot and poisonous.

"Ring the bell," the high magistrate said, and the cork on her mouth loosed and Bell screamed.

"Close the book," the high magistrate said, and fairy glamour passed over Book's eyes and smoothed them away.

"Snuff the candle," the high magistrate said, and struggling to contain him, the soldiers of the Inquisition slit Candle's throat.

He crumbled to his knees shedding fringe and feather, and his head hit the flagstones and burst. A smell of beeswax and ripe summer wafted from it, and then the body was cold.

The man in the box screamed and did not stop screaming, and Bell wanted to scream for herself, but her throat was empty now and her tongue would not obey. She fell to her knees and dug kidskin into the rough-grouted stones of the Grand Cathedral.

"So be it," the priests intoned, and the mass dispersed at five past midnight.

B ell led Book home, weeping all the way, to his loft above the racetrack. The garret was stuffed with shedding paperback novels; their pages filtered the light of the rain-streaked slanting windows. She brewed him weak tea in a battered tin kettle and sat him down at table. The tablecloth was stained with ink.

He fumbled for it tentatively, mewling in the back of his age-spotted throat. Bell took off her gloves and put her hands on his, guided them to the chipped china mug bought decades ago from some tourist shop down the coast. Glaze chipped off as she wrapped his hands around it, left a long scratch, fingertip to thumbpad. Blood welled and she sucked the wound, still weeping in noiseless gulps.

When dawn came the skin where Book's eyes had been melted away, and he opened new dark eyes, quick as ferrets. "You've been crying," he said, and she nodded. Her voice burned in her throat again, warmed it like a heartbeat.

"We can't do this again," she croaked in a voice that had been made to sing not scream, and Book nodded.

Bell went back to the dress shop. Her manager scolded her for the scratch on her hand. She wore demure black lace gloves to work until it healed, a seamed line that curved her hand into a fist when she slept. Book went back to the mold-dampened secondhand shop where he spent his days presiding behind the counter, fingering paper and the curve of illuminated letters. He stared at the coin his customers gave for yellowed textbooks too long, the faces of sheepish men who asked him the odds for whole minutes. People avoided his eyes: too young and nervous.

Nobody saw Candle.

The snow melted. Green and careful shoots wended through the soil into the air, budded, burst. The tree in the centre of the Cafe Mariposa bloomed with pink Japanese blossoms, white apple blooms, drunken lavender lilacs, crocus, and mint. New pegs grew from the trunk to hold hats and capes and light spring wraps, and each was tipped with roses.

Bell and Book met in the Cafe Mariposa when the weather broke for certain. The tree stroked her hair with lilypetal fingers when she took off her cloche to hang it up. Book was shaggy and ragged and wore no hat or coat. There was an inkstain on his earlobe.

"I've been calling him night and day," Bell said. There were pouchy shadows beneath her eyes.

"I've been writing him every morning," Book said, and took her hand.

"What if he didn't come back?"

The wind coming through the patio heard and fell flat on the tiled floor.

"We've a job," Book said doubtfully. "It's why we're here. It's why they haven't called us back up yet."

Unless there's nobody left to call us back, Bell thought for the five thousandth time, and didn't speak it. Some things were too terrible to speak.

One day I won't come when you call me, the wind mimicked, and Bell shivered at the touch of winter. "We can't do this again," she said, and led him out of the Cafe Mariposa.

The dress shop where fine ladies bought ermine-trimmed capes lay north, along cobbled avenues lit with converted gas streetlamps, where tinsel fluttered in the wind every month of the year. The junk shop where students prowled through Book's tailings lay east, through drab apartments and noodle shops where the painfully young quoted philosophy to each other all night. Bell and Book went west, west where the gutters clanked with needles and the lonely walked the streets, hungry for love or drink or junk.

They stopped where a workman stood eyeing the whores, across the street from their long-limbed display, stuffing hands in his pockets and taking them out again.

"We're looking for Candle," Bell said like a flute. "He lights up the world wherever he goes."

"I know a Candle," the workman sighed, "but she's a woman, a beautiful woman with a gown that's crimson and green."

"He—she, whichever," Bell snapped. "Where has he gone?"

"I wish I knew," he said sad-eyed, "but ask the whores; I met her walking with them, and her eyes were nothing like the sun . . ."

They crossed the street. Book shuffled and kicked garbage with his cracked wingtip shoes. A crumpled wrapper hit a drunk slouched between buildings, and he railed at them in a voice like hours upon the rack.

"We're looking for Candle," Bell said nervously, plucking at her skirts. The whores were bright and painted just like him, but it was false and made her ache deep down in her gut. "He is varicoloured as a peacock and arrogant and sweet and men and women both would do anything to hold him."

"We know a Candle," they murmured seductively, and Book shifted and hopped foot to foot. "But he is not varicoloured but dun grey, and not arrogant but cowed, and went into the Dark House to die."

Bell swallowed tears and clenched hands in her skirts. "Where?" she asked, and they pointed.

The road curved south. The road curved through the projects, the falling-down Old Quarter, the factories and cemeteries and emptied into the yard of the Great Cathedral, screaming-stone spires melting and cracking in the damp spring air. There was a guard at the churchyard door, armed with guns, leather, a chain, a frown. Book gave him a damp, crumpled roll of small bills and they passed inside.

The doors of the confessionals were cut into counters,

and a row of black-suited madams stood within with keys and cashboxes, sour lemon eyes.

"We're looking for Candle," Bell said, low and tired. "He burns too fast, and he stings the back of your throat when he's almost gone, and you lie awake wanting him at night even so."

"I know a Candle," the madam said, "but he is with the Marquis, and you'll have to wait your turn."

She gave them a number on a plastic card. They waited.

"I . . . I forgot how bad it was," Bell whispered in Book's inkstained ear as the flagellants came and went, trailing love-sweat and tears across the stones of the Great Cathedral.

"We all did," he whispered back. The crypt lurked below them. It gnawed cold at their toes. He took her hand and squeezed it. "Not your fault. It's our job. They wouldn't have given it if it was . . ."

He could not finish.

A loinclothed novice called their number, and they followed him up the slippery stairs of the hollowed cathedral towers. The stained-glass windows had been smashed long ago, back when the inquisitors were put to the sword, and nobody had replaced them. A few fingers of spring rain gusted through the jagged remnants.

Bell and Book found Candle curled up on a bed, bleeding onto black satin sheets that wouldn't show the stain. He shuddered when the door opened. The wounds were already closing.

"You're alive—" Bell blurted.

"I'm alive," he whispered, arms wrapped around dimpled knees. "I'm alive. I'm alive."

Bell stripped off her white springtime gloves and touched his cheek with her bare hand, nails dark red and trimmed boy-short as to not catch and pull fine silks. "You're alive," she gasped and pressed him close.

He was Candle. He was not made to die.

"I love you," she whispered, "I love you, I always have."

"I don't love you," he said dully, and hid his eyes behind her sleeve.

"S'okay," Bell said, and ran her other hand through his hair. It was bound and garlanded with thorns. She picked them out one by one. They stung her fingers to bleeding. "We weren't made for this. We're not this anymore."

"Bent to it," Candle said, and flickered the cold of the tomb. "It's our job now. Got no other."

He was cold, too cold. His hair lay rank with smoke.

It set her to burning.

"Never again," she told him fierce as trumpets, and he sagged into her arms.

She took him home to her flat over the Aniseed Bakery, where old men drank strong coffee in quail-egg cups and told the same stories daily about the last war. She fed him figs and strong cheese, champagne and lobster, and sang him lullabyes in her crow-voice when he shook at night. She hung his room with peacock feathers; they swayed in the breeze and swept rose and poppy petals in tea-leaf patterns on the floor.

She lay awake when he slipped in at three, four in the morning, and stripped off his paints and pearls and torn pantyhose, and ached as he hummed hearthsongs.

On Midsummer morning he stayed out until seven, past sunrise, and brought in the post with him. Bell sat at the kitchen table with a mug of weak tea, stirring it this way and that with her lace-covered index finger. "What's that?" she asked, alto. The bitterness seeped through her fingers and soured the tea.

Candle held it out between fingernails painted like galaxies. It was tied with a ribbon, musty, yellowed, stamped with symbols in running black ink.

"From Book," she said, and put on her boots and hat.

Bell, Book, and Candle met at the Cafe Mariposa, and

Book hunched over the wrought iron table. Ladybugs fluttered around his balding head and landed, freckled with concern.

"There's word," Book said, and squeezed his old hands in hers. They came away bloody.

"Book," she said, mouth open. "What's happened?"

"I lost a bet," he said, and closed his eyes—Book never lost bets. The seams between lid and lash were so thin she thought they did not exist. "They made me call."

Bell caught her breath. It tasted like a poison scream deep in her throat. She looked up at Candle's eyes, and the life in them flickered, guttered, dimmed.

"Run," she choked.

Wool-coated men blocked the door to the Cafe Mariposa, even though it was high summer. Wool-coated men lined up on the patio, a masked and cloaked barrier between the glass-dangle birds and the street. Bell backed against Candle and Candle picked up Book. They had not been called for centuries: she'd watched the inquisitors put to the sword and wept, oh help her, *wept* for the loss of their purpose.

Where had they all *come* from?

Somewhere behind them struggled a young man, bound at wrist and ankle and roughly gagged. His terror straightened her spine. "We've come," Bell said automatic, and clamped her hands over her mouth.

The high magistrate smiled. She could see it through his mask. She could see through his flesh and bones. "Do you serve?" he asked, and the cream on the tables soured.

"Run," Candle whispered, and levered into the tree.

Bell dug one leather-booted toe into the gaps of the hatstand tree and climbed. Rose-thorns pricked her stockinged legs. Bell grabbed the knobby hat hooks of generations past, levered herself up between the rivers of moss, the beetles that fished them and lived on their shores. Candle flitted upwards like a burning rainbow, Book slung over his shoulder, birds querying anxiously into his delicate pierced ears. The inquisitors swept in after them, dangled their prey on a hat-hook, displacing a thin shawl printed with acres of puffy-clouded sky. Thorns thickened and spiraled about them, tugged at her feet, blocked out the light.

Candle reached down and hauled Bell into the nest of branches of the Cafe Mariposa's tree. The thorns closed around them and sealed the exit. Bell, Book, and Candle huddled together in the waving, endless leaves and breathed hard.

"Do you serve?" the high magistrate called, and she quivered.

"You speak," Book whispered, arms cradling his slit belly. "Just don't answer."

Bell pressed her palms against her ears and shut her eyes tight tight, clamped her lips down on the words that centuries of ritual had hardwired onto her tongue. She shook her head once, twice, focused on the jerk and fly of her short-cut hair instead of the burn in her throat.

Won't. She thought. *Never again.*

Where had they all *come* from?

The acid bubbled up into her mouth. It was going to burn her voice out, it was going to scorch her throat for good and she'd never sing again even in a voice mutilated from centuries of screaming—

"We serve," she choked out, and wailed as the ritual took her.

"Keep her quiet," Book hissed—he scribbled and scratched, dipped pen in his own seeping blood to keep it wet and live.

"We separate him, together with his accomplices and abettors—" the magistrate said, and the tree shook with anger, leaves raining down in a rustling diving assault. "Ring the bell."

Weeping, she opened her mouth to speak, and the words were stopped by Candle's lips upon hers. Candle's tongue in her mouth. Candle's hands on her waist.

"Ring the bell?" the high magistrate called, a fearful note in his voice, but she felt nothing but Candle's kiss.

Bell spoke. Book carried messages, saw, described, deciphered. And Candle—Candle burned. Candle's kisses warmed her to the centre, set her hips rising below his flower hands, shuddered through her like the end of a spell of rain. His hands danced upwards, splayed and expert upon her breasts, and the doom receded from her throat.

She smelled cinnamon and honey and baking on his skin. He lifted her skirts with one practiced caress.

"Ring the bell—" might have come up plaintive, and then Book notched a satisfied note in pen and blood in his battered notebook, and silence. The pen dripped red-black on the page, and Book's book looked much bigger for a hot, fevered moment: millions of pages and dates and names, the cover all of spidersilk, the ink blotting out each name sooner or later until it was pages and pages of night sky.

Candle parted her legs, and the tree shuddered with her as he pressed inside.

"Once I was an angel with a bright sword," she gasped, whispered, wept. "Once I was a guard on the road to the city, at the gate to the city, and I stood alone and burned. Once I had a voice that sang not screamed, and wings of powdered silver and when they scratched me I did not bleed but sunlight poured out of the holes in my flesh and I would have swept down flaming and singing and they would fall upon their knees with the alleluia chorus—"

"Shh," Candle whispered back into her mouth. "Shh."

When it was done she lay curled-up in the arms of the tree, feeling its slow sap heartbeat spiked with the scent of tea leaves and time, the faint clinking of dishes and the hiss of a barista machine. When it was done she shook herself like a cat and sat up, summer light filtering through the branches onto her hand. Candle leaned against a branch opposite, looking cool and sleek as ever, his golden hair touched with flame.

"There's no word," Book said, still holding his stomach. The bleeding had slowed. He sat better now.

"Thank you," she whispered, to him, to both of them. "I couldn't have . . . I couldn't have not spoken."

"That's why we work together," Candle said, and wiped the kisses off his soft, hot mouth.

Bell, Book, and Candle were to meet for the five thousand and fifty fourth time on the eve of summer turning to autumn, with the leaves just yellowing at the tips on the broad avenues between Dry Street and the open plains. Bell did not call; there would be no word. But she went down to the Cafe Mariposa.

She ordered a Korean drink of cinnamon and honey and sipped it slow; it reminded her of the taste of Candle's skin. It reminded her of the smell of his bedsheets, which she had not changed since the night they slew the Inquisition, since the night he sauntered out the door of Cafe Mariposa and did not return for his feathers and pearls. She slept in his alcove now, restless with the inadequacy of her own skin. But if she thought of him, sometimes, it was enough.

Book had not seen him. Bell had not seen Book. He never lost a bet, and he had lost one somehow, and would not speak of how or why. All she knew was that the tattered Great Cathedral had burned from the bottom up in the week after midsummer, and pages, thousands of pages swirled in the air like ash and settled upon its gutted corpse.

They were keeping something from her.

But she'd remembered wings.

Book came into the Cafe Mariposa with a new hunch to his walk, his pocket stuffed with pawn tags and a track card in his hatband. The newspaper was folded under his arm with his brown leather notebook, and a hardcover romance peeked out between its pages. He sat at the wrought iron table and dropped his parcel on its glass top.

"Bell," he said, and ordered a double shot of whiskey. He looked old. But his wrinkles were smiling.

"Is he coming?" she said, with a catch in her voice.

Book shook his head. "It doesn't say."

They waited.

At five to midnight Candle swept through the door on the arms of two girl-children barely old enough to drink, their dark eyes shining with his reflected light. His legs were wrapped in knotted silk scarves and his torso bare and muscled, and he wore no hat but a vineyard wreath, which he hung on a hook on the World Tree as he passed its thick trunk by. He stroked their hair and sent them to the counter with a wink and a wave, then perched backwards on his wrought-iron chair, cradled its back between his thighs.

"What's the word?" he asked, with a saucy wink and a bow to the Count three tables down.

"No word," Book breathed, and sagged back in his chair.

"No word," Bell said, and took his hand. "Wick, you'll—"

He kissed her hand elaborately and something moved in her throat. "I'll see you next month," he said, and stood, and lovers took each others' hands and snuck away to the rooms veiled in silk and gauze in the hotel upstairs.

Bell, Book, and Candle left the Cafe Mariposa just before close.

Bell sung the changes all the way home.

THE TARRYING MESSENGER

by Michael J. DeLuca

Pedals pumping, her breathing steady, Molly crests the hill, downshifts and coasts across the desert plateau.

Rhythm. Perpetuity. The whirring, watch-like mechanism of a ten-speed bike, kept from obsolescence and the verges of rust by meticulous care. The comforting, controlled bend of a pair of straight braids in hot, dry wind. The necessity of holding her mouth firmly closed to keep out the dust. The intensity of coloration imposed upon bulbous red boulders by prescription sunglasses, and the wash of white that intrudes from beyond the edge of the lens. Molly thinks of the scientist whose job it is to make vibrant and dynamic the bleak images from the surface of Mars, and how she herself, via those tinted lenses, performs the same task.

A highway sign sails past, like a fellow satellite on a different trajectory. A town rises out of the earth's curvature: heat-shimmers, irrigation, green landscaping made fantastic by contrast with the pale colors of the desert. And on the town's outskirts, high atop sandstone cliffs like courses of bricks laid by the hand of God, a man-made structure gleams—all stark, straight lines and perpendicularity, concrete and glass. Art in conflict with nature. A church.

Below it, a parking lot full of windblasted cars, sparkling. Tourists—of whom Molly does not count herself one, though she has never been to Sedona before and does not mean to stay. She isn't here to leave her mark upon the landscape, or to capture part of it to take home. She's just a traveler.

Molly angles away from the highway, tracing the smooth curve of the white line exactly, the ten-speed's wheels holding to it like a rail. She squeezes the brakes. Her sneaker scrapes against pavement.

A water fountain. It bubbles up hot and slowly grows colder. Molly reminds herself not to drink too much. She fills her water bottles, though she has to queue up again with the tourists for each one.

She tightens the straps on her saddlebags, walks the bike to the foot of the stairway where tourists wait to ascend the face of the cliff. A small crowd collects there: Germans, Texans, Japanese, children kicking at pebbles, babies sagging in the heat.

And in their midst, an angel. Golden. Rigid. Immobile, strapped by its legs to the bed of a truck. It stands with knees bent and wings half-spread, as though just arriving, or about to depart. In one hand it carries a trumpet, in the other a scroll. A messenger.

Molly cranes her neck, muscles pleasantly sore from the posture of cycling. The steeple, stark white against the cloudless sky, surmounted by nothing. She imagines the angel up there. The end of its journey. Nobody will see it from this close again. From those distant, gilded lips, no one will hear its message.

Another week and Molly's summer journey will end at the Pacific. A plane ride home, then back to her parents and school. The thought scares her. She has grown too accustomed to motion.

Hydraulic brakes blast. A tractor-trailer pulls in off the highway, carrying a crane. Squat Navajo workmen push the crowd back from the angel, setting up cones.

She feels faint, lightheaded. Too many miles, in too much heat. The angel swims before her eyes. She decides, in the interest of safety, to allow herself a rest.

Molly hitches a ride into town. She sits in the rear of a pickup, the soles of her sneakers pressed together, one hand gripping the crossbar of the bike. She stretches her thighs, the tips of her braids tickling her shins. The broken red cliffs and the church recede. She sips water, already tepid, and thinks about the mindset of the West—of the kind of society that could exist among such spiritual landscape, yet feel the need to interrupt its beauty with a monument to God. The people riding in the cab of the pickup, a couple with a toddler—she wonders what makes their own mindset so different from hers. On the East Coast, churches are small, unassuming. It's the ideas they enclose that betray them.

In town, she buys lunch: avocado, sprouts and pickles on a crunchy baguette, iced green tea sweetened with agave. She retreats with her meal from the too-cold air conditioning, sits at a table on the sidewalk. Red rock mountains rise in the distance at either end of the long, main street. Rows of Tibetan prayer pennants strung between phone poles. A shop sells turquoise, woven blankets, kachina dolls; another beside it, astrological symbols, crystal pyramids, recordings of waterfalls. She visits these places, touching objects, looking the proprietor in the eye because she feels obliged to, because that's what her trip across the country is supposed to be about. Truth versus indoctrination. The real versus the preconceived. She left the ten-speed locked outside the bank, but she carries the bike helmet with her, swinging from her wrist. It reminds her of her transience here— that none of what she does or sees need stick, or mean anything at all.

"You have a glow about you," says the plump Latina lady in the crystal shop. "An aura of detoxification and change."

Molly laughs nervously. "What, like I'm pregnant?" The joke comes out meaner than she meant.

The lady smiles thinly and explains about auras. How they're particularly visible in the desert air, the same way the stars at night seem magnified. "Your body is expelling toxins on both the physical and spiritual planes. There's a buildup of negative feeling in your chakras that has suddenly begun to break free."

Molly brushes at her arms. Pedaling in desert heat, her pores produce not sweat but salt, a whitish haze on clothes and skin. "I've been riding a bike across country."

"For how long?" asks the lady.

"Not long enough."

"That would explain it." The lady places a tumbled gemstone on a silver chain around Molly's neck. "Rhodochrosite. It's believed to foster acceptance and serenity during periods of radical change."

The shop has mirrors everywhere. Molly hides a sour face. It's a pink stone. Pink, with white impurities, and a startling streak of black. Makes her think of her mother. She can't buy anything anyway. No room for trinkets in her budget, let alone room in her bags. She starts to pull it off. The lady gently grabs her wrists. "I'm sorry. I can't let you do that. Negative energy, you understand—its release contaminates all those around you. I'm not asking you to buy the pendant. In fact, why don't you take it? A gift. Otherwise, I'm afraid I'll have to ask. . . . Please get out of my store and don't come back."

Speechless, Molly drops the pendant back around her neck.

On the way to the door, she passes a bulletin board full of ads for psychics, reiki, acupuncture. Hot springs excursions. Horseback tours of the canyons, Hopi ruins. A white flyer, pinned at the center of the board, shows a drawing of the church on the cliff. In the drawing, the angel is already in place atop the spire—just a stick-figure really, except for the wings. A halo surrounds it like a lens flare.

Temple of the Line
Celebrate the Raising of the Angel
Sunday Service at Dawn

She pushes through the door into the heat. The pink pendant sparkles.

She imagines the church service inside that giant white monolith—windows behind the altar opening on desertscape, scraggly clusters of evergreens, red buttes. Someone in a robe, attempting to assign it a meaning different from the one she's come to on her own.

What day is it? Time blurs, spent rolling down the highway to wind and the whirr of gears. She waits for the bank sign to come around. *107° F. 1:12 PM. Sat., Sept. 6.*

A man strolls by in a sandwich board, his shadow sharp against the sidewalk. The words on the board warn of Armageddon, with an illustration of a landscape in flames. A big saguaro cactus going up like a devil's fork. Molly hasn't seen saguaros yet—not far enough south. Anyone who takes Revelations at face value must necessarily be immune to irony.

He catches her eye, or she catches his.

Molly breathes in, steady. Just some crazy prophet. Trying to hand out pamphlets and failing, repelling passersby as though surrounded by a magnetic field. He even looks like Jesus.

"This is it," he's saying, his voice projecting like a circus barker's. "Yep, the end of the world. Want to know how I know? We've broken our trust with the Lord. He gives us dominion over His creatures, asks us to care for His creation, and we do? Make golf courses out of deserts. We shouldn't *be* here. God made deserts as a place of trial, of holy cleansing. He made them beautiful to give us hope during punishment. Jesus came to the desert when he doubted. Moses and his people wandered here for forty years. Now we turn our deserts into resorts. The rich flock here, and the desperate follow. In Revelations, God threatens to punish us for our arrogance, to turn the skies black and the seas to poison. We beat Him to it. *This* Eden is artificial, a false and fragile paradise. We ourselves are raising the Sign of our end! You all have seen it: this new Temple of the Line, with its paralyzed messenger angel, borne to earth by its own weight—the weight of greed and indifference!" He lifts a sheaf of the white flyers in his fist, tears them down the center, throws them into the street. "Repent! Damn you people, repent!"

Molly is a person of conviction too. She just never managed to distill her convictions to a size that will fit on a t-shirt. This man has found a way around that. His t-shirt is almost the size of a billboard.

She falls into step beside him.

His eyes widen, crow-footed and gray through the panes of her sunglasses. The sandwich board hobbles his gait, trips him up every few strides. Molly has never engaged with a crazy prophet before. In Boston and New York, it's easy enough to look the other way. But this is the point of her journey, isn't it? An attempt to understand.

She forces her fingers to quit fiddling with the rhodochrosite stone. "What's your name?" she asks.

"Daniel."

"Do you really believe in all that, Daniel?"

His face reddens. Molly realizes that she's questioned the faith of a madman. She braces herself to be called harlot, Jezebel. Her fingers tighten on the helmet strap, ready to clock him if she has to.

His shoulders slump. "Doesn't it sound like I believe it? Am I not convincing?"

"No. . . . I mean, I believe that you believe it. I even agree with you, mostly."

"Mostly. Well, you seem to be the only one." He sighs. Tosses the rest of his flyers in the trash. "Which part is it you disagree with?"

"The God part," she says.

"God is the point."

"Well, that and your methods."

He kicks at his sandwich board. "Hmm. Very wise." She is surprised to find this prophet capable of sarcasm.

Daniel's voice is raw from shouting at the sinners. She gives him what's left of her tea. They talk about belief, the natural world. Whether it's more profound for beauty to arise out of meaningless chaos or a divine clockmaker's plan. He shocks her by quoting the Koran.

Assuredly the creation
Of the heavens
And the earth
Is a greater matter
Than the creation of humankind;
Yet most people understand it not.

He says he came here from the Northwest, from Portland. To preach. This is his pilgrimage, his trial.

Molly explains she came here looking for perspective. There's something about where she grew up, who she grew up as, that she can't help but question. Her father the preacher. Her mother. Their faith.

Daniel offers to show her his own perspective.

It feels dangerous opening up to him, even this tiny bit. She's alone in the desert with some crazy doomsayer. With whom she happens to agree. The pendant swings.

They stop in front of the bank for Molly to collect the

ten-speed. She hangs the helmet from the handlebars.

He takes her to his pulpit: a little patch of wilderness surrounding a dry creek at the north edge of town. Sage, dust, a lizard or two, until a roadrunner appears at the top of the draw. A housing development encroaches: clay roofing tiles, uniform landscaping, smooth curbs. A mile away across the desert to the east, cars pull in and out of the church parking lot, points of blinding sunlight reflected in plastic and glass.

Daniel shrugs out of the sandwich board, climbs up on an outcrop of rock. "In other parts of the world, people come to such a place to pray. They walk, some for hundreds of miles. They make offerings they can't afford. Here people come to take pictures."

Underneath the rocky overhang, a sleeping bag. A military-surplus olive sack. A cross wedged into a crevice.

While he preaches God's word to the emptiness, Molly turns the bike upside-down on its handlebars. She checks the pressure in the tires, oils the dust out of the gears, readjusts the left front brake pad an eighth of an inch. She listens to him proselytizing the creatures of the wilderness. Like Saint Francis, preaching to birds on the roadsides because he knows they won't talk back.

The clank and shudder of the crane through dry, sweltering air. The angel dangles on a wire, flashing gold as it ascends.

"Are you going to the service tomorrow?" she asks.

The crow's feet around his eyes wrinkle like cracks in parched earth. "You think I'd abase my faith to *that*? They make it out to be a messenger from God. Then they imprison it in gold. They freeze that benevolent expression to its face. They petrify the Word upon the angel's lips! To honey-coat the message of the Lord? Worse than gilding a lily. How could I worship under a symbol like that?"

Molly flips the bike upright, resettles the saddlebags

astride the rear wheel. "Know thy enemy?" she says. "I'm going."

"Then I'll see you there. I'll stand outside the doors of that false temple and preach! I'll turn people away. I'll convince them. That angel—if you could unseal its lips, and somehow get that trumpet to them, it would herald the coming of the End."

Molly swings her leg over the crossbar. "Yeah."

"Don't try to tell me you don't believe it—in a few years you won't be able to ride a bike through this town without dying of heat stroke. A few years after that, God will turn this whole place back into a real desert. Lifeless. Like the deserts of the moon."

That's the trouble, Molly thinks, with wearing your convictions on your sleeve. Or on a sandwich board. Even when you're right, it makes you look crazy. And then how can you ever convince anybody?

She doesn't say it, though. It would come out sounding cruel.

Everything is so much easier to take in, orbiting past it on a bike at uniform speed.

Evening approaches. The angel, mounted in its high place, gives off a color like molten rock that sunglasses do nothing to mitigate. Most days, she'd be long gone by now, halfway to the next town, the gears whizzing beneath her, wheels glued to the white line.

Molly checks into a motel across from a mini-golf course. She digs a crumpled summer dress out of the bottom of the saddlebags and irons out the wrinkles. The motel-room door, half open on an evening surprisingly cool. Grasshoppers singing in the waste grass between the putting greens and the desert. The pink stone, dangling from her neck, its color muted.

She finds her cellphone in a zipper pocket. She calls her mother.

"Molly? Anything wrong?"

"How's Dad?"

"Better, I guess. You've been gone a long time. But he's still mad, if that's what you mean."

"Mom, I'm going to church tomorrow."

"Really. Why?"

"I don't know. To make you happy?"

"Well, that's a nice thought—but Molly, your father doesn't need you torturing yourself on his behalf. And neither do I. We've accepted that you're not interested in faith. You've made that abundantly clear."

"Mom, I *want* to go."

"Oh you do. Why? Is it one of those old mission churches? I bet that would be a great cultural experience."

"No, it's. . . ." She doesn't know why she's going, why she's staying here the night instead of some campground way out in the hills. She's stalling. Because she doesn't want to go home. "Have a good night, Mom. Love you."

"Okay. I love you too."

She can't bike to the church. The dress would rip, get caught in the gears. She can't ask for a ride; she doesn't want to expel any more of her toxins on this town's spirituality than she already has. It's only a few miles from here to the church. She can walk, if she gives herself time. It won't mean waking up much earlier than usual.

She sets the clock alarm by the bed. When it buzzes the next morning, she dresses. Hesitates a moment over the pendant, in the end puts it on.

The sidewalks emanate faint heat. The bank sign says *Sun., Sept. 7. 64° F. 4:16 AM.* Her sandals swing from her fingers. Her sneakered footfalls make no sound.

The lady from the crystal shop was right about the stars. As the town shrinks behind her, the predawn sky presses close, crowding in against the cliffs. The Andromeda galaxy, spinning overhead. Betelgeuse and Capella on the horizon. The pale line of the highway. A hundred satellites sail past in an hour.

It feels funny to walk such a long way. Her steps come too easily without the pedals to resist her.

At the midpoint between night and dusk, a silhouette, small and thin, distinguishes itself from the shadow on the highway ahead of her. A person. Daniel maybe. She quickens her pace, tries to catch him.

The stars and galaxies fade. A rosy glow, white-streaked like rhodochrosite, insinuates itself upon the sky. Daniel's silhouette sharpens, then disappears.

In the parking lot of the temple, Molly passes the pastor's car, the empty flatbed and the crane. No sign of Daniel. She sits on the steps and switches her sneakers for the sandals.

People begin to arrive and file into the church. Baggy eyes, expectation. No Daniel to deter them. Molly expected more of him. She fiddles with the pendant, almost wants to shout at them herself.

The dark, curving outlines of the angel's wings against the sunrise. The slowly growing sheen of gold. Giving up on Daniel, Molly takes a place at the back of the line.

Inside, four immense panes of glass impose a frame upon the desertscape in the shape of a towering cross. The bright line of the dawn progresses across the red boulders and juniper like the raising of a shade, accentuating contours, valleys, crags.

Molly finds a seat among the cramped pews. She feels tiny. Alone. Like sitting in a planetarium after the projector goes off, when the floor lights come up and the canvas behind the cosmos is revealed. The people around her make murmurs of awe over the hum of the central air. Molly shivers, rubs the goosebumps from her arms.

The pastor enters, silk vestments rustling. A pale face unnaturally young. He taps the microphone. Behind him, the glorious, red-golden vista of broken hills and sage and otherworldly buttes is as still as though it were a shoebox diorama, and Molly thinks that whatever he says, she won't be able to forget the frame around it, the stark filter of holiness, like the knee-jerk impulse of the scientist afraid he'll lose his funding unless he dyes the Martian desert the color everyone expects.

The sun breaks the horizon, spilling light directly into Molly's eyes. She squints; she left her sunglasses behind.

Then he speaks, and it's worse than she imagined. The crisis of faith—Christ in the wilderness. The sermon Molly's father threw at her back as she fled.

Throw yourself off, the devil keeps saying. Throw yourself off the cliff.

She stands abruptly, both hands in front of her eyes to block the light. Her legs bump awkwardly against the knees of the people between her and the aisle. The crystal shop lady sits in the back row dressed in white, her face beatific. Molly covers the pendant. She hurries through the doors into the morning.

Her sneakers are right where she left them, behind a rock by the top of the stairs. And the angel is still there, at the top of its pinnacle, never to fold its wings or fly or blow its trumpet, frozen in its posture of change. Molly wriggles her toes as she steps out of her sandals. By the time she gets back to her bike it will be hot again.

Molly crouches, her back to a boulder. She ties the laces of one sneaker, switches to the other. The angel sparkles. She's thinking of that silhouette on the road before dawn. Thinking about angels and auras and belief and air conditioning and how none of it compares to the feel of the sun.

Then a black shape appears against the white concrete of the church steeple, like an afterimage left on her eye by the sunrise. She blinks and tilts her head. The shape resolves into a man, climbing up that sheer white face towards the angel.

Daniel. She stops the word in her throat, afraid of distracting him, of making him fall.

No handholds, no purchase, at an angle steep and

tapering. Yet he keeps climbing, all the way to the tiny platform at the pinnacle. He grips the angel's ankle. He pulls himself up onto the disc at the top of the spike. He looks the angel in the eye. Defiance. A challenge.

Molly gawks. He's decided to act instead of speak. Something's changed him—was it her? She leaves the left sneaker untied.

Daniel grasps at the scroll and horn, tries to wrest them from the angel's grasp. He wants to take them for himself. To be the messenger. The angel resists. The dull figure and the glittering one shift and totter, circling, trading feints and lunges like two wrestlers on a Grecian urn. Their strength is evenly matched. Likewise their determination. It only remains for one of them to make a misstep.

There's too much glare to tell who falters first. The angel beats its wings, but the feathers are fused, the weight of the gold too immense. Daniel yells something incoherent. Triumph.

They fall. The crash of their impact echoes from the buttes.

Molly clambers over the boulders. Her loose sneaker trips her up; she loses it. Her foot slips, and red rock rips skin from her knee. It stings. She leaves a little blood behind.

Where the flawless concrete meets the rough sandstone, she finds Daniel's body, shattered. There's nothing left of him to cry over or comfort. Her tears are toxic, swallowed up by the parched earth.

There was life inside him. Bones, a heart. Conviction. The angel was hollow.

The scroll is just a lump of metal. It will never unroll, and if it did, what would be written there no one could read or comprehend. But the trumpet . . . Molly picks it up, looks through it.

The trumpet is real.

Soon, the pastor and his congregation will rush from the

church. Molly will have been the only witness. What should she tell them? What will they think?

Her mind conflates her father and the frozen angel, Daniel and herself. Her bike, back in Sedona, casting its motionless shadow over the manicured grass of the mini-golf course. Her braids, dangling straight in the windless desert morning. Her heartbeat, inexorable. Blinding sunlight. Blood trickling down her knee.

Molly scrambles, slips and stumbles over the boulders and back to the doors of the church. She waits, balanced, uneven, on one sneakered and one stockinged foot.

The doors swing open, and she lifts the trumpet to her lips.

THE OCCULTATION

by Laird Barron

In the middle of playing a round of Something Scary they got sidetracked and fucked for a while. After they were done fucking, they lighted cigarettes. Then, they started drinking. Again.

—My God. Look at that, she said. Her mouth sagged a little.

He grunted like he did when he wasn't listening.

—Hey! I'm creeped out, she said.

—By what? He balanced two shot glasses on his lap and tried to avoid spilling tequila all over the blankets. He'd swiped the tumblers from the honky tonk across the highway where he'd also scored the X that was currently softening their skulls. The motel room was dark, the bed lumpy, and she kept kicking restlessly, and he spilled a bit regardless. He cursed and downed his in one gulp and handed her the other glass, managing not to burn her with the cigarette smoldering between his fingers.

She accepted her drink, took a deep sip and then held the glass loosely so the edge cast a faint, metallic light across her breasts. She exhaled and pointed beyond the foot of the bed to a spot on the wall above the dead television. —That, she said.

—What?

—That! Right there!

—Shit. Okay. He dragged on his cigarette, then poured another shot and strained it through his teeth, stalling. —Pretty weird.

—Yep, pretty weird is right. What *is* it?

He made a show of squinting into the gloom. —Nothing, probably. You trying to torch the place?

Ashes crumbled from her cigarette and glowed like fallen stars against the sheets. She swept them into her palm then into the now empty glass. —It just freaks me out.

—You're easily freaked, then.

—No, I'm not. I'm the only girl in my family who watches horror movies. I don't even cover my eyes for the scary parts.

—Yeah?

—Hell yeah. I don't spook. I don't.

—After some consideration I think it's a shadow.

—That's *not* a shadow. It came out when you were doing the story thing.

—See how a little bit of light from the highway comes in under the blinds? Shadows all over the place.

—Nope. I'm telling you, it came out while you were talking.

—Oh, then it's gotta be a ghost. No other sane explanation. Woooo-ohooooo!

—Shaddup. I need another shot.

—Want this? Couple swallows at the bottom. He sloshed the bottle back and forth.

—Gimme. She snapped her fingers, then grabbed the bottle when he swung it close.

—Wait a sec, we'll solve this right now. He leaned against her, reaching across their bodies for the bedside lamp.

—No!

—Huh? What's the matter?

—Don't do it.

—I'm trying to turn on the light, not cop a feel.

—Go ahead and cop a feel, but leave the light alone, 'kay? She thumped the bottle against his arm until he retreated.

—Whatever. Jesus. Got any more cigs?

She fumbled a pack of cigarettes from the nightstand, lighted one from hers and handed it to him. —Last one, she said, crumpling the pack for emphasis.

He slid toward his edge of the bed and slumped against the headboard and smoked in silence. A semi rumbled past on the interstate and the blinds quivered against the window frame. Outside was scrub and desert. The motel lay embedded in the implacable waste like a lunar module stranded between moon craters.

—Don't sulk, she said.

—I'm not.

—Like hell.

—I'm not sulking.

—Then what?

—I'm looking at the wall. Maybe you're right. Maybe it's something else. Why can't we turn on the light?

A coyote howled somewhere not too far off. Its cry was answered and redoubled until it finally swelled into a frantic, barking cacophony that moved like a cloud across the black desert. —Holy shit, what's that? he said.

—Coyotes, she said. Scavenging for damned souls.

—Sounds fucking grandiose for coyotes.

—And what do you know? They're the favored children of the carrion gods. Grandiosity is their gig.

He laughed, a little strange, a little wild, as if echoing the animal harmony. —So, what are they doing around here? Going through a landfill?

—Maybe you drew them in earlier with your howling.

—Bullshit. They can't hear that. All the way out in the tumbleweeds?

—Sure they can. Howl again. I dare you.

—If coyotes sound this bad, I'd hate listening to jackals. Or dingoes. Remember that news story, years ago, about the woman on the picnic with her family?

—*'A dingo ate my baby!'* God, that's awful. But comical in a horrible way.

—It isn't comical in any way, honey. You're scaring the children.

—Please. Nobody really knows what happened. The kid's mom probably offed her, you ask me.

—There's a great relief. Why do so many parents kill their kids, you think?

—Lots of reasons. Don't you want to strangle the little fuckers sometimes? Like those shits on the flight when we went to see your parents? What a mistake that was, by the way. That one girl kept kicking my seat so hard my head was bouncing. And her mom. . . .

—Ha! It was fun watching you get so mad, though.

She didn't answer, but sat rigidly upright. She trembled.

—Honey? He rubbed her back. —What's the matter?

—Go ahead, she said. Her voice was small.

—Go ahead and what?

—Turn on the light, she said in that small voice. Her cigarette was out and the darkness gathered around them, oily and deep. Faint illumination came through the blinds like light bleeding toward the bottom of a well, a dungeon.

—*You* turn it on, he said. —You're right there.

—I can't move.

—What the hell are you talking about?

—Please. I'm too scared to move, all right? She was whining, borderline hysterical. She enjoyed being frightened, savored the visceral thrill of modulated terror, thus Something Scary, and thus the What If Game (What if a carload of rednecks started following us on a lonely road? What if somebody was sneaking around the house at night? What if I got pregnant?), and thus her compulsion to build the shadow, the discolored blotch of wallpaper, into something sinister. As was often the case with her, a mule's dose of alcohol combined with sleep deprivation rapidly contributed to the situation getting out of hand.

—Fine. He flopped across her lap and found the lamp chain with his fingertips and yanked. The chain clicked and nothing happened. He tried several times and finally gave up in disgust. Meanwhile, her left hand dug into his shoulder. Her skin was icy.

—Owww, he said, pushing toward his side, happy to get away.

—I knew it. She turned her head so her mouth was closer to his ear and she could kind of whisper. —I knew the light was going to crap out on us. We're alone in here.

—Well, I hope so. I wouldn't like to think some big hairy ax murderer was hiding under the bed.

—I already checked. She chuckled weakly and her icy talon found his bicep now, though somewhat less violently. She was almost calm again. —I looked for Anthony Perkins hiding in the bathroom, too.

—Good! Did you scout around for a peephole? The night clerk could be in the next room winding up his camera. Next thing you know, we're internet porn stars.

—That'd suck. She'd begun to slur. —Man, I hate the desert.

—You also hated Costa Rica, if I recall. Who hates Costa Rica?

—Tarantulas. Centipedes. I hate creepy crawlies.

—Who doesn't?

—Exactly! Thank you! There's a species of centipede, Venezuela, somewhere in South America, anyway; it's as long as your forearm. Eats bats. Knocks them outta the air with its venom-dripping mandibles, and bang! Bat Surprise for dinner.

—You're super drunk. I thought I had most of the tequila.

—Yep, I'm off my ass. Some cowboy bought me like eight shooters while you were in the bathroom. You were in there forever.

—Come again? he said, scandalized.

—Down, boy. He didn't grope me. He just plied me with booze on the off chance I'd let him grope me later. No biggie.

—No biggie? No biggie? Was it that stupid looking sonofabitch in the Stetson? The guy who couldn't stop ogling your tits?

—You're describing half the bar. Who cares? I gave baby Travolta the slip and ran off with you!

—Awesome.

They lay there for a time, she playing with her lighter, grinding short, weak sparks from the wheel; he listening for the coyote chorus and keeping one eye on the weird blotch of shadow on the wall. Both of them were thinking about the story he'd half told earlier about his uncle Mo who'd done a stint with the Marines and had a weird experience during shore leave in the Philippines; the Something Scary tale that had been so sublimely interrupted.

She said, —Maybe I'm a little intimidated about the Filipino strippers. I can't pick up a pop bottle with my pussy. Or shoot ping pong balls outta there, either.

—Those girls come highly recommended, he said. —Years of specialized training.

—Sounds like your uncle sure knew his way around Filipino whorehouses.

—Wasn't just the whorehouses. Those old boys went

crazy on shore leave 'cause that far out shit was front and center in just about every bar in town. They were dumbass kids—pretty fortunate nobody got his throat slit. According to Mo, a bunch of the taxi drivers belonged to gangs and they'd cart drunk soldiers into the jungle and rob them.

—Enough about the whores and thieving taxi drivers. Get to the scary part. If there's anything more disturbing than Marines slobbering on bottles some whore has been waving around with her cooch, I wanna hear it.

—More disturbing? Uncle Mo told me one about these three guys in Nam who snuck into a leper colony to get some ass. Back then, I guess the locals put the immediate family in the colony whether they were infected or not, so the fellows figured there had to be some prime tail up for grabs.

—Ick! Moving on . . . .

—Okay, R&R in Manila. Mo and Lurch, a corpsman from his platoon, were whooping it up big time; they'd been drinking three days straight. Barhopping, y'know, and eventually a couple party girls latched onto them and they all headed back to this shack by the docks the guys were renting. A rickety sonofagun, third floor, sorta hanging out over the water. Long story short, Mo's in the bedroom and the girl is smoking his pole. His mind wanders and he happens to look out the window. Across the way, through the window of this other crappy house, there's a naked Filipino broad getting her muffin dusted by some G.I.. Talk about symmetry, eh? It's raining like a cow pissing on a flat rock and a sash is whacking around in the wind, cutting off the view every few seconds. The broad grins over at Uncle Mo and she reaches up and covers her ears. Then she just lifts her head off her shoulders. Mo's standing there, straddle-legged and slack jawed and the woman's head keeps on grinning at him and her lips start moving. She's laughing at him. He notices there's something coming out of her neck, like a beak, or who the fuck knows what, 'cause the shade is flapping, see. Meanwhile the other grunt is going to town on her pussy, oblivious to the fact this freak is tucking her head under her arm like a bowling ball.

—And then?

—Then nothing. End of story. Mo and the stripper went back to the main room and drank some more and blazed the night away. He came to forty-eight hours later when his platoon sergeant dumped a bucket of water on his head and kicked his ass back to the ship for the clap inspection.

—Clap inspection?

—After shore leave all the grunts had to drop their pants so an NCO could check them for VD. Heh-heh.

—What a crock of shit, she said. —That's not even scary.

—Sorry. I made the last part up. The part about Mo getting a BJ while the hooker and the other dude were getting busy across the way was true. I think. Uncle Mo lies about stuff, so you never really know.

She groaned in disgust. —Where'd you even get the idea?

—I dunno. Popped into my head while I was lying there. Figured it would get a rise outta you. He laughed and poked her arm, dropped his hand to her leg.

She pushed his hand aside. —Now that that's over. Check this out: I found something odd earlier, she said. —A bible.

—Lots of motels have bibles lying around, he said.

—And Jack Chick tracts. He was studying the shadow again. —You know, that thing *does* resemble an insect. Thought it had wings earlier, but I dunno. Can't see shit in here. Wait a minute . . . It's a water stain. This rat hole leaks like a sieve, betcha anything.

—The bathroom wall is rotten. I was sitting on the toilet and felt a cool breeze. I could stick my fingers outside. Freezing out there.

—Peephole, he said. —For the desert cannibals. There's an abandoned atomic testing range a few dunes over. History Channel did a documentary on them. So I hear.

—I dunno about that, but what I do know is something poisonous coulda crawled in any old time and made a nest, could be waiting to lay eggs in our ears when we fall asleep. If that's the case, I gotta tell you, twenty bucks a night seems like a rip-off.

He chuckled.

—Why are you laughing? she said.

—Earlier, I was pissing and noticed something a bit fucked up.

—I think you might have an enlarged prostate.

—The hell are you going on about?

—Frequent urination is a sign of an enlarged prostate. Don't you watch infomercials? They could save your life.

—Anyway. I'm taking one of my apparently frequent pisses, when I notice there's no toilet paper. Like the gentleman I am, I find another roll in the cabinet and get ready to put it on the hanger rod. All for you, snookums.

—You *are* a gentleman, she said.

—Yeah, I raised the seat and everything. I pulled the rod out and set it aside. Unfortunately, I dropped the toilet paper and it went flying out the door and I had to chase it down, wadding the unspooled paper as I went. Man, you could trace pictures with that stuff. It's like one-ply.

—The moral of the story is, shut the door when taking a piss.

—No, that's not the moral of the story. There's more. I go back just in time to watch a big-ass spider squeeze itself out of the rod and scurry into the sink. Thing had a body maybe the size of a jawbreaker; red and yellow, and fleshy, like a plum. It was so damned hefty I could see light reflecting in its eyes. Then it took off down the drain. I think it was irate I screwed with its cozy little home. He had a laugh over the scenario.

—For real? she said.

—Oh, yeah.

She thought things over for a bit. —No way in hell I'm going back in there. I'll pee behind a cactus. A jawbreaker?

—Hand to a stack of bibles, he said, wiping his eyes and visibly working to appear more solemn.

—The bible! She half climbed from bed, groped for the dresser, and after a few anxious moments came back with something heavy and black. She snicked the lighter until its flame revealed the pebbled hide of a small, thick book.

—What kind of bible is that? he said.

—Greek. Byzantine. I dunno, she said. Gilt symbols caught the flame and glistened in convoluted whorls and angular slashes; golden reflections played over the blankets, rippled across the couple's flesh. The pages were thin as white leaves and covered in script to match the cover design. Many of the pages were defiled by chocolaty fingerprints. The book smelled of cigarette musk and mothballs. It was quite patently old.

—This has got to be a collector's item. Some poor schlep forgot it here. He turned the book over in his hands, riffling the pages. No name on it . . . Finders-keepers.

—Hmm, I dunno. . . .

—Dunno what?

—Whether that's a good idea.

—Billy will go apeshit over this thing. Besides, I owe him a hundred bucks.

—I don't care if Billy goes apeshit over antiquarian crap. That's what antiquarians do, right? You owe me the hundred bucks, anyway, motherfucker.

—Don't you want to know what it is?

—I already know what it is; it's a bible.

He shrugged and handed the book over. —Whatever. Do

what you want. I don't care.

—Great! She tossed the book over her shoulder in the general direction of the dresser.

—Man, you really are so wasted.

—Gettin' my second wind, boy. I'm bored.

—Go to sleep. Then you won't be bored.

—Can't sleep. I'm preoccupied with that spider. She's in those rusty pipes, rubbing her claws together and plotting vengeance. Go kill her, would ya?

—You kiddin'? It's pitch dark in there—she'd get the drop on me.

—Hmp. I'm chilly. Let's screw.

—No thanks. I'd just whiskey dick you for half an hour and pass out.

—I see. You won't kill a predatory bug, but you'll club our romance like a baby seal. Swell.

—Wah, wah, he said.

It had grown steadily chillier in the room. She idly thumbed the lighter wheel and watched their breath coalesce by intermittent licks of flame. The shadow above the television had become oblong and black as the cranium of a squid. She raised her arm and the shadow seemed to bleed upward and sideways, as if avoiding the feeble nimbus of fire. —Odd. More I think about it, this thing didn't appear until after you started your story earlier. Then there it was. . . .

—I called the shadow forth. And summoned the coyotes. Go to sleep. He rolled over and faced the opposite wall.

—Hell with this. I need a cig. Honey.

—Don't honey me. I'm bushed. He pulled a pillow over his head.

—Fine. She flounced from the bed and promptly smacked her shin on the chair that had toppled over from the weight of her jeans and purse. —Ahh! She hopped around, cursing and fuming and finally yanked on her pants and blouse, snatched up her purse and blundered through the door into the night.

It was cold, all right. The stars were out, fierce and prehistoric. The dark matter between them seemed blacker than usual and thick as tar. She hugged herself and clattered along the boardwalk past the blank windows and the cheap doors with descending numbers to the pop and cigarette machines by the manager's office. No bulbs glowed along the walkway, the office was a deep, dark pit; the neon vacancy sign reared blind and black. Luckily, the vending panels oozed blurry, greenish light to guide her way. Probably the only light for miles. She disliked that thought.

She dug whiskey-soaked dollar bills and a few coins from her purse, started plugging them into the cigarette machine until it clanked and dispensed a pack of Camels. The cold almost drove her scurrying back to the room where her husband doubtless slumbered with dreams of unfiltered cigarettes dancing in his head, but not quite. She cracked the pack and got one going, determined to satisfy her craving and then hide the rest where he'd never find them. Lazy, unchivalrous bastard! Let him forage for his own smokes.

Smoke boiled in her lungs; she leaned against a post and exhaled with beatific self-satisfaction, momentarily immune from the chill. The radiance of the vending machines seeped a few yards across the gravel lot, illuminating the hood of her Volkswagen Beetle and a beat to hell pickup she presumed belonged to the night clerk. She was halfway through her second cigarette when she finally detected a foreign shape between the Volkswagen and the pickup. Though mostly cloaked in shadow and impossibly huge, she recognized it as a tortoise. It squatted there, the crown of its shell even with the car window. Its beak and monstrously clawed forepaws were bisected by the wavering edge of illumination. There was a blob of skull perhaps the diameter of a melon, and a moist eye that glimmered yellow.

—Wow, she said. She finished her cigarette. Afraid to move, she lighted another, and that was tricky with her hands shaking so terribly, then she smoked that one too and stared at the giant tortoise staring back at her. She thought, for a moment, she saw its shell dilate and contract, in rhythm with her own surging heart.

The night remained preternaturally quiet there on the edge of the highway, absent the burr of distant engines or blatting horns, or the stark sweep of rushing headlights. The world had descended into a primeval well while she'd been partying in their motel room; it had slipped backward and now the desert truly was an ancient and haunted place. What else would shamble from the wastes of rock and scrub and the far off dunes?

She finished the third cigarette and stuffed the pack in her jeans pocket, and with a great act of will sidled the way she'd come; not turning her back, oh no, simply crabbing sideways, hips brushing doorknobs as she went. The tortoise remained in place, immobile as a boulder. The cosmic black tar began eating a few handfuls of stars here and there, like peanuts.

Once at what she prayed was a safe distance, she moved faster, counting doors, terrified of tripping in the dark, of sprawling on her face, and thus helpless, hearing the sibilant shift and crunch of a massive body sliding across gravel. But she made it to the room without occurrence and locked the door and pressed against it, sobbing and blubbering with exhaustion.

He lay facedown in the middle of the crummy bed, his naked body a pale gray smear in the gloom. She went to him and shook him. He raised his head at a drunken pitch and mumbled incoherencies. He didn't react to her frantic account of the giant tortoise, her speculation that it might be even now bearing down upon them for a late night snack, that the world might be coming to an end.

—Goddamn it, wake up! she said and smacked his

shoulder, hard. Then, as her eyes adjusted, she saw tears on his cheeks, the unnatural luster of his eyes. Not tears; sweat poured from him, smoked from him, it saturated the sheets until they resembled a sloughed cocoon. The muscles of his shoulder flexed and bunched in agonized knots beneath her hand.

—There's been an incident, he whispered.

She wrapped her arms around her knees and bit her thumb and began to rock ever so slightly. —Baby, I just saw a goddamned turtle the size of a car in the parking lot. What incident are you talking about?

—It wasn't a water stain. You were right. It's a worm, like a kind that lived in the Paleozoic. The worm slithered off the wall when you left, made a beeline right over here. . . . He pushed his face into the sheets and uttered a bark. —Look at the wall.

She looked at the wall. The ominous shadow was gone, melted away, if it had ever been. —What happened? she said.

—The worm crawled up my ass and there it waits. It's gonna rule the world.

She didn't know what to say. She cried softly, and bit her thumb, and rocked.

—I'm high, he said. His entire body relaxed and he began to snore.

—Oh, you jerk, she said and cried shamelessly, this time in relief. No more pills with tequila chasers for her. She wiped her nose and curled into a ball against his clammy flank and fell unconscious as if she'd been chloroformed.

When she awakened it was still very dark. They lay spine to spine, her leg draped over his, her arm trailing over the edge and near the carpet. His body twitched against hers the way a person does when they dream of running, flying, being pursued through vast, sunless spaces. She closed her eyes.

He shuddered.

Something hit the floor on the opposite side of the bed

with a fleshy thud. Her breath caught and her eyes bulged as she listened to the object slowly roll across the floorboards in a bumpy, lopsided fashion. This was a purposeful, animated movement that bristled every hair on her body. She reached over her shoulder and gripped his arm.

—Psst! Honey! It was like shaking a corpse.

Quietly, muffled by the mattresses, someone under the bed began to laugh.

THERE IS A MONSTER UNDER HELEN'S BED

by Ekaterina Sedia

Moth flutters against the billowing curtains—white on white—and Helen knows it's there only because of the sound its wings make, quick little beats, dry and rustling. Helen imagines the moth scream in a silent high pitch.

Helen wants to get up and untangle the little wings carefully, avoiding the powdery scales, but she cannot let her feet touch the floor. She imagines the cool wide boards, polished to a smooth shine, so good to slide across in her white socks she has to change every day now—but that's for daytime, when monsters are asleep and sated, and retreat under the floorboards and behind the wallpaper covered in deceitfully bright flowers. All monsters sleep behind the flowers, in the narrow interstices between the wallpaper and the drywall, under the nodding shadows of printed daisies and poppies.

But at night they wait for Helen, and she does not dare to set foot on the smooth floor. The moth flutters, and Helen digs herself deeper under the covers.

Helen has to go to the bathroom. The monster senses her restless shifting and breathes heavily, moving closer to the edge, its claws scrabbling on the wood of the floorboards. Helen can hear the wet gurgling of its saliva and phlegm, and shivers. She will wet her bed again tonight.

Helen's new mom, Janis, listens to the sounds upstairs. The circle of yellow light from the lamp clings to the shaggy rug Janis wants removed but never gets around to.

Her husband Tom follows her gaze with his own and smiles sheepishly.

"How long do you think until she learns English?"

Tom shrugs. "Children pick up languages pretty fast."

"But she's . . . older." Janis says. There is carefully hidden disappointment in her voice. She tries to love Helen; most of all, she tries not to regret her decision to adopt her. She did not want to wait for a younger child to become available, not in that horrid hotel with frozen pipes and non-flushing toilet, not in Siberia, where snow covered the ground in October. She grabbed Helen and ran back to the semblance of civilization in Moscow and then back to New Jersey—much like one would grab a sweater one did not particularly like, just to not spend another hour in a mall. She now regretted her panic, she regretted—even though she would never admit it to herself—bringing back Helen and not someone else. She is older, and like so many orphanage kids, she has developed an attachment disorder, or so her psychiatrist said.

She is a pretty child though, Janis consoles herself. Thin and blond, with dark blue eyes that have a habit of staring at any adult with thoughtful intensity, as if sizing them up for parental roles. But everyone said how pretty she was. Janis sighs and returns to her reading. It's a parenting book, something she never thought she would be reading.

There's rustling upstairs, and both Janis and Tom look

up, as if expecting to be able to see through the vaulted ceiling.

"Should we check on her?" Janis says.

Tom shakes his head. "She's old enough to sleep by herself."

Janis remembers the orphanage—ten beds to a room. Helen is not used to being by herself.

"She better not wet her bed again," Tom says.

Janis nods. The book is not helping.

Helen thinks back to the day when the monsters first appeared. She had to go to the bathroom, and she felt (or imagined) a quick touch of hot breath when her feet touched the cold linoleum tiles of the orphanage floor. She listened to the even breathing of eight other girls—one had been recently adopted, the youngest, who went home with her new mom and dad. There were no monsters and no hidden breathing, just a general unfairness of the situation: the longer one waited for the parents to show up, the smaller one's chances grew.

Helen went to the door, into the long hallway lit by dead fluorescent lights, and all the way to the bathroom where the toilet gurgled habitually.

On her way back, Helen heard voices—husky voices of the older boys, too old to be adopted, too young for the vocational training school where they would be sent once they turned fourteen. The boys everyone knew would grow up to be bad, and already well on their way to fulfilling the expectations. Helen pressed against the wall and listened to their whispers and laughter.

She passed the door of her dormitory and peeked around the corner. They were by the lockers, five or six of them, and there were no adults in sight.

Helen can see it now: there is a girl with them—Tanya, who is older than Helen. She is ten, and she hangs out with the boys; she smokes and drinks with them after the lights-out. But they do not act as her friends. Tanya is crying.

The boys push her against the solid wall of the lockers, and Helen imagines how the cold metal feels against a cheek wet with tears, the faint smell of green paint lingering since last summer.

The boys tell Tanya to shut up, and press harder, her face and chest flat against metal; they lift her dress and pull down her underwear, they force her legs open.

One of the boys, red-headed, cold-eyed, puts his hand between Tanya's legs; his shoulder is moving as if his hand is searching for something, and his breath is loud in the silence broken only by the occasional sob. He then pulls down his pants and presses against Tanya who cries more as he thrusts with his hips. He steps back and another boy takes his place. Helen thinks she smells the sea, of which she retains a faint memory—she was only two when her real parents took her on vacation.

She stepped away from the corner and ran to her room on light feet, barely touching the linoleum. She ran to her bed and then the monster lunged. She felt its fetid breath on her knees, its clawed hands grabbing her ankles.

She cried and wrestled free, and dove under the covers; until morning she dreamt about cold eyes and sharp claws sliding up her legs and forcing them apart.

Janis tries to be a good mother; even as she finds Helen awake and curled up among the bunched and wet sheets, she does not scold. She only sighs and tosses the soiled sheets into the hamper. She then tells Helen to go eat breakfast.

At the table, Helen is still subdued but wrinkles her nose at slices of toast—she does not like Wonderbread, she misses the chewy thick slices with a golden crust. Janis makes a mental note to pick up some loaves of Italian bread, and butters the toast for her impossible girl.

"Eat," she says, even as Helen stares at her with

uncomprehending eyes. "We're going to see the doctor."

Helen smiles at that word. "Papa," she says.

Janis shakes her head. "No. Nyet. Tom is your papa," she says. "Not the doctor, not any anyone else. You can't choose your family, you know."

Helen does not understand, but Janis does, and she mentally admonishes herself to practice what she preaches, to remember this little adage. Like it or not, she is stuck with Helen; she's not going to return her like an unloved puppy to the pound. If only she were easier to love.

Janis shakes her head and cleans the table. She nudges Helen up the stairs, and she goes, obedient, to brush her teeth and put on her clothes. Helen does everything quickly, the motions precise and fluid, trained by half a decade of synchronized grooming, dressing, and eating. She makes her bed neatly with hospital corners—even though she still seems baffled by the second sheet instead of the white cloth envelope enclosing the blanket that so vexed Janis during her hotel stay in Siberia.

Janis drives to the doctor. In this part of Edison, there are many Russians and other Slavic nationals—she can hear their rough, guttural speech reaching for her through the open car window, trying to drag Janis back to the snow-covered town in Siberia, run down buildings parasitically attached to some industrial monstrosity of secretive purpose.

Helen, on the other hand, perks up and sticks her head out of the window, smiling and waving. Janis purses her lips and pulls her inside, and rolls up the windows. Helen has to learn English, not to cling to a misplaced remnant of the life she had left.

The doctor is Russian too—he laughs with an avuncular roll, and reassures Janis in his heavily accented English. He takes Helen to his office on the third floor of the office building, where the windows offer up a view of the adjacent strip mall.

Janis follows even though she cannot understand them. They seem to conspire against her—the doctor at his ostentatious mahogany desk (he sits next to it, not behind it) and Helen, sunken into a plush red chair, a box of tissues thoughtfully placed on the small stand by her elbow. Janis sits awkwardly on an uncomfortable ottoman by the door, feeling like a poor relation, an unwelcome intruder.

The doctor and the girl look at her simultaneously, laugh, and resume their conversation. What an ugly language, Janis thinks. There are no tissues by her ottoman.

Helen likes the doctor, the same way she likes all bearded men with calloused hands and a faint smell of cologne and leather clinging to them. She wishes for a new father like that— not her current flabby, pasty one. Helen knows that despite what the doctor says, the family is not permanent—she remembers children who went home with their new parents, only to be returned and given to different ones. The trouble is, Helen does not want to go back to the orphanage where the monsters are relentless and walk freely at all hours. She prefers the ones that stay under the bed and sleep during the day. Helen devises plans to become a monster herself.

"Why are you unhappy?" the doctor asks. His eyes behind the lenses of his spectacles are kind. He often asks this question.

Helen shrugs.

"Aren't your parents nice to you?"

"They are," she says. "They are nice."

"What's the problem then? Do you miss your friends?"

"No." She shakes her head. She does not miss anyone. "I want new parents."

"Some would say you are lucky to have the parents you do. They give you everything you want."

She nods. She knows she is being ungrateful—always

has been, even back in the orphanage where she was lucky to have a roof over her head and a bed to sleep in, where she did not have to freeze to death in the streets. "I know."

"Then what?" The kindness in the doctor's voice cracks, about to let something else through. "What's the problem?"

"There is a monster under my bed," she says. "It wouldn't let me go to the bathroom."

"Is this why you wet your bed?" the doctor asks.

Helen feels her cheeks grow hot—she cannot believe Janis has told on her. Her eyes flash indignation, but the doctor does not notice.

"What kind of monster is it?" he asks.

Helen hikes up her trouser leg and shows him deep bruises the color of plums, the wide gashes barely healed over, running from her kneecap to the top of her white sock. She hears Janis gasp on her ottoman.

Then the doctor starts asking Janis questions Helen does not understand. She only hears fear in Janis's voice, and feels guilty. Now she knows about the monster too, and probably worries.

Janis looks at the newspaper clipping the doctor has photocopied for her. Some are printouts of the internet articles, and Janis wonders if he collects this stuff and why. But she knows the answer—there are enough of these adopted children and their anxious parents to pay for his office and the mahogany desk and the red plush chairs. Of course he collects the clippings about child murders.

Janis reads the small, too dark print of a poor photocopy, she looks at the photograph that doesn't look like a child's face—just a Rorschach of black and white planes; it's such a bad copy of the picture. Could be a little boy with black pools where his eyes should have been.

She reads the articles—they all say the same thing. An

adopted child beaten to death by his parents in Switzerland. Countries and names change from one article to the next, but the story is the same—beaten, dismembered, thrown out of windows, moving vehicles, off bridges. She flips through the clippings, face after face after face in severe black and white. Janis cries then, not for them but for Helen.

The monster growls so softly it sounds like a purr. Its claws tap on the floorboards like castanets. Helen sits on her bed hugging the bruised knees to her chest.

The doctor did not seem to believe the story of the monster, and instead seemed to think that her mom and dad were the ones who hurt Helen. He even said that if they beat her, she should tell him that now and the police would find her new parents. While the proposal seemed tempting, Helen decided that lying was still wrong. The monster growls louder, reminding her of her mistake.

Helen cannot sleep and she thinks back, to what she can remember of the orphanage—so much of it is fading from her memory already. But the monsters she remembers, their long shadows stretching across the chipping walls. The nannies tell her that these are not shadows, just stains from the age-old plumbing leaks. Just blemishes of an unknown origin. They rumble in the pipes, they spread in the puddles of gray light that move across the floor of the classroom as the day wears on. They hide under desks and chairs in the common room, they follow the children outside to the swings and the monkey bars.

The monsters look out of the eyes of the parents who come to take away children; they all speak unfamiliar languages. They look out of the eyes of the nannies and especially the older boys, all teeth and clawed fingers. Helen avoided them and kept her head down, dreading the day she would be tall enough to push against the lockers.

She dangles her foot off the bed and pulls it back up right

away, teasing the monster. She hears it lunge and miss and dig its claws into the floorboards. Its breathing is heavy now, upset. If she weren't so afraid, she would've descended to the floor and let the monster devour her—every bone, every morsel—and lick the floor clean of blood with its red tongue, rough enough to strip the paint and varnish off wood. Her parents would find no trace of her, as if she simply vanished from the world.

It would be a good death, she thinks, not at all like the girl in the orphanage, found hanging off the curtain rod, her red tights wrapped around her neck. Helen remembers her purple tongue teasing between white sharp teeth; she remembers the missing incisor and the swollen tissue squeezing through the gap. Or like the boy who snuck off to go swimming in the lake a few kilometers away. They brought him back, blue and naked and wet like a creature from a horror movie. Like a monster.

She dangles the edge of the blanket and hears the tearing of fabric. She pulls back the long twisting shreds. She hears the footfalls on the staircase, and hides the torn blanket from sight. She pretends to sleep as the door squeals open and Janis stands in the doorway. Helen feels her worried look with the back of her neck.

"This is ridiculous," Tom says, and turns off the TV to illustrate his seriousness on the matter. "They think that we are hurting her?"

Janis nods and shows him the clippings. They do not say it out loud, but they both are thinking the same thing: these children are impossible, they are messed up and they cannot be fixed. They do not speak English, and yet they demand, they want things, they require tutors and psychiatrists, and their medical bills are piling up. The orphanages have the secret policy of adopting the most damaged children abroad, and Janis cannot decide if it is out of kindness, trying to get them help they cannot get at home, or cynicism, getting rid of the defectives and the unwanted.

She thinks of the people in the adoption agency and the orphanage staff, and she does not know if those people even know their own motives. She only knows that the doctors at the orphanage give all the children a clean bill of health, afraid to spook the potential parents. In any case, they find out soon enough.

Helen came with a heart murmur and bed wetting; the latter does not seem too bad compared to the congenital heart defect that is too late to fix. But even that fades in comparison to her acting out and scratching, to her fears, to her reluctance to let them touch her. Even that fades in comparison to the unexplained bruises and cuts.

"I think she did it to herself," Tom says. "The doctors checked her out before—there wasn't a problem then. Maybe she fell or banged against something in the playground?"

Janis shakes her head. "I don't know. But those bruises . . . they look like fingerprints. Adult fingerprints, and nail scratches." She draws a deep breath, dreading the question she has to ask. "Tom. . . . You wouldn't . . . "

He looks at her open-mouthed, not indignant, just surprised. "No. Of course not." Of course not, Janis scolds herself. How could she even think that?

He stares at her, clears his throat. "Janis, we really need to talk."

She knows what it's about—the child is a problem, like the children in the clippings. The problem. They never fought before, never suspected one another of anything unsavory. They used to have leisure and spare cash, they never used to argue like that. Janis just cannot bear to think about admitting defeat, to tolerate the smug *I-told-you-sos* from family and friends. "It's different when it's your own," they will say. "What did you expect? She's too old, too mixed up. It's not the same as having your own baby. It's sad, but you can't save them, Janis, you can't save them all."

She thought she could save just one, but even that is apparently too much for them.

"Yes," she says out loud. "We need to talk. Let me just check on her."

Helen squeezes her eyes shut and waits for the woman to close the door, cutting off the thick slab of light reaching in from the hallway. The light makes the monster retreat into its den somewhere between the bed and the floorboards, where its eyes glow with quiet red ferocity in the darkness. She wants to ask the woman—Janis, mom—to leave the door open, to put the lights on, but she cannot, and she cries silently, her salty tears sliding down her cheek and into her hair, soaking into the pillow.

The woman does not leave. Instead she comes in and sits on the bed, the white texture of her cable-knit sweater exaggerated by the light from the hallway and darkness inside the room. It is cold tonight—the cold has finally caught up with Helen. It chased her across the unfathomable chasm of the ocean and nine hours of flying through the air over the stationary clouds. The autumn is here now, and there are no more moths fluttering in the curtains.

Helen peeks between the tear-soaked eyelashes, and the beam of light twinkles and breaks into a myriad of tiny stars. The woman looks back at Helen but does not smile like she usually does when their eyes meet. Instead she sighs and strokes Helen's hair. She feels the moisture under her fingertips, and she looks like she's about to cry herself.

Helen considers opening her eyes completely but decides against it and squeezes them shut, feigning sleep. If she looks at her new mom directly, she will start talking, and then Helen would cry in earnest at her inability to understand, to explain about the monsters and shadows and fear.

Helen wants to talk about summers in Siberia—so short and so intense, so full of high-pitched whining of mosquitoes and the smell of pine trees oozing fresh sap, of spongy bogs studded with butter-yellow cloudberries. About the lake where the runaway boy drowned but which becomes transformed by a cloudless blue sky overhead into a swath of precious smooth silk surrounded by soft, succulent-green branches of firs.

But Helen cannot explain these things and she forces her eyelids tighter together, until her eyes burn.

Janis gives up and rises to her feet, the springs of the mattress squeaking in relief. The door closes behind her, cutting off the light.

In the darkness, there is shifting and stirring. Helen watches the sheet of wallpaper peel away, admitting a thin beam of bluish light into the room.

Helen sits up and peers into the widening gap—carefully at first, wary of the monsters. She sees a small man, no bigger than a cat, crouching on the other side of the wallpaper barrier. His withered narrow face looks at Helen over his shoulder, and then he turns away and draws on the inside of the wall—a chain of tiny cranes, dwarfed by the shadows of daisies and poppies. They seem paler on the other side but alive, nodding in the invisible breeze.

Helen pulls the sheets of the wallpaper apart, and she sees a bright blue lake surrounded by yellow-needled larches. The monster crawls from under the bed and stands beside her, panting like a dog, the black fur between its wing-like shoulder blades bristling. Helen is surprised to not be afraid of it anymore.

The monster leaps into the gap and Helen follows, timid at first. She turns to look back and watches the wallpaper fold back with a quiet rustling and grow together, fusing. She sees the ghostly flowers, and behind them—her room, a shadow image from a magic lantern.

The monster growls and bounds ahead, then stops and waits for her by the tiny man and his cranes, which are flying in place, their wings sweeping up and down in a graceful motion. She watches them for a while, never moving and yet flying south among the daisies and poppies which are still blooming despite the autumn and its cold fingers reaching even behind the wallpaper, where the monsters sleep during the day.

The monster barks and laughs and leaps to the right, then to the left; then it gallops toward the lake, looking over its shoulder, inviting Helen to follow. Helen sighs and walks through the fallen leaves, rubbery under her white socks, she walks to the lake where a blue boy with sharp teeth is waiting for her, the monster by his side like a hound.

PALISADE

by Cat Sparks

There are four Ann Elisabeths in my father's house. He claims he loves them equally, but all I've ever been certain of is that he never felt love for me, Luisa Alice, his true biological child. Yet he persists in requesting my presence at his table on those occasions he summons dinner guests. The Ann Elisabeths are spared such tedium, all but the precocious six-year-old, who has the run of the mansion and the surrounding gardens. That single Ann Elisabeth needs three nannies to keep her in check. With ruddy cheeks and golden ringlets, she is the darling presented to his friends, trained to sing and recite poetry when the brandy is served after dinner.

My father's guests must surely know she is a stint, doomed to a life locked in perpetual childhood, yet not one of them has ever made an unfavourable remark. All but the hardest hearted of visitors declare the child incurably adorable.

Still, I have heard my father claim her as his daughter often enough, a barefaced lie easily caught out by the Indiras or the Vazquenadas or the Temelkovs, returning every visit to find a six-year-old in place. Stinting is illegal on all the worlds but ours. There are no laws on AmberJade. People settle here in order to do as they please, the dense jungle canopies and savage hurricanes giving cover from prying eyes. Even the missionaries have given up on this place. Were it not for my physical condition, I would have left it behind long ago. I would have abandoned my father to his horrible bugs and his elaborate dinner parties; his slaves and his precious darling Ann Elisabeths.

I do not care for the Vazquenadas family. There are far too many of them, each one more heartless and stupid than the next. Every year I pray that their sleek silver ships might ignite upon entry, or crash in a magnificent orgy of grinding metal and flame, yet my gods are from the old world, my prayers ineffectual in this hostile alien landscape.

They enter the dining chamber together, all thirteen of them including retinue. Goran Vazquenadas, patriarch, obese beyond measure and little used to walking; his chalk-skinned wife Makayla, her hooped skirts emblazoned with sapphires. Their sons and daughters are a sorry mix of their parents' physiques, garbed in an assortment of outlandish fashions.

Father has me seated next to little Aelira Vazquenadas, instructed to amuse her with my swallowtails. I sit still and quiet in my embroidered dinner gown. I shall not speak unless I am addressed directly.

Aelira is too young to be of consequence, and many thoughts weigh heavily on my mind tonight. I will not break my concentration without purpose. As I sit here enduring their vulgar small talk, a message waits for me on the Link, back upstairs in my Autumn suite. A message from Harmon, my dearest, most forbidden heart. The only person I have ever loved.

As the waiters serve a dainty entrée of slivered Kryl and

Kucha eggs, I feel my father's cold stare press against my skin. I do not let my discomfort show. I know what he expects of me. Aelira watches as I wave my hand and a cloud of holographic swallowtails materialise above her head. She squeals with delight, abandoning her food to swat at them with small, splayed fingers.

"Damned ugly things," declares my father, his gaze still harsh upon my skin. "Useless for export. Too short-lived. Too dull."

"But they are the cleverest creatures," I explain, my voice as steady as stone. "They seek out the lower forks of Tunjuk trees to build their cocoons, using the close-knit branches as barriers against the storms. After fifty days of cosseted hibernation, the little things push free of their wrappings to burst into the light, only to die soon after their eggs are laid."

Aelira, a bug-eyed thing herself, with pasty flesh and insipid rosebud lips, pays scant attention to my words. All she wants to do is crush the fluttering creatures between her palms. She does not seem to understand that they are holograms.

Named for the butterflies of old Earth, my swallowtails remind me of a world I've never been to, a life I've never led. Some days the skies above the house are filled with great swirls of them, buffeted ever upwards by gentle gusts of wind.

"Razed this patch of jungle with my own bare hands," boasts my father loudly. He flexes his fingers as he speaks, his eyes now on the Vazquenadas girl.

"Our world is named AmberJade," I tell her, conjuring a planet hologram and setting it to hover in the empty space above my swallowtails. "A bright green jewel inlaid in velvet darkness. Such a pretty sphere; all cloudy oceans and barren rock, with a slim habitable belt running the length of its equator."

The world turns and I point to show Aelira where my father's mansion lies. I tell her of its eighty rooms sectioned into four wings, each named for a season; an old world conceit as there are no true seasons here. Just the thrashing hurricane winds and the relative calmness of the pauses between the storms.

"We are safe," I say, explaining how the buildings nestle amidst a hundred acres of jungle clearing, protected from regrowth and any number of other hostile incursions by an electronic palisade. The only creatures permitted within its barrier field are those whose biological signatures have been programmed into its recognition software.

I have been warned never to stray beyond the palisade's protective field by my father himself and the succession of servants who raised me to adulthood. The jungle, I am told, took my mother's life when I was young. An unfortunate accident. She wandered beyond the palisade's blue-green tint and lost her bearings. The jungle claimed her as its own. My mother's name was Ann Elisabeth. The stints are all that remain of her now, but I will never recognise her gentle face in those abominations, even if, as my father claims, they were cultured from her living cells.

In any case, I cannot walk far, and I am frightened of the crawling horrors my father traps and breeds for export: bugs as big as my two fists, with glittering carapaces and stinging tails; things with as many heads as legs or jaws that can pierce metal. Collectors of such things pay high prices for them, specimens both living and preserved.

I keep well away from the sturdy holding tanks, terrariums and taxidermy studios where my father's slaves toil.

Safe within the palisade, I watch the jungle pulse and bloom on screens, lying in the soft grass knowing nothing flying in the air, nor crawling through the soil can harm me. The palisade keeps the storms at bay, and I lie beneath the sky at night, protected from all danger, dreaming of Harmon as the lightning tears apart the clouds.

My beloved Harmon lives on a small moon circling Bellady; the farthermost planet in our solar system. So far away from AmberJade that the signal relay takes a full twelve minutes to deliver its message via the Link and receive one in return. Thus, our conversations are stilted and paused. This fact makes me choose my words more carefully than I might were our communications instantaneous. I strongly suspect it is this very constraint that caused our love to grow. The words we share are precise and considered. We do not waste our words on frivolous things.

Like me, Harmon suffers certain imperfections of form— dangerous imperfections that cause him to shun physical society. I determined early on in our confidences never to ask him why he could not walk, nor why he rejects prosthesis, even though there are worlds which permit their use. I sensed there was more than discomfort involved. Harmon would have told me had he wanted his reasons understood.

We have grown so very close, my Harmon and I. We met in a Linklounge three years ago, and over time I have come to trust him like no other. I treasure his communications more than anything else in my world.

My father knows nothing of Harmon, or my secret desires. He will never grant me a dowry. But I know where my father keeps his gold. There is nothing I would not do to be with Harmon, nothing I would not give him were the power in my hands.

My swallowtails flutter around me as we speak on the Link, arranging themselves in patterns to suit my mood. I do not show Harmon the private sensorium I have fashioned from his words: the close-ups of his gallant features; snippets of his laughter, firm, yet comforting.

"I love you, Luisa Alice, as I have loved no other. One day we shall run away together."

One day indeed. When the Link is down, I walk the

length of my sensorium with eyes closed, enveloping myself in the sound of his voice, immersing myself in his presence, wishing his arms around me. I fantasise about stealing a ship and flying it all the way to Bellady's moon to embrace my love. The Link is the key. It holds all the information I need. With it, I could teach myself to pilot. With my father's gold I could buy a silver ship.

When the second course arrives—Jester beetles in their shells served with comb grass and raspberry jus—I push my plate aside. Such pretty shells, named for the red and blue diamond criss-cross patterns on their backs. The Jester beetle feeds on the flesh of other beasts. They prefer the meat of the living to carrion, which is why my father has such a lucrative trade agreement with the Vazquenadas family, who have been in the bioweapons industry for at least a century. I do not want to know what the beetles are used for.

My father laughs loudly with the Vazquenadas elders. I have watched him grow grotesque and wealthy off this planet's vicious spoils. In my tenth year he purchased a consignment of prisoners from a judicial contractor in receivership. Those poor unfortunates were sent out into the jungles of AmberJade to hunt for the peculiar bugs that fetch such high prices on other worlds. A task previously assigned to automatons, but they performed uneconomically in the humid, sticky air or in the wet, often breaking down, or rough-handling the delicate specimens to the point of rendering them useless. Human hands are so much more gentle, human skin more resilient to the rigours of jungle climate.

The prisoners adapted quickly to their new life. Some strayed into the jungle. Father let them go. They soon learned that there was little palatable food beneath the alien canopy—but plenty of creatures willing to feast on them. The ones that crawled back to the palisade in the following weeks were butchered before the others as a warning. I remember the blood stains on the grass.

I am not supposed to think about such things. I am supposed to smile at my father's guests and be grateful for the protection of the palisade. I spend most of my time on the Link ensconced in debates with my university friends, discussing the poems of Chartres and Dessiqa; the plays of Modine, the sculpture of Poussen-Yang and Rudiliere. I speak to them through a platinum blonde avatar, with bronzed skin and elegant limbs. Harmon is the only one who has seen my true face.

The thought of leaving my home fills me with apprehension. Despite the enlightened, intellectual circles in which I move, there is always the possibility of exposure. AmberJade, ungovernable as it is, harbours all manner of practises and beliefs not permitted on other worlds. On Sheredon, Ellah and non-secular Carnis Major, the malformed are not allowed to live.

I am never lonely. I have my friends, my swallowtails, my dreams and my secret love. My life is illuminated with the love of Harmon, the man I hope to name as my husband, despite the relentless cruelty of my father.

As the third course is served, I hear whispering amongst the waiters. They do not seem to care that I am listening. Over time I have become invisible to their eyes. It is only my father they fear. They say that Daria is missing. Baby Ann Elisabeth's nanny; a skittish girl, forever flirting with the pilots. Her bed has not been slept in these past two nights.

Daria is the prettiest of all the nannies. I suspect my father molests her but I have never caught him at it. Her predecessor lasted a year before hitching a lift back to Sheridon on an export trader's barge. Who could blame her? Pretty girls should be out there travelling among the worlds, not trapped in the perpetual pink-and-blossom twilight of a stinted baby's nursery.

The two fourteen-year-old Ann Elisabeths do not require nannies. They inhabit my father's offices in the Summer and Winter wings. He keeps one girl handy to each suite where they perform embroidery and cross-stitch. Sometimes they swap places. He can never tell the difference between them.

Father visits the nursery once a week. He never sees the baby in the same outfit twice. Daria is skilled at her work. She manages to teach the baby a new trick for each visit: picking up the kewpie rattle and shaking it for daddy; smiling at daddy when he walks into the room; crawling towards the sound of daddy's voice; stumbling a few clumsy steps.

But each old trick is forgotten by daddy's next visit. Baby Ann Elisabeth has never even mastered walking. Father hoped for more, but the growth retardant process is not precise. When it comes to stinted babies, a few months can make such a difference.

Stint nannies know they don't have to try too hard; visiting day is all that matters. Nannying is a good appointment for a working girl, but being fondled by my ugly old father can't be pleasant.

But Daria is missing! Suddenly I realise my chance has finally come! Pretty Daria must be planning to run away. No ship has departed Amberjade in the past few weeks. The girl must still be here somewhere. There's no need for me to learn to fly a ship. She knows all the offworld pilots by name. Daria and I will escape together and flee to Bellady's moon.

I must act immediately. Harmon must know of my plans. Keen to avoid the tedious ritual of the six-year-old stint's singing, I slip from the table unobtrusively. No one bothers me as I leave. The men are drunk, the women screeching over small holographic amusements. My swallowtails are forgotten.

As I make my way back through the autumn wing, my mind floods with possibilities. *I will steal some of my father's gold. He will not miss a little of it—it will be several days before he sobers up and notices I am missing.*

I climb the staircase and hurry through the house as fast as I am able, all the way through my Autumn rooms to my Link portal. It activates as I enter, pulsing warm and red, the colour of my heart. The air fills with the scent of rose and jasmine, an olfactory hallucination. Such plants cannot thrive in this planet's bitter soils.

A message awaits, as I knew it would. I am bursting with excitement. I nod for it to play, stand back and hold my breath. No, I will not wait another moment. Words will tumble from my lips in a delicious garble. He will not have to hear them to know what I intend because my manner will tell it all.

When the Link connects my darling Harmon stands before me.

He stands.

I pause, sensing the wrongness, not understanding what I'm seeing even as I'm seeing it.

He stands.

There is no blanket shielding Harmon's supposedly damaged lower body. He smiles, and an undercurrent of unfamiliarity taints his voice. My Autumn suite grows deathly cold, rose and jasmine draining from the air.

This man is not *my* Harmon. This man has his face, but nothing else of him is the same.

His hair is coiffed, his clothing finer and his mannerisms much more aggressive than those of the man I know.

"Arna Maria, my dearest love," he says. "I ache for you. If only we could be together. I would take you to see the grand touring exhibition of Rudiliere's sculptures on Ellah, and then to the library on Gizienne. Why must we live so far apart? When will this torment end?"

Arna Maria? Who is she? A friend from the university Linklounge, perhaps?

"I love you, Arna Maria, as I have loved no other," says Harmon. "Will your father not agree to our marriage? Soon I will have gold. Plenty of it. We can go anywhere we want."

My breath catches sharply in my throat. *"I love you, Arna Maria, as I have loved no other."* I know this line by heart. The very same words he has used on me. The *exact* words, as if taken from a script. A script he no doubt reiterates as many times as amusement dictates.

I fall to the floor, clutching at my chest. He has sent the wrong message to the wrong woman—how many of us has he accumulated in his Link harem? Is his error accidental, or an intentional act of cruelty? Harmon, my lovely Harmon, is a fraud.

"Say it to my face," I whisper, all my dreams in ruins. Say it to my true face, not this cold, projected likeness. *I will steal a ship from the Vazquenadas. I will fly to Bellady's moon and discover the truth for myself.*

I feel my heart burn and shrivel. I am no longer in control. I find myself limping through my father's mansion, eyes blurred with tears, my mind consumed with the hideous image of my darling Harmon smiling at another woman with love that was supposed to be all mine.

Daria. Where is Daria? She will know which of the pilots can be trusted. I will make her take me with her. We shall escape from my father as he drinks himself to senselessness downstairs.

My uneven footsteps echo loudly on the polished marble floors. Room after useless room, yet I feel invigorated through my tears. Driven forward by my pain and confusion. *Surely my Harmon does not mean those words? I have misheard him. Misinterpreted what he said, that is all.*

Above the sound of my own anguished cries I hear another little voice. Instinctively, I head towards it, pushing through double gilded doors. A sickly stench assails my nostrils. Something putrid. Horrible. The wailing is much louder now, and I recognise it suddenly; the crying of a baby.

I find the infant through another doorway in the spring suite nursery. Baby Ann Elisabeth lies screaming in her crib in a mess of her own excrement, a drip feeder taped crudely to her arm. She looks to have been in this condition for some time. Where is nanny Daria? And then it strikes me that this is Fourthday—three whole days away from my father's scheduled visit. Daria could be anywhere on AmberJade. My father would never know. So long as the baby is healthy for daddy's visit, no one cares what happens on the other days.

I lift the squalling bundle from the crib, detach her from the apparatus, wipe her as clean as I can manage with the corner of the sheet. I pull a fresh towel from the linen closet and wrap her tightly.

The stench is indescribable. Covering my nose, I run from that awful place. My father will have to be informed. Daria shall be found and banished in disgrace.

I must find my father and present him with the filthy, squalling stint. I will demand he pay proper attention to his house and change his self-indulgent ways. I shall demand a ship of my own, and a pilot to fly me far away from this horror and decadence.

Baby Ann Elizabeth continues to howl as I carry her through my father's house, through room after empty, pointless room till we reach the grand dining chamber. I will display the dirty stint before his precious dinner guests. Let them all smell its neglect. Interrupt the recital or the pretty song, or whatever he has the six-year-old performing for that troop of drunken Vazquenadas baboons.

I push open the double lacquered doors with my shoulder. The dining room is empty, the table still laid but the dishes abandoned. A butler whose name I do not know steps up to greet me, a crisp white linen draped over one arm.

"Would Miss Luisa Alice care to partake of

refreshment?" he asks.

I lift baby Ann Elisabeth from my shoulder and present her to the butler.

"Take this to my father," I say as calmly as I can, but I know my voice is wavering. If the butler thinks my request bizarre, he makes no obvious show of it. He lifts the squalling stint-child from my arms.

I wipe my hand across my face and find it damp with tears. My clothing reeks, and I realise that I am so terribly tired. I sit in the nearest chair, pick a crumpled napkin from the table and use it to mop my brow. Beside the napkin, a full glass of red wine that I drain in one gulp. I do not normally care for wine but I must have fortification if I am to face my father and demand a ship.

The wine spreads warmth through my veins. My thoughts begin to focus. I *must* have a ship. I will fly to Harmon and demand an explanation of his actions. It is only when I reach for a second glass that I remember his other words. *Soon I will have gold. Plenty of it.* Surely he could not be referring to *my* gold; the gold I plan to steal from my father? Where is my father and his revolting guests? Where has everybody gone?

I stand and walk the length of the dining chamber, through the double lacquered doors and through a further identical set. Servants bustle around me cleaning up the detritus of the evening's festivities. Nobody speaks a word.

I find one of the Vazquenadas on the balcony fucking an underbutler. I turn my face away—I have no quarrel with them. The rest of the family staggers about in the garden below. I only want to speak to my father—what those degenerate foreigners get up to is their own business.

I cannot locate him in any of his regular haunts. I find only the Summer and Winter stints huddled together, whimpering. They will not tell me what is wrong. Has news reached them already of baby Ann Elisabeth's neglect?

I wander through my father's house opening door after door until I come at last upon his bed chamber—a room I have been forbidden to enter, a room I have never given any thought to at all, until this moment.

The door is not locked. My father is accustomed to obedience. He never locks any of his rooms.

Through the door, I see my father in his four-poster bed. Alongside him, sprawled across red silk sheets, a fifth Ann Elisabeth—a child somewhere in age between the six-year-old and the Summer and Winter stints. Nine perhaps, maybe ten. She is naked. Her lips and cheeks are rouged, her eyes lined with jet-black kohl. She wears gold bands around her wrists and ankles. She smiles wickedly as I enter my father's room. Our eyes lock and I see that her heart and mind are devoid of all emotion: no happiness, no light, no love.

There were five Ann Elisabeths in my father's house but now there are none. There is only me, Luisa Alice, the child he never wanted by the wife who abandoned him and ran into the jungle rather than endure another moment in his presence.

I have cut the power to the palisade. Smashed the generators with an iron bar. The skies above the house, once filled with my precious swallowtails, will soon be humming with the dark wings of other flying creatures. Abominations with stingers, barbs and fangs. Jester beetles and other monsters with a taste for human flesh.

Already the jungle has begun its steady creep towards my father's house. Liana vines entwine themselves around my father's butchered corpse. Within a week the marble steps will be cracked and broken, no longer visible from above. Within two, it will be impossible to tell what kind of structure once stood here. The grasses will thicken with tentacles and roots, the soils seethe and churn with carnivorous microbes.

I have freed my father's slaves. Some of them have

ransacked the house and run into the jungle. A few of the hardy ones may survive this time. The others have joined the servants in commandeering the Vazquenadas' silver ships. I watch their contrails blaze across the sky as soft flames of dawn kiss the horizon.

The hangars are empty, the Ann Elisabeths all dead. I killed them, as I myself should have been killed all those years ago, spared the indignities of this pointless existence rather than mutilated with my father's machete blade in an effort to spite my faithless mother.

I stand here now before the Link, trying to compose a final message to Harmon. My embroidered dinner gown is soaked with blood. I want to tell him of the pain he has wrought, but in the end I will send no message. I will say nothing. The encroaching jungle will speak for me. It will tear this mansion stone from stone, wiping our human stain from its memory forever. The jungle will have the final word. It will cover my father's wicked bones, claiming the gold he and my heartless Harmon loved above all else. It will leave no trace of poor Luisa Alice and her beloved swallowtails.

THE WOMAN

by Tanith Lee

1. The Suitor

Down the terraces of the Crimson City they carried her, in her chair of bone and gold.

The citizens stood in ranks, ten or twenty men deep.

They watched.

Some wept.

Some, suddenly oblivious of the guard, thrust forward shouting, calling, a few even reciting lines of ancient poetry. They were swept back again. As if a steel broom could push away the sea of love.

But Leopard did none of these things.

He simply stood there, looking at her. At *Her*. He thought, and even as he thought it he chided himself, telling himself he was quite mad to think it, that her eyes for one tiniest splinter of a fractured second—met his. *Knew* his—knew *him*. Knew Leopard.

But then the chair, borne by its six strong porters, had gone by.

All he could see were the scarlet, ivory and gold of its hood, and the wide shoulders of the last two bearers.

Many of the citizens had fallen on the ground, lamenting and crying, cursing, begging for death. Like a tree which had withstood a lightning strike, Leopard remained on his feet. He was upright in all senses, bodily, mentally, in character and in his moral station. Also sexually.

For he had seen her. At last. His predestined love.

The Woman.

In the village where he had grown up, the birth of Leopard had been a great disappointment. He had been aware of a coldness among his family from an early age. By the time he was six, his mother was dead of bearing another son, and Leopard began to see neither he, nor his newcomer brother, were liked.

One day, when he was a little older, and had been playing 'catch' with the boys on the flat earthen street, under the tall rows of scent trees, Leopard heard one of the village's pair of ancient hags muttering to her sister: "Accursed, that boy. And, too, the infant boy that came after him." "Why's that?" quacked the second hag. "Ah. The mother was frightened by a leopard when she carried that *older* one. So he was turned into something useless." "And the infant?" "Think of *his* name," said the first hag. Then both old women nodded and creaked away into their hut. Leopard felt ashamed. He had vaguely thought he was called Leopard for the beast's silken handsomeness and dangerous hunter's skills. It would seem not. While his poor little brother, Copper Coin—had Mother been scared by a piece of *money*?

Copper Coin, however, rather than cursed, actually proved very useful later on, when he became popular for his beauty, and their family grew both respected and well-off.

Today, several years after, Leopard removed himself from the crowd and strode away along the wide white streets of the Crimson City, to the wine-house Copper Coin now owned. Leopard had a thing of wonder to tell Copper. Leopard's heart buzzed and sang within him.

A single enormous scent tree reared outside the wine-house; it was somewhere in the region of three hundred feet tall. At this season it rained down orange blossoms that smelled of incense and honey.

Patrons sat in the courtyard to catch the perfume on their hair, skin and clothes. And while they did this of course, ate and drank. Trade was bustling.

Inside, Leopard had to wait. His beautiful brother was occupied for another quarter of an hour with a favoured client.

Leopard drank hot green alcohol and ate two or three river shrimps roasted with pepper. Seeing who he was, the food and drink were on the house.

Then the client, dreamy-eyed and flushed, rattled down from the upper apartment. He passed Leopard without seeing him though Leopard had met the man before. He was a prince of the High Family of the Nine, immensely rich, always courteous and good-natured. But also he was crazily in love with Copper, and usually came out of the bedroom in a trance, between shining joy and dark despair. This morning Leopard sympathized. For now he, Leopard, was also insane with love.

The servant took Leopard upstairs.

Copper, just fresh from the bath and belted in a dressing-gown of embroidered white silk, lay on a couch. His hair, worn some inches longer than any merely male man would wear it, coiled over his shoulders, gleaming black as sharkskin.

"Gorgeous as ever," remarked Leopard, between praise and banter. "Prince Nine tottered down, almost dead of love."

"So I should think. We were together three hours. It

wouldn't look good for me, would it, if he pranced out bored and burping. But you," added Copper, "you're pale as a marble death-stone."

Leopard stared at Copper. Then Leopard went and kneeled at his brother's feet and laid his head in Copper's lap. Murmuring gently, Copper stroked Leopard's own hair, shortly thick as a cat's fur. There was nothing sexual between them. Copper had become like a mother-sister for Leopard at about the same time Copper also found his own inner femaleness.

"Ssh, what is it, darling?"

"Oh gods of the seventy hells—"

"Don't invoke that uncouth nasty mob."

"The eleven heavens then. Oh Copper, Copper—Did you know?"

"Know what, my baby?"

"*She* was shown in the city today."

"The *Woman*? Gods, yes, I'd forgotten. No wonder half my best lads' clientele was absent. Damn it, there was I cursing them. And they too stupid to remind me."

Leopard shook, but with laughter.

He sat up and gazed into his brother's exquisite and surprised face.

"Listen, Copper. *I* applied."

"You—my own spirit! *When?*"

"Last Rose Moon."

"Three *months* ago? And all this while you never told me—"

"I was afraid I'd be thrown out from the first examination. But I passed them all."

Copper sank back on the cushions, fanning himself.

"Wait, sweetheart. You go too fast. I'm staggered as an old hag on her last legs."

Leopard gripped his hand. Glowing with pride, he detailed every contest he had entered, and passed, always well, and often with the brilliant coloured inks of his competency and genius marked on the scroll. There had been reading and writing, in which, though village taught, he had had the luck of erudite masters, and the added learning Copper had later bought for him. There had been philosophy and debating too, humour and drama. There had been the art of painting, and the arts of war—cross-bow, staff, moon-sword and bare fist. Finally he had had to compose a love poem of four lines only, each line containing only four words. Leopard modestly said he did not believe his own work one twelfth as good as others he had seen inscribed on the judges' parchment, but by then he had also been physically examined by physicians and dentists, some of his skin and hair, his urine, blood and saliva scientifically evaluated. Lastly his semen was checked, having been gathered after the use of a certain drug and a dream, as he had thought, of The Woman herself. Only the finalists of the examinations were ever given this hallucinogen, but after it he could not recall what she had been like, the goddess of his orgasm. Now, naturally, he need not wonder for today he had seen her in person. Her eyes had—surely? unbelievably?—rested on him in turn.

In a restrained tone Copper observed, "And they allowed you to stand close to the road where she travels by in her chair. Only finalists may stand so near. Or the most wealthy, they say, who can afford to buy places. But, Leopard, my sweet one—these contests concerning The Woman occur only once every year—"

"I know. And now *you* know why I've lived in this city for a year, the parasite beneficiary of your bounty, and never a hard word from you though I earned myself not even a single bit of lead."

"I've plenty." said Copper, "why should I mind—yet Leopard—Leopard—"

Leopard raised his proud young head. "Say nothing to bring down my mood. *Nothing.* Don't tell me how many others have almost won her, yet failed the Ultimate Test. Say *nothing* of that."

Copper lowered his eyes. The kohl on his long lashes glistened. They might have been wet with tears. "I say only this. One hundred men have died, in only the brief years *I* was here in the Crimson City, because of The Woman, and the Ultimate Test."

"I love her," said Leopard.

When he spoke of love, which was a common enough word and a concept often enough employed, love's very soul seemed to brush across Copper's elegant reception chamber.

Copper Coin had been named, at birth, for the copper coin their mother had bribed an itinerant hag to fix in the neck of her womb and stopper her, following the previous birth of Leopard. It was rumoured their mother had told the hag, "I can endure no more. I can *bear* no more." But the hag, though a villainess, had nevertheless been also either inept or cunning, and the coin had not saved Mother from conceiving, carrying and ejecting her last son, even if his advent killed her.

Copper had always, though glad to have been given life, felt very sorry for their mother.

Not himself desiring women, which he found a blessing, Copper had space to respect and pity them. Even the old ones— especially they perhaps. And even The Woman, maybe, the demon-goddess, cold and distant as some far off planet, whose surface, if ever one *did* reach her, smashed men like brittle dragonflies on her rocks of razor and adamant.

The sky was green as young-grape wine.

Alone, Leopard stood on the roof of his lodging. Below, his city room, a cell equipped with a pillow, a writing-stand, and the fixtures for elimination and ablution in one corner, had also a ladder which had often led him up here.

He watched evening stars like molten silver burst from

the greenness. So love was. So it seared forth from the dusk of life.

Leopard had dimly heard of The Woman in the Crimson City since the age of six. But, at sixteen he *heard* with more than his ears. Thereafter he had had only one goal, which he kept secret from all who knew him closely, until this day.

Now Copper had been informed. And now Leopard had beheld, in flesh, not two arm's length away in front of him, The Woman.

Oh, to win her, to retain her—which must be impossible.

Yet to see, to have, and *then* to lose her—also impossible.

In the balance of the gods of balances, his weighted hopes and dreads must lie level tonight.

He had visited various temples about the city, sometimes passing other finalists he recognized, or they him, each man nodding politely, heart hidden yet well understood. He had travelled the white streets for miles, and made his offerings lavish, financed by Copper's generosity. And Copper had said nothing more. And yet, at their parting, Copper's perfect eyes truly had been full of tears, like diamond pearls. Such beauty.

If only Leopard had loved men, as Copper did.

But no. Leopard loved women—loved The Woman.

Nothing else would do.

Even if so many other hundred thousand men had perished, Leopard believed he alone would prevail. He would pass the Ultimate Test, have her and keep her. *Him* she would love. But too, of course, he knew such a thing could never be. He could only become one more shell smashed upon her steely beach. One more dead, useless man.

2. The Lover

U nlike the dusk, the dawn was a peach. The moisture of it
put out the blazing stars yet lit the lioness of the sun, who
leapt up high above the city.

"Oh, Sun Lady, give me my dream. . . ."

Leopard climbed the three hundred marble steps to the
Palace. He did this alone. For no finalist of the examinations
ever made his final journey in company with any others.

Leopard noticed, despite the haze which seemed to
envelope him, and the burning turmoil inside him, how the huge
vistas of the city fell away and away. Long avenues and
dwellings with roofs of carmine, purple or jade-green tiles;
squares where fountains restfully played and gold and amber fish
swam in pools among the lotuses; gardens of scent trees or
sculpted pines and cedars . . . the world of the city, flawless and
mathematical, grew less significant, nearly of no importance. So
death must be, decided Leopard, strong enough he did not need
to pause on the great stair for breath, only now and then to
glance back and downward. For death too would be to leave the
colourful world of life, ascending to some heavenly plain—or
otherwise falling, of course, into some abysmal hell.

His reflections then were quite appropriate.

Who climbed this stair to the Palace of The Woman
would indeed afterwards enter a heaven, or a hell.

At the vast doors guards were absent. Servants drew him
in like a welcome guest.

For many hours he was prepared, bathed and massaged,
dressed in costly robes, given to eat and drink light and ethereal
foods of great nourishment and strange pale wines.

Leopard grew calm through these ministrations, but in
the way of one deeply shocked by some colossal calamity or
happiness. Even though such an event still lay before him.

Of the other finalists there was never any sign, and no

mention. This day, this night, were unique to Leopard, as to each finalist there was given always one such passage of hours in light and darkness.

During which he would undergo the Ultimate Test, and win or lose The Woman, and his life.

In the last recent years, a hundred dead, Copper had told him. Leopard had been amazed there were so few. None had ever won her. None.

In the afternoon, flocks of pink birds flew round and round the upper arches of the Palace where Leopard was now standing. He did not see them.

Before him lay a door of bronze inlaid with gold.

It opened after only half an hour.

No one remained on the gallery save Leopard, and in the room beyond the door, there would be only one. She.

He seemed to move through air, weightless as a ghost. He crossed the threshold. The door drew slowly shut at his back.

The Woman sat on a golden chair, with her feet on a footstool shaped like a crouching elephant.

Her hands rested on her knees. Every finger had a ring of silver or gold and assorted jewels. She wore also a wig of indigo hair, plaited with blue gems.

She seemed neither pleased nor dismayed at the sight of Leopard. He found he could not fathom her expression. But then he was stunned by her wonderfulness, by her female aura and her sexual glory.

He greeted her ritually, and musically spoke aloud for her his four line poem, then knelt on the patterned floor to await her commands.

Silence snowed heavy as old blossoms.

He smelled incense and perfume from his clothing.

Partly afraid to go on gazing at her, he stared at the floor and the painted animals there began to waver before his eyes.

"Oh, get up," she barked suddenly in a hoarse high little voice. "Rise from your knees before you faint. So many of you do. How I dislike this fainting. Get *up!*"

Unsteadily yet quite gracefully Leopard obeyed her.

"Your poem's thought clever," she said. "That use of the one word *see* three times, then a fourth time but altered. How admirable. I suppose. Well," she said. She reached her small plump hand towards a silver side-dish and selected a sugared plum. She ate it slowly, looking at him.

And her cold-sheened eyes slid over him. *They* were entirely expressionless, like pieces of opaque black slate. Over and over him the slate eyes slid.

How wondrous she was.

Oh gods, he could hardly bear it—and already in a kind of desolation, fearful she did not like him, even so his sex was upright and ready, the most potent weapon of love.

"Come here then," she said. "Since you must."

He went to her, stood there, standing once again in every sense.

"Well," she said, her shrill voice rather more dull, "take off your garments. Let me see what you are, you—what do they call you?—*Leopard?*" And at this, his name, she laughed, more shrilly, like a flute warped by rain.

And yet *he* laughed as well, vibrantly, loving her mockery even, loving *her*, and burning.

Naked, Leopard was a man like a perfect statue, made of satiny tawny wood polished smooth as glass. Wide-shouldered, slim, every muscle well-developed yet lean. He shone in the icon of his body, which had the form of both fighter and dancer. On his chest the two jewels of his nipples, themselves erect, were the colour of the purest beer. At his groin the short black pelt resembled, in its silkenness, the thick silk hair upon his head. And from his groin also rose his succulent phallus, blushing and firm as the most edible fruit. He had no flaw. And his face too was a marvel. Where his brother Copper was transcendently lovely, Leopard was incandescently handsome. And while his parted lips—he was breathless with terror and lust—revealed the whiteness of his teeth, his large dark eyes revealed the flames of longing, and perhaps some aspect of his soul.

The Woman regarded him with care. Then she pushed herself off her seat and puttered all around him. She observed him front, sidelong and back, scarcely blinking. Were her own eyes pitiless? Like a reptile's? Surely merely a trick of westering light.

She was not tall, The Woman.

The top of her blue-wigged head was level only with Leopard's ribcage.

Behind him still, she grunted.

He was afraid to turn, in case this sound of hers indicated some annoyance—or disappointment—*dismissal.*

He trembled.

Out of one of his luminous eyes a single tear dropped like silvery jasper. Yet even now his eloquent phallic erection stood its ground. His brain and heart might quake; this rose-gold warrior, primed with battle-juice, was too forthright and too wise yet to surrender.

Perhaps—could it be?—*its* instinct, if not the man's, had picked up from the short round woman who patrolled the vicinity of Leopard's splendour, some secret scent of answering desire . . .

"Oh," eventually said The Woman, at Leopard's back, "very well, then. Over there. The room behind the lacquer doors."

"Lady—do you mean—"

"I mean we'll go to the couch and do what's to be done."

And then The Woman turned and waddled away, and Leopard, dipped in fires, followed her.

A mong his self-educations. which as an adult had come to include singing, fighting, drama and philosophy, Leopard had not neglected to add the arts of love. He had learned these, as with the others, from the best teachers, who taught him everything at one remove. And he had then practiced all alone, over and over. "Beware," they had told him. "If *ever* you should enact these things with a real subject—that is with a *woman*—it will be as it is also when you fight. For in love too your lover, male or female, is unwittingly your opponent, striving to overthrow you. But you must subdue your ardour and yourself remain the master. And, whereas in battle you must kill with force and pain, in sex you must kill with delight. *That* death's a very different matter."

And Leopard, his goal—her—had fully learned and then practiced with total dedication.

Now therefore, even as he saw The Woman take off her clothes, even her wig so her hair fell forth, he kept the confidence of a great mage, whose power sweeps in on him at his instruction. The more mighty the odds against self-control, the more mightily controlled now might Leopard be.

So at last, assured, he went to her, and leaning over her, measured and gauged her with his learned hands and fiery eyes.

T hree hours was the time Copper had quoted for his companion, Prince Nine.

But Leopard and The Woman entered a timeless zone. Which in fact lasted the rest of the day, all one night, and some space of the subsequent morning.

Leopard coaxed and seduced and adored and magnified The Woman. With acts not words he laved her body with caresses, used on her a musician's hands, a poet's mouth like velvet, a tongue like streams and feathers and bees, a sexual organ like a magician's tireless and world-ordering wand. Again and again he brought her to the prolonged spasm of ecstasy.

Sometimes even she might emit a squeak of pleasure, though generally she was noiseless in culmination, only the ripples of her loins and belly giving evidence of achievement.

How he loved her.

Her fat, barrel-shaped form with its sallow, coarse, slightly blotchy carapace of skin. Her shapeless breasts. The thin hair that meagrely clad both her head and the heavenly, wide gate between her short legs. He loved her spatulate hands and ridged nails, and the nails of her toes from which the paint had worn, leaving them like ten square and striated rocks. He loved her teeth, which were so charmingly discoloured, and her sugar-sour breath. The ordinary non-profundity of her face. Her arrogance and indifference he loved too, though they lashed him with tragic fear of failure. And her gelid eyes. Even these—though they condemned him, surely.

Ah gods, even in victory over the reluctant, grudging climaxes of her body, Leopard at last heard the lament of approaching defeat.

Long before the night wore out, the red dawn—no longer peach but bloodied wine—he knew in his heart's heart he had not won her. And never could. None could.

None.

3. The Reject

All that day-night-day, Copper paced his apartment.

It comprised three rooms and a private courtyard on the roof. He went from one area to another, climbing up, descending, walking, turning. Now and then he touched something. A small statue of a dancing lion, a cup of black onyx, a little dagger of twisted wood Leopard had carved and given him when Copper was only five years old.

Copper wept. Chided himself and blotted up his tears. Cursed Fate and The Woman, cursed life and the world. Flung himself in a chair, wrote down his thoughts without coherence, got up and paced again, wept again, chided and blotted and cursed—again. Again.

Gods knew, if only Leopard had loved only men. There were male men who did so. Some of Copper's nicest 'lads' were like that, and those like Copper, if not pretty enough to make their way, came to such gallants for solace. One indeed had married a male man from Copper's wine-house, and they had lived happy now three whole years.

But Leopard was only Man.

So many men, despite dalliances with their own gender, were only—Men.

And so: The Woman of the Crimson City.

Copper knew, despite his hopes and wishes, and Leopard's glamour and virtue, that The Woman would not want him for long. She had never wanted any of the ones who devoted their dreams to her and then passed all the required examinations but one. For to meet and make love with The Woman was the Ultimate Test. No man had *ever* passed it. Evidently. Or she would not be there still, hung like an over-ripe yellow fruit, cruel and evil with her thorns, on the tree of human longing.

How the gods must hate mankind, to do this to them.

The hours ground away under Copper's pacing, weeping and cursing.

About sunfall, the man he had sent to watch the Palace's Lower Gate bounded up Copper's stair and beat on the door.

"What's happened, Heron?"

But Heron was crying. His tears spoke loudly, in an uncouth bellow.

"So then," said Copper, gripping in his own emotion, "did he emerge from the Gate?"

"Yes, oh yes—oh gods, I've seen old gentlemen whose white beards brushed the earth, whose backs were humped with age like a camel's—and they walked more sprightly than your brother, lovely Leopard."

"Where did he take himself?"

"Towards the bank of the river—"

"*And*—?"

"And my companion, Lamplit, our best runner as you know, sped after and caught him. Then Tomorrow, my other friend from next door, ran up too. They took hold of him and are bringing him here now. But slowly. He can barely move, Copper Coin."

Copper whispered a curse then that curled up the air of the apartment. The sun too seemed to wither in it and threw herself off over the precipice of the horizon. Dusk veiled everything. Nightingales and tweet-birds sang from the tall scent tree outside.

One more hour later, when the sky was black and the bright windows and rosy lanterns of the city showed the path, Lamplit and Tomorrow helped Leopard into Copper's reception chamber.

"Drink this."

"Nothing. Please. Give me nothing."

"Darling Leopard. It's myself offers the drink. Look. Do you see me? Your brother. "

"I see you, dear. But take the cup away. The dead need no food, no water."

Finally, persuaded to one sip, the kindly soporific in the drink took its effect.

Leopard was laid on the second bed, his head on pillows of silk.

But even sleeping, his face was old, and ruinous. He looked like a man who must soon die.

The physician came. This doctor was of high quality and learning, but once Copper told him why Leopard was distressed and ill the physician bowed his head. "I shall do whatever I am able. But I also had a brother once. This was thirteen years ago.

He too went after The Woman, and won through to her. When she cast him out he lived only two months. We watched him night and day in case he tried to poison or hang himself. But in the end, without assistance of bane or rope or blade, he simply died. It was through his death I set myself to learn medicine, to understand the windings of the human intellect. But I doubt I can help you, or your brother."

"She's vilely wicked," said Copper, "The Woman. A demoness sent up from the hells to destroy us."

"Perhaps," said the physician.

Then Leopard woke up and the physician set to work on him. Seven days, and the nights between them, trudged by.

Then seven more.

Copper went on with his usual duties, but refused all those clients he normally had pleasure with. He explained to them privately that he could experience no pleasure at this time. Only Prince Nine was permitted to arrive frequently, and he simply to talk with Copper, gratis, to steady him and try to ease his sorrow.

In the end Leopard began to be seen. He would walk in the courtyard or sit there quietly on his own. At evening, sometimes, he would dine at the communal table of the wine-house, if not in Copper's apartment.

Regular customers treated him with care, and with respect and sympathy. If they were jealous of his having been a finalist, and briefly winning The Woman and lying with her, they curbed themselves. Decidedly they could see where his moment of success had afterwards dragged and abandoned him. He seemed quite soulless. He seemed part dead.

One evening a newcomer entered the wine-house, and sat down at the main table. He was an older man, of fine physical appearance, and perhaps a philosopher.

He spoke directly to Leopard, in an actor's clear voice. "So you are the unlucky fellow who fucked the great bitch in the

Palace?" he said.

Instantly silence deafened the room.

Heron, who had been eating, got up without a word and went straight to knock at Copper's door, despite the fact Copper was just then entertaining a prince of the High Family of the Ninety-Two.

Leopard however raised his head and looked at the newcomer.

"I am he. But she is not a bitch. She is beautiful, and by me beloved, and will be so until the day of my ending."

"Very well," agreed the philosopher, if so he was. "Very well. Maybe she is a bitch since only circumstances have made her one. As also time has made her older and fatter. But I think a snake gave her such cold eyes."

Leopard lowered his gaze. He did not reply.

The philosopher went on, in his clear and reasonable voice, "Surely you, or some of you here at the very least, must understand *why* men venerate and think such a creature wonderful?"

A man cried out: "Because she is *The Woman*."

"Just so," said the philosopher. "The *only* woman. That is," he amended, "the only known woman yet living in our city, or in the existing world, who has not yet died of the excessive bearing of male children, or grown into an ancient hag." A vast sigh, nearly a groan, curdled from the room-full of men. It passed on into the courtyard, where the other men had, many of them, risen and come to see who spoke such words. It drifted up to balconies of the wine-house and surrounding buildings, and was echoed back from them. It fled along the white streets and found some kind of other echo always there, in every masculine throat, in every masculine mind. For there were only men in the Crimson City, as the philosopher had stated. Men who were feminine or men who were male, and some who were gifted with both states, and those who were young or old. Or there were a few old, old women who had somehow survived relentless decades of child-bearing, scorned and sworn at on every occasion, which had been by now every occasion without exception, that they had produced, rather than a daughter, yet another son.

Beyond the Crimson City, did the curdling echo of the groan strike out even there, like a cold fist beating on the surface of a cold metal gong, and the reverberation unfurling, on and on? Probably so. For in all the land about, in the towns and villages, in the farthest places, still there were only the differing types of men, male men and female men, or men of both persuasions, and young men, and old men, and dead men in graves with death-stones over them like white fallen pieces of the lonely masculine moon.

And even the hags maybe heard the sigh, the groan. Even the dead women in their own graves that bore each the symbol of the barren blazing sun, the dead women burned away by bearing only men.

While outside the borders of this land, the other lands. All the same. All, all, the same.

For some years ago, about the time that the mother of Leopard and Copper Coin had herself died, the very last of all the women yet able to conceive a child, had perished.

With the last of such deaths, all chance of change died too.

And now there were only the men and the hags. And the female sun. And She. The Woman in the Palace.

When Copper tore down the stair, Prince Ninety-Two deserted above in the upper rooms, it was Tomorrow who ran quickly and caught hold of him.

"Stay, Copper—stay, stay—look there. Do you see?" And Copper halted, and his pale face went more pale and his eyes widened.

For there Leopard was, held in the arms of an unknown newcomer to the house, a man neither old nor young, but handsome and well-dressed, perhaps a philosopher, and with an actor's voice. Leopard was weeping his heart out as since returning here he had not wept. And the philosopher raised his face and glancing at Copper said, softly, "Don't fear it. I am his brother too, his brother in this most bleak of miseries. For I also, long before, was a finalist in the Crimson City. I also won The Woman, lay with her, lost her, failed at the Ultimate Test. A man who wandered in an earthly hell some while. But sense came back to me, and that hell faded. I lived. As Leopard may live. There is more to life than love. I am the proof, am I not, that not all men die who fail with her."

Copper felt his heart clutch, as if a dagger had gone into it. For he sensed that here at last might be the single other man in all the world who could give back to Leopard a reason for existence. And passionate hope had stabbed at Copper's heart, and bitter envy had cloven it.

"Do what you must," said Copper. And offered the stranger his most beautiful and generous smile.

Then he kissed his brother on one temple, and left him in the keeping of the unknown man. And in the hands of the gods too, where all things may lie, whether they wish it or not.

4. The Woman

High above the terraced streets, the squares and courtyards and gardens, The Woman stood in a long room without a single window, lit only by tall lamps in the shape of flowers. She wore a plain garment, her hair tied back in a knot. She was barefoot on the cool painted floor. Once pink birds had sung here. But one day she had opened a door and let them go free. They had never entirely forsaken her. They still flew about the upper arches and nested in the roofs. How wonderful, she had always thought, The Woman, their magical power of flight.

How old was she when first they brought her here? Quite young, she believed. Five, seven?

She had never been certain of her age.

She was the first and last daughter of a peasant woman called This Fern.

This Fern had birthed The Woman, and been made the heroine of her village, for only recently that year the otherwise last known female child, a girl of eleven years, had died in the far north, of stomach trouble.

But This Fern also soon died, after a bear attacked her at the edge of the forest. Everyone hunted the bear, to kill it, but it was gone, and so of course was This Fern. The Woman had only been two years old then. She could not remember her mother, though they had given her her mother's possessions, her festival robe and her festival shoes, her wooden comb and earrings of tin, and one of her teeth, which had been knocked from her mouth ages before and preserved in a small black box.

These artifacts The Woman still possessed. Now she kept them in a chest of carved and perfumed cedar-wood inlaid with silver, and with a ruby on its clasp.

Men in authority had brought The Woman to the Crimson City. In the Palace she was trained, vigorously and often unkindly, to be a woman. That is, an important woman. That is, The Only Woman.

When, at the age of fifteen, she had fallen in love, or fancied she had done so, with one of her malely inclined tutors, he was beaten almost to death and exiled from the city.

His own feelings she never learned.

Probably he was as crazily infatuated as she.

But she was never sure, nor if he recovered from the beating and the exile.

At sixteen she began to be shown in the city.

Then, seeing young men sometimes of extraordinary attractions, gazing at, or fainting at the sight of her, she herself often lost her heart.

But she had been thoroughly lessoned by then in her role, and theirs. Since seemingly—and soon irrevocably and definitely—she was the last young human of her gender—only those with the highest qualities of looks and skills would ever be allowed to approach her.

During this era, The Woman still had one female attendant, a hag who had been almost seventy when The Woman first met her.

The hag, Ochre, was never very polite and never pleasant to her charge, let alone affectionate. The Woman supposed Ochre had been selected for her unappealing acidity because, after all, Ochre was ancient, all of her kind were by then, and must soon die. Bereavement of her would therefore be less distressing.

But the hag was presently caught anyway mixing ground glass into The Woman's food.

Taken off to be stoned somewhere or other below the Palace, Ochre screeched that The Woman was a demoness, a curse not a blessing on the city. After this, inevitably, no further hags served in the Palace.

Later, when the first waves of lovers, having passed spectacularly well in the examinations, began to approach The Woman and she, as instructed, made love with them—initially loathing the act, which hurt her and also seemed grotesque—another unfortunate thing was discovered. The Woman did not ever conceive. Since tests had been made as well on the semen of all the young male lovers, and it was both wholesome and fertile, the fault must lie with The Woman's body. But as she was The Woman, and the last woman of all women, it was concluded it could not be her fault, even after several quite horrible procedures to which she was subjected in order to 'awake' her womb, proved useless. A general decision asserted that the wicked hag Ochre, prior to the episode with the glass, had already succeeded in somehow poisoning The Woman and so negating her reproductive knack.

With maturity The Woman learned to enjoy the sexual act.

In the beginning, she herself read manuals of love she had been taught to read—and practiced such arts with the waves of lovers. But their frenzies of joy and gratitude frightened her.

She ceased to be active during sex, even restricting her cries at climax, for a similar reason.

At the start she had continued to fall in love and to wish to make a permanent union with this man or that.

But in the Palace the men in authority, who by that time grew old themselves, male hags who frequently went absent in death, had told her she might *never* choose any man above another. To choose one over all the rest would doubtless see him murdered. At best the city would riot and lose its collective mind.

Originally it seemed, the rite of the examinations to find the best, and the making of love between that best and herself, had been organized in the hope of children. Some of which, if the gods were tender, might be daughters.

But of course Ochre, or something or other, had forestalled that plan.

Now therefore the Woman's only value was in her female presence, which must at intervals be revealed, offered and *given* to occasional males.

Until her own demise, this was all The Woman was to be for.

A vision, a goal, a sop. And a method of the most vicious rejection.

Partly she was to represent hope, still, and partly she was to teach that all women were worthless, evil, thus unregrettable. While the dying out of the human race, which now almost without a doubt was unavoidable, could be blamed on the female kind. Also too, perhaps, she was to demonstrate that death, and the death of humanity, might be no bad thing.

In these elements she was like a goddess.

For gods were cruel. They made hells as well as heavens, and all the earthly ills.

Having walked about for a while in the restful windowless room, The Woman sat down on an ivory bench.

She drank a little apricot wine.

She ate a sugar biscuit.

The enormous and never ending depression that now informed most of her days, and usually sleepless nights, came crouching up the floor and rubbed its flank against her consciousness.

Listlessly, resistlessly, she greeted it.

She did not want the riches of the Palace, nor the extreme—unreal—power she had been given. She did not really even want sex any more, let alone the intermittent torrents of young men who came to her, singing poetry, caressing and coaxing, their delicious kisses less than the momentary sweetness of a biscuit.

She might love none. She loved none.

She might choose none. She chose none.

She sent them away, and they threw themselves in the river and drowned, or slit open their veins or swallowed venom.

Oh, she did not *dare* give her heart now to any man. She would be loving a ghost. A thousand ghosts. Death itself.

So. The Woman did not want wealth or sex or ecstasy or worship or love.

Was there anything then that she wanted, longed for?

Yes. Yes.

The Woman wanted her mother. Sometimes even The Woman would daydream that This Fern, fresh up from her grave, would walk into the room. She would not be phantom, nor skeleton. She would not even be old. No, no, This Fern would be about The Woman's own age. Whatever age that was.

But it was more than that, of course. Not only that she wanted the mother she had never known. It was *women*— Woman—The Woman wanted. Not for sexual love, never that. But . . . to talk to. To laugh with. To be with. Oh gods, women about her, easy and familiar, different and the same. Desire? Entirely. The desire of the lonely one for its other self. Here in the Palace high above the Crimson City and the world, The Woman sat on her bench of bone, pining, lamenting, slowly dying—for her own kind.

> *Gods who see me*
> *When her I see,*
> *See I have become*
> *As a seeing god.*

Translated from the poem by
Leopard

A MASK OF FLESH

by Marie Brennan

Sitting alone in the green heat of the forest, far from the road and any observing eyes, Neniza began to craft her mask of flesh.

She started with her toes, for the face would be the hardest part. Toes, feet, legs; the gentle curve of hips. She would have dearly loved to shape for herself the slender, delicate body of an amantecatl, but it would never work. Oh, she could take the form easily enough, but the amanteca were not common caste, and she could never hope to mimic the ways of court folk well enough to pass. Instead she crafted the petite, pretty figure of a young alux peasant. Someone innocent of city ways. Someone who could catch the eye of the lord.

Her father had taught her this work, their art, after her horrified mother saw what she had birthed and left it in the woods. He wished she were still a son, Neniza knew, wished she had not changed into a daughter. Daughters were dangerous things. But his own words had done it, telling the story of what happened to their people. Waking the anger in her. The priests spoke of the wet season and the dry season, the season of giving and the season of taking. For her people, it was no mere abstraction. Their bodies reflected their souls.

Perhaps her father could overlook the wrong they had suffered; Neniza could not. She had not told him where she was going, what she intended to do. He believed they should stay out of sight, accept the hidden existence left to them—never mind that he himself went to town all too often, to court the women of other castes, perhaps to sire more children for them to fear. It was all right for *him*.

But not for her. Not so long as she remained female. She was too dangerous.

That means I'm powerful, Neniza thought, and began to work on her face.

She made it a young one, and attractive, wondering as she did so if it looked anything like her mother. Her father would never say. Neniza had nothing to know her by, no way to pick her mother out of the countless aluxob working the fields, and if she were to go to town without her mask of flesh, her mother would never acknowledge a thing like her as offspring. Every time she made an alux face, she told herself it was her mother's, and every time it was different.

Bushy, soft hair above a round and cheerful face, with eyes the fresh green of new corn. The mask was complete, but Neniza hesitated. Her father would warn her against this, if he knew.

Her father had proved his weakness many times over.

Neniza pulled clothes on over the fleshy nakedness of her body, loincloth, skirt, and a shawl broad enough to hide her arms, then forced her way through the trees to the road.

The city almost made her turn back.

Neniza had been to town before, disguising herself as a woman of one common caste or another, mingling into the crowds she found there, but her first sight of the city showed her how little that had prepared her.

The huge stone walls took her breath away, towering upward in interlocking blocks of carefully-dressed limestone. The tangle of forest had been cleared in a broad swath around them, so the sun hammered down on the line of aluxob with their grain and vay sotz with their packs of goods to trade, all waiting to pass through the gates. Neniza joined them, thirsty and footsore; she was unused to walking barefoot and masked on the hard, pounded dirt of the road. A few of the other travelers glanced at her incuriously, but most disregarded her, intent on their destination. She was grateful for their inattention.

Inside the walls she found a clamoring chaos that took the breath right out of her lungs. Smells, sights, sounds, people pushing at her on every side, dogs underfoot, jostling elbows, flapping birds tethered or in cages, sellers shouting, strangers of every caste packed in like ants, and over it all, rearing above the flat level of streets and houses, the imposing heights of the temple and palace mounds.

Neniza stared upward, transfixed, and then stumbled and nearly fell when a passing kisin rammed into her. He continued on without apologizing, while the flow of people buffeted her this way and that, until she lurched up against the mud-brick wall of a potter's shop and stopped to catch her breath.

She could no longer see the palace mound from where she stood, and it was probably just as well. With her goal not dominating her vision, she could calm herself, take slow breaths, reassert her self-control before she ventured back out into the stream of people flowing through the lanes and plazas of the city. They wore shawls and serapes woven in many colors, with beaded fringes of carved wood or even coral, that would have been unimaginable wealth in the villages she knew. It was too much for Neniza to take in. She flinched every time someone brushed up against her, which was often. Never before had she put her mask to such a test, and it was hard to trust that it would hold.

No one gave her a second glance, though. Why should anyone pay attention to a young alux woman, lost in the mass of people swarming through the city streets?

By the time she arrived at the foot of the palace mound, she was breathless and faint, and for the first time she experienced doubt. This was no place for her. She belonged out in the trackless expanses of forest, where the fields and towns had not yet pushed the wilderness back. She belonged in solitude, away from contact with others except when she chose to bring herself near them. She was meant to deal with people singly, not in flocks.

Alone at the base of the mound—for the people of the city did not come here unless they had reason—she bit her lip and looked upward.

The wide steps of dressed limestone led up, and up, and up. The arched entrance to the expanse of the palace mound faced westward, opposite to the main temple, so that the setting sun scorched its carved facade with scarlet light. Two figures stood on either side of the arch; she could not see them clearly at this distance, but their muscled outlines and the spears in their hands marked them as guards. Once past them—if she passed them—she was committed. Or so she told herself. Once she attained the heights of the palace mound, she would not turn back.

Neniza took a deep breath, wiped her sweating brow, and began to climb the steps.

The guards did not move as she climbed past the carved and painted murals of the lord's triumphs against his enemies, but the instant her foot touched the level surface of the smaller landing just below them, their spears snapped across to bar the arch.

Neniza jumped at the movement, even though she had been expecting it. The guards, of course, were ocelotlaca, and she had never been so close to such before. They stood half again as tall as her small alux form, and their muscles slid smoothly beneath the jaguar spots of their fur. They wore loincloths, arm-bands, headdresses of beads and shells; nothing stood between them and harm but their own teeth, claws, and weapons, their skill in battle.

They needed nothing more.

"State your business," a melodiously bored voice said in accented Wide Speech. Within the shade of the archway, just behind the spears, stood an amantecatl. He was dressed in elegant court finery, with golden ear-spools and a pectoral of turquoise and jade. Still, Neniza told herself, he must not be very important, if he were assigned the tedious duty of the palace entrance.

She slid her hands beneath the opposite edges of her shawl, crossing her arms and bowing as she knelt on the hot stone. "I have come to wait in the plaza of the Honored One, in hopes that he will listen to my words."

The amantecatl sighed. "You're going to wait a long time."

Neniza nodded, eyes fixed on a near-invisible seam where two blocks of limestone joined together. "I understand."

"No, you don't," the amantecatl said, and then muttered something in unintelligible Court Speech. "But you may enter, if you wish to waste your time."

A wooden clack as the ocelotlaca tapped their spears together and withdrew them. Neniza rose, bowed again, and hurried through the arch into the plaza behind.

They had grown careless. They believed the threat was long gone. They had not demanded to see her hands.

The amantecatl's words were true. Neniza lost count of how many days she spent waiting in the petitioners' plaza. She knew only how difficult it was to keep her nature disguised, living so closely with others.

She did not need food, but she had to hide her lack of need, and water was a constant concern. Others ran out of provisions but would not leave; they traded sexual favors to the palace-mound inhabitants who came by the plaza, in exchange for what they needed. It was one of the many sacrifices that kept the world functioning. But Neniza, female as she had become, dared not imitate them.

Nor could she maintain the mask forever. Her first task, upon reaching the plaza, was to find an alcove sufficiently sheltered for her to hide in when she felt her flesh failing. The plaza was ringed by buildings, and the petitioners went among them, but privacy was hard to come by.

Still, she endured. She had climbed the palace mound and passed the guards; that meant she could not turn back.

Life in the petitioners' plaza was not a simple matter of waiting. However long Neniza had been there, others had waited longer, arriving after the last visit the lord had made to this place. There were even a few desperate souls who had been there when he came, but had not received the gift of his attention; they stayed on in the fading hope that their fortunes might improve. They were few in number, though. Most who were not heard the first time lacked the determination to go on waiting.

In the plaza, Neniza saw people of every caste. Hairy kisin, owl-eyed chusas, vay sotz with gifts they hoped to give the lord, and at least a dozen aluxob, whose company Neniza avoided. Even some of the noble castes were there, startling her with their presence. Over time she came to understand that not all amanteca and ocelotlaca had courtly rank, that some of their kind had fallen out of favor to the point where they made their way in the cities as commoners, selling their skills to others.

People of every caste except her own.

There were none left in this domain, save Neniza and her father. Still, she found herself searching, looking at the hands of everyone in the plaza, until the day she realized that she was *hoping* to find another, hoping to convince herself that she did not need to be here. It was a desire born of weakness, and so she dug it ruthlessly out of her heart and cast it away. She would not be like her father, and let what had happened pass without consequence.

So she waited, hiding beneath her mask, until her luck finally changed.

"All kneel! All kneel! Kneel before the Master of the House of the Dawn!"

The voice rang out over the petitioners' plaza from the balcony that overlooked it. Neniza glanced up long enough to catch sight of several amanteca, draped in glorious feathered robes and gold jewelry. One, standing forward of the rest, was serving as herald. This much she saw; then, like everyone else, Neniza threw herself to the ground, prostrating herself on the hot stone.

Everything fell silent as the last person grew still. In the hush, they could all hear the measured steps above. The lord of the land had come at last.

The amantecatl spoke again. "Today is not a day for petitions."

What? Neniza thought, and heard someone near her sob once before stifling himself.

"The Revered Lord has come for another purpose," the amantecatl went on. "Four dawns from now begins the feast of the Flayed God, on the day Thirteen Leaf. On this great festival depend our hopes of fertile fields, the growth of the corn which feeds us all. The Elevated One has come here today to seek a maiden to serve as the Rain Bride. The woman so honored will be guaranteed a place in the highest heaven, and the petition she brought with her to this place will be granted. Remain as you are, and he will choose from among you."

Neniza's mind raced as she heard footsteps descending to the plaza. More than one set; of course the lord would not come down here himself. It would be the amanteca, searching among the petitioners for suitable candidates.

She was suitable.

And if they chose her. . . .

She could wait for another day, but there was no guarantee the lord would ever hear her petition, let alone grant it. This would bypass uncertainty entirely—but at a price.

I knew what I risked, coming here, Neniza thought, trembling with excitement and fear. *I always knew.*

She prayed silently as the footsteps ranged up and down the plaza. People said of her kind that they could manipulate others, driving them to think with passion instead of reason. Even Neniza didn't know if it was true. Her father would never answer when she asked—afraid, perhaps, of what she might do with it as a daughter. If it were possible, she had no idea how. But she prayed, as if her thoughts could reach the minds of the amanteca searching the plaza. *Choose me, choose me, choose me. . . .*

One set of feet stopped not far away. Neniza ceased to breathe.

A rustle of feathered robe, as if the amantecatl were gesturing. From above, a soft, sibilant response in Court Speech, and Neniza's skin tingled at the sound of the lord's voice.

"Maiden," the amantecatl said, "the lord favors you."

Neniza risked the tiniest shift of her head. And she saw that the amantecatl was gesturing, not at her, but at a young alux woman less than a pace in front of her.

No. This may be my only chance.

"I beg your forgiveness for my presumption."

The words came out before Neniza could even decide whether to speak or stay silent. All around her, she felt others jerk in horror; they would have edged away, had they not feared to move. As well they might. Neniza would have taken back the words, but she could not; there was nothing to do but speak on.

She lifted her head just enough to speak clearly. To look up would only ensure her death, with the lord standing above. "I beg your mercy. But the woman you have chosen is no maiden."

It was true. Like many others in the plaza, the alux had lain with men in exchange for food and water. How much it truly mattered, Neniza couldn't say—surely they'd chosen wrongly before; was that what caused the drought years?—but having heard it so publicly, the nobles could not ignore her words. Everyone here knew the alux was no virgin, and to choose her knowingly would be to undermine their faith in the festival.

Dead silence had followed on her words. Neniza's muscles ached with tension as she waited. Then a chiming rustle as the amantecatl stepped over the prostrate body of the alux he had been considering.

"Are you a maiden?"

"Yes," Neniza said. *Possibly the only one here.*

The amantecatl said something in Court Speech, not to her. A pause, and then the lord responded again. Was he angry? Amused? Neniza strove to read past the alien, unfamiliar facade of his words, to the mind behind it. She might have just killed herself, and achieved nothing in doing so.

"Very well," the amantecatl said. "You will become the Rain Bride."

She wondered, in the four days that followed, whether the alux whose position she'd taken hated her. The lord's gift to the Rain Bride, the granting of her petition, meant nothing to Neniza now. She would get what she wanted regardless. The alux might have lost her only chance. But petitioners went home again, once they had spoken or given up, and Neniza knew she herself would not. One always made sacrifices, one way or another.

Her status meant she was treated well, even lavishly. It almost became a problem. They brought her delicacies to eat, and she had to find a way to dispose of them without suspicion—not the peccary meat that villagers might eat in the wet season when food was abundant, but jaguar and eagle, the noblest animals of earth and air. For drink she had delicate wines of honey and fruit; her experience with them was limited, and the first night she drank rather too much. But she maintained her mask, and no one suspected.

Before dawn on the final day, an escort of eight ocelotlaca woke her and took her to be bathed.

Low-ranking amanteca had the job of preparing her. Neniza feigned blushing modesty and managed to wash herself, so that no one would examine her too closely. The higher-ranking artisan who took over once she was clean focused on things other than her hands, painting her breasts and belly and groin, draping her in "clothing" that was nothing more than sweetly chiming jewelry, dressing the soft bush of her hair with hibiscus flowers. The blossoms were an unexpected sign of the wealth and power that surrounded Neniza, for they did not bloom in the dry season, and the rains, of course, had not yet begun.

They prepared her, and Neniza curled her hands into fists to hide them from casual eyes. Let them think her nervous. *I am not afraid.*

The procession was dizzying. Her escort carried her palanquin, while twenty more ocelotlaca formed a solid wall that kept the crowd from her. They descended from the palace mound and crossed to the temple mound, and it seemed the entire city was there to see, for the feast of the Flayed God was second in importance to none.

She climbed the temple mound alone, on her own two feet, with the jaguar-men standing guard below. The carved and painted murals on each temple riser showed the gods in their glory, forming the miracles of the world. At the top, following the priests' instructions, she walked four circuits around the worn stone of the exterior altar, then went into the blessedly cool darkness.

Neniza had never seen the inside of a temple. The space was smaller than she expected, given the imposing facade, but it still dwarfed the village shrines she had seen on a few occasions. The back wall was taken up by a hammered gold image of such intricacy that she could not make out half of it; only the World Tree, dominating the center, was clear to her. Copal incense smoked from censers in the four corners, musky and strong. The smell, more than anything, brought home the reality of what she was doing. Copal was the scent of religion. Copal, and blood.

She lay down on the interior altar and waited.

Outside, the clamor of the crowd gave way to melodious singing. The lord's procession was approaching. Neniza listened, every fiber of her body tight. The clack of spear-hafts: the lord had descended from his palanquin, and the ocelotlaca were standing guard. The chime of jewelry: he was outside the door. A sustained note from the chorus: the lord was performing the rite of bloodletting, piercing his tongue. She could smell the acrid tang as he burnt the strips of bark-paper now wetted with his blood.

Then he entered the temple.

A petitioner in the plaza could not look at the lord of the land. The Rain Bride could. Neniza sat up on the altar, and saw what she had come so far to find.

They said he could take the form of a tremendous serpent, but right now he was shaped like a man. A tall man, sleekly muscled, without the heavy shoulders of an ocelotlacatl.

His skin glimmered, scales reflecting the faint light inside the temple. She could see nearly all of that skin; he wore a loincloth of jade and gold, and a pectoral, and a drape of pure white cotton hung from his arms, but his body was mostly bare. There was no hair on him anywhere, not even the smooth curve of his skull, but behind him, rustling as he shifted, Neniza could just see the iridescent quetzal feathers that ran down his back.

The sight of him, permitted to her as it was, still sent her to her knees. "Master," she whispered, and slid from the altar to the floor.

The quetzalcoatl who ruled the land came toward her, one sinuous step after another. His presence was overpowering. Not a deity to equal the Flayed God, or any of the others honored in the rituals of the year, but not a person, either. Not like those who waited outside.

Least of all like her.

His voice startled her: not Court Speech, but heavily-accented Wide Speech. "Rise, Rain Bride," he said. "Today we are wed."

And so the ritual began.

He would ask for her petition later, when they went outside to complete the ritual, so that it could be publicly heard. But all Neniza wanted was this, here, now: to lie with him, just once. Peasants begged it sometimes, for fertility. The Rain Bride did it for duty.

Her entire body trembled as she rose to her feet, but not with fear. Standing all but naked before the lord, her nature awoke within her. The nature her father fought so hard to keep in check, for fear of what it would do. Male or female, whichever form they took, all of their caste felt it. For males, in the wet season, the passion was different. Safer. Kinder.

Neniza was female, in the dry season, and she was not kind.

She reached out for the feathered serpent, bold with the

power that was in her, and drew him toward her, onto her, as she laid herself once more on the altar. Even had this not been their purpose here today, he could not have resisted her. She cried out as he entered her, not in pain, but in triumph.

As he moved above her, she felt her power envelop him. Women of other castes rarely if ever wanted what the males of her kind gave them—the strange, unnerving children they birthed—but it was a gift, freely given. Neniza's rage inverted that power: she gave nothing, and took everything.

Blood dripped from the lord's mouth where he had pierced his tongue. She licked it off her own lips, tasting his life in that blood, feeling it in his body as he rode her. Feeling it flow from him into her. The sensation was intoxicating, exhilarating; she grew drunk with that power, and a laugh built deep within her.

The feathered serpent shuddered above her, spine rippling like water. She put one hand on the scales of his chest to support his weight.

And he froze, staring at the fingers of her hand.

He tore himself free of her more quickly than she could follow, slithering down from the altar to the temple floor. *"Show yourself to me!"*

His voice struck her like thunder. However much she despised him, however much he despised her people, she was a woman of his domain, and he was her lord. She could not refuse his command. The power of it forced the mask of flesh from her at last, revealing what lay beneath.

Skin and muscle gave way to wood. The soft, lush body of a young alux woman dissolved, leaving behind the roughly-hewn form of a xera, like the toys children would sometimes carve for themselves before their mothers saw and took them away to be burned. In shape like a person, but not of flesh, and each hand bore only four fingers, mute testimony to the lesser, inferior, outcaste nature of her kind. She could hide anything with the mask, except that.

He bellowed something in Court Speech, and with a clattering rush the ocelotlaca were there, weapons out. Neniza did not care. She knelt on the floor where his command had left her, and she laughed.

"I am no Rain Bride to be sacrificed," she said, proudly baring her wooden face to them all. "There is no skin to flay from me, no heart to cut out. Your rains can come or not; I do not care."

"I will sacrifice you anyway," the quetzalcoatl spat, his words almost unintelligible through his accent. "I will burn you, as I burned your people."

Her rage could not overcome the power forcing her to kneel, but she snarled and jerked against it. "My father told me what you did. Yes, we live—you will never be rid of us. Not so long as one male of our kind lives to sire more xera on your women. We are *always* fertile. It is our gift." She laughed again. "But I am not male. Not since I heard the tale of what you did, and knew what it is to want to kill. Where my father gives, I take. And I have taken your life. Within three days you will be dead. Burn me; I am of wood. But I have no blood from which to take your power back."

They bound her there inside the temple, and gagged her so she could mock the lord no more. He sent the priests to choose another maiden from the crowd at the base of the mound; Neniza watched as the quetzalcoatl took her on the altar, then listened as they finished the ritual outside. The girl asked for her family to be cared for. The lord promised to honor her request. Then they cut out her heart and flayed the skin from her to bring the rains, because that was how the world worked; everything that mattered was paid for with sacrifice.

Listening to the drums that followed in the wake of the girl's screams, Neniza wondered if her own blasphemy had tainted the ritual beyond repair. Would there be drought, famine, death?

She did not care. All that mattered was that the lord would not be there to see it.

The signs were already beginning to show when he returned that night. His sleek face was drawn, his delicate scales dulled. The spark that had been in him was in Neniza now, and nothing could take it back.

But they tried. They dragged her from the temple mound back to the palace, and there they ritually abused her wooden body, piercing and splintering it as if she were an enemy noble captured in battle. Neniza laughed at the ironic honor.

She could not bleed, though, and so in the end they did as she knew they must.

The quetzalcoatl stepped in front of her as they hauled her up. She could see the pyre looming large behind him, and shuddered uncontrollably. Watching her fear, the lord said in grim tones, "You may yet escape it. Restore me, and I will spare both you and your father."

Her father? Neniza would have spat in his face, if her wooden mouth had any moisture in it. She was dry, so dry. Her father was a coward, soft and wet and weak. She would give nothing for his life.

"Take her," the quetzalcoatl snarled at last, his smooth voice distorted with rage and despair.

They dragged her to the pyre and bound her at its peak, and soon the flames danced up around her, licking eagerly at her dry wooden form. She began screaming, then, and did not stop.

But as she burned she saw, through the smoke and the wavering air, the lord's withered feathers, ghosting to the ground. And no one, not even Neniza, could tell then if she was screaming or laughing.

SEVEN SCENES FROM HARRAI'S *SACRED MOUNTAIN*

by Jennifer Crow

I.

I first saw the sacred mountain as I lay in the blood between my mother's legs. There are those who say this cannot be; that an infant sees only blurs, vague hints of color and form. But to this day, the smell of blood makes my stomach churn, and I remember—as clear as the sky on a summer morning—the broken pyramid, dark in the frame of the window. I recall the hushing sound of silk, a whisper from the coming night as they covered her body, and the sound of my father's weeping. He never cried again—never in my presence.

XX.

The mountain watches over fools, and the peasants say a man who sleeps in the mountain's arms will come home a poet or a madman. Nothing is said of women; perhaps they are thought too practical to fall to the mountain's embrace. Or it may be that the fools who call themselves wise do not believe a woman can be a poet, and that her madness is an ordinary thing, built of thwarted love and the steady drone of days. But my first love went up to the mountain. She cut short her hair and put on her brother's clothes, and I watched her figure grow smaller as she walked up the mountain's flanks. She dwindled to nothing. I waited at the window for a day, two days, five. But only the mountain remained. I never saw my love again.

LXXV.

The summer the great ship appeared in the sky, the mountain burned. Smoke crowned it, blurred the sharp edges of its broken face. The thick, oily sap of the red-leaved thorn tree flared slowly, but burned long. For months the thorn trees died in flame, and the silver body of the ship reflected them, the scarlet and orange light reflected like a searing glance. We watched the black line creep down the mountain's sides, the promise of destruction ever closer. On the last day of summer, with rain only a memory on our parched skin and in the dry wells and dusty courtyards, the chief judge laid himself on the steps of the temple and his eldest son folded his mantle of office and set it out of reach. And then that son took a knife born from the mountain's heart and cut his father open. We watched the life flow out of him. In three days the rains came, a season too late, and as we buried the chief judge, the ship reflected the red silk of his bier and vanished. But unlike my love, it would return.

CCCLX.

My first wife insisted we move house. She saw the mountain as a threat; she never believed that I would not run to it some night and leave her bereft. She wept tears stained red by the tarrac-earth she used to highlight her eyes. She lay in front of the door at night, even after we moved, in case the mountain-fever came upon me unawares. I confessed to her that I was no true poet, that I had no desire to risk madness for art. But she clung to the ties of my robe whenever we left the house, and even the slow festivals of the winter months I could not attend alone. Such lack of trust dooms a life. The swelling sickness ate her from within; four days after her death, I returned to my family's home.

MC.

Though I swore never to approach the sacred mountain, once I broke that word, or near enough. My daughter, my light, fell ill, some slow poison in her heart that wasted her bit by bit, a fading out of life. Her skin smelled of flowers past their bloom, her hands felt cold against my fingers. I sang to her, all the old songs, the ones that sob in the throat. The chief priest came, and the chief judge, and they smoked the room with incense and ordered the spirit of illness to depart. The herb-woman brought poultices and tisanes, and still my daughter faded like a painting left too long in the sun. At last I walked out into the red sunrise and turned to face the sacred mountain. It waited, the snow on its brow like a sign of age and wisdom. I walked into the hills, listening for its song, but I heard only the birds and the wind, and at last, by the stream that runs down from the eastern side, I stopped and drank and then turned back. By the time I reached my home, the girl had died. And I took up my pen and began to write.

MCCXXV.

When the snows melt and the wind from the south freshens, an old man's thoughts turn to war. Thus it was that I lifted the red banner with my brothers, and we marched—with the young men in a frenzy of passion beside us, and their lovers trailing behind—around the skirts of the mountain toward the city of Xerane, with its tarnished silver domes and equally tarnished morals. Under the broken dagger of the mountain, we slew their finest men and were slain in turn. In the end, they tore down our red banners and sent the survivors home. They asked for nothing but peace; we gained nothing but honor. The mountain waited in my window, a fire burning near the peak. I watched it for days, but it never died and never spread. When I showed it to the chief judge, he said the souls of our dead burned on the mountain.

MML.

The sky ship has returned with its brothers, and their red lights are searing away the top of the sacred mountain. Shorn like a harlot, it still watches over the city. But my time is past, and I wish I had not lived to see this day. I close this book, and stroke its red cover, and lay it aside. Tonight, I will wait for the mountain's last call. And when that voice comes to me, I will turn my face one last time toward the remnants of its glory, and walk into darkness on its slopes.

OBLIVION: A JOURNEY

by Vandana Singh

Memory is a strange thing.

I haven't changed my sex in eighty-three years. I was born female, in a world of peace and quietude; yet I have an incomplete recollection of my childhood. Perhaps it is partly a failure of the imagination that it is so hard to believe (in this age of ours) that there was once such a place as green and slow as my world-shell, Ramasthal. It was the last of the great world-shells to fall, so any memory of childhood is contaminated with what came after: the deaths of all I loved, the burning of the cities, the slow, cancerous spread of Hirasor's culture-machines that changed my birth-place beyond recognition.

So instead of one seamless continuum of growing and learning to be in this world, my memory of my life is fragmentary. I remember my childhood name: Lilavati. I remember those great cybeasts, the hayathis, swaying down the streets in a procession, and their hot, vegetable-scented breath ruffling my hair. There are glimpses, as through a tattered veil, of steep, vertical gardens, cascading greenery, a familiar face looking out at me from a window hewn in a cliff—and in the background, the song of falling water. Then everything is obscured by smoke. I am in a room surrounded by pillars of fire, and through the haze I see the torn pages of the Ramayan floating in the air, burning, their edges crumpling like black lace. I am half-comatose with heat and smoke; my throat is parched and sore, my eyes sting—and then there are strange, metallic faces reaching out to me, the stuff of my nightmares. Behind them is a person all aflame, her arms outstretched, running toward me, but she falls and I am carried away through the smoke and the screaming. I still see the woman in my dreams and wonder if she was my mother.

In my later life as a refugee, first on the world of Barana and after that, everywhere and nowhere, there is nothing much worth recalling. Foster homes, poverty, my incarceration in some kind of soulless educational institution—the banality of the daily struggle to survive. But there are moments in my life that are seared into my mind forever: instants that were pivotal, life-changing, each a conspiracy of temporal nexuses, a concatenation of events that made me what I am. That is not an excuse—I could have chosen a different way to be. But I did not know, then, that I had a choice.

This is the first of those moments: the last time I was a woman, some ninety years ago in my personal time-frame. I was calling myself Ila, then, and doing some planet-hopping, working the cruisers and blowing the credits at each stop. I found myself on Planet Vilaasa, a rich and decadent world under the sway of the Samarin conglomerate. I was in one of those deep-city bars where it's always night, where sunshine is like a childhood memory, where the air is thick with smoke, incipient violence and bumblebees. I don't remember who I was with, but the place was crowded with humans, native and off-world, as well as mutants and nakalchis. There was a bee buzzing in my ear, promising me seven kinds of bliss designed especially for my personality and physical type if only I'd agree to let the Samarin Corporate Entity take over half my brain. I swatted it; it fell into my plate and buzzed pathetically, antennae waving, before it became non-functional. Somehow I found this funny; I still remember throwing back my head and laughing.

My fingers, slight and brown, curved around my glass. The drink half drunk, a glutinous purple drop sliding down the outer surface. Reflected on the glass a confusion of lights and moving shapes, and the gleam, sudden and terrifying, of steel.

There was a scream, and the sound of glass breaking that seemed to go on for ever. This was no barroom brawl. The raiders were Harvesters. I remember getting up to run. I remember the terrified crowd pressing around me, and then I was falling, kicked and stepped upon in the stampede. Somehow I pushed myself to safety under a table next to a stranger, a pale woman with long, black hair and eyes like green fire. She looked at me with her mouth open, saying one word:

"Nothen . . ."

A Harvester got her. It put its metal hands around her throat and put its scissor-like mouth to her chest. As she bled and writhed, it rasped one long word, interspersed with a sequence of numbers.

Her body turned rigid and still, her face twisted with horror. Her green eyes froze in a way that was simultaneously aware and locked in the moment of torment. It was then that I realized that she was a nakalchi, a bio-synthetic being spawned from a mother-machine.

The name of the mother-machine is what pushes a nakalchi into the catatonic state that is *Shunyath*. When they enter Shunyath they re-live the moment when that name was spoken. Since the nakalchis are practically immortal, capable of dying only through accident or violence, Shunyath is their way of going to the next stage. Usually a nakalchi who has wearied of existence will go to one of their priests, who will put the candidate in a meditative state of absolute calm and surrender. Then the priest will utter the name of the mother-machine (such names being known only to the priests and guarded with their lives) so that the nakalchi may then contemplate eternity in peace.

For first-generation nakalchis, Shunyath is not reversible.

That is when I realized that this woman was one of the ancients, one of the nakalchis who had helped humankind find its way to the stars.

So for her, frozen in the state of Shunyath, it would seem as though she was being strangled by the Harvester all the rest of her days. No wonder she had asked me for Nothen, for death. She had known the Harvesters had come for her; she had known what they would do. I remember thinking, in one of those apparently timeless moments that terror brings: somebody should kill the poor woman. She was obviously the target of the raid.

But to my horrified surprise the Harvester turned from her to me, even as I was sliding away from under the table to a safer place. While the Harvester had me pinned to the floor, its long, flexible electrodes crawled all over my skin as it violated my humanness, my woman-ness, with its multiple limbs. Through the tears and blood I saw myriad reflections of myself in those dark, compound eyes, from which looked—not only the primitive consciousness of the Harvester, but the eyes of whoever manipulated it—the person or entity who, not content with finding their target, fed like a starving animal on the terror of a bystander. In those eyes I was a stranger, a non-person, a piece of meat that jerked and gibbered in pain. Then, for a moment, I thought I saw the burning woman from my memories of childhood, standing behind the Harvester. This is death, I said to myself, relieved. But the Harvester left me a few hair-breadths short of death and moved on to its next victim.

I don't know how many they killed or maimed that night. The nakalchi woman they took away. I remember thinking, through the long months of pain and nightmares that followed, that I wish I had died.

B ut I lived. I took no joy in it. All that gave my mind some respite from its constant seething was a game I invented: I would find the identity of the person responsible for the Harvester raid and I would kill them. Find, and kill. I went through endless permutations of people and ways of killing in my head. Eventually it was no longer a game.

I moved to another planet, changed my sex to one of the Betweens. Over the years I changed my body even further, ruthlessly replacing soft, yielding flesh with coralloid implants that grew me my own armor-plating. Other people shuddered when I walked by. I became an interplanetary investigator of small crime and fraud, solving trivial little cases for the rich and compromised, while biding my time.

It was already suspected that the man responsible for the Harvester attacks that terrorized whole planets during the Samarin era was no other than the governing mind of the Samarin Corporate Entity, Hirasor. The proof took many years and great effort on the part of several people, including myself, but it came at last. Nothing could be done, however, because Hirasor was more powerful than any man alive. His icons were everywhere: dark, shoulder-length hair framing a lean, aristocratic face with hungry eyes; the embroidered silk collar, the rose in his buttonhole. It came out then that he had a private museum of first-generation nakalchis locked in Shunyath in various states of suffering. A connoisseur of pain, was Hirasor.

But to me he was also Hirasor, destroyer of worlds. He had killed me once already by destroying my world-shell, Ramasthal. It was one of the epic world-shells, a chain of island satellites natural and artificial, that ringed the star Agni. Here we learned, lived and enacted our lives based on that ancient Indic epic, the Ramayan, one of those timeless stories that condense in their poetry the essence of what it means to be human. Then Samarin had infiltrated, attacking and destroying at first, then doing what they called "rebuilding": substituting for the complexity and beauty of the Ramayan, an inanely simplified, sugary, cultural matrix that drew on all the darkness and pettiness in human nature. Ramasthal broke up, dissolved by the monocultural machine that was Samarin. I suffered less than my fellow-citizens—being a child, I could not contribute a brain-share to Samarin. I grew up a refugee, moving restlessly from one inhabited world to the next, trying and failing to find my center. Most of the ordinary citizens of these worlds had never heard of the Ramayan epic, or anything else that had been meaningful to me in that lost past life. In my unimaginable solitude my only defense was to act like them, to be what they considered normal. When the Harvesters invaded the bar, I had been living the fashionably disconnected life that Samarin-dominated cultures think is the only way to be.

Hirasor was so powerful that among my people his nickname was Ravan-Ten-Heads, after the demon in the epic Ramayan. Near the end of the story, the hero, Ram, tries to kill Ravan by cutting off his heads, one by one, but the heads simply grow back. In a similar manner, if a rival corporation or a society of free citizens managed to destroy one Samarin conglomerate, another would spring up almost immediately in its place. It—and Hirasor—seemed almost mythic in their indestructibility.

What I wanted to do was to find Hirasor's secret vulnerability, as Ram does in the epic. "Shoot an arrow into Ravan's navel," he is told. The navel is the center of Ravan's power. When Ram does so, the great demon dies at last.

But Samarin, and with it Hirasor, declined slowly without my help. An ingeniously designed brain-share virus locked Samarin's client-slaves—several million people—into a synced epileptic state. After that Generosity Corp. (that had likely developed the virus) began its ascent to power while the Samarin Entity gradually disintegrated. Pieces of it were bought by other conglomerates, their data extracted through torture; then they were mind-wiped until the name Samarin only evoked a ghost of a memory, accompanied by a shudder.

But Hirasor lived on. He was still rich enough to evade justice. Rumors of his death appeared frequently in the newsfeeds for a while, and a documentary was made about him, but over time people forgot. There were other things, such as the discovery of the worlds of the Hetorr, and the threats and rumors of war with that unimaginably alien species. "Give it up," said the few people in whom I had confided. "Forget Hirasor and get on with your life." But finding Hirasor was the only thing between me and death by my own hand. Each time I opened my case files on him, each time his image sprang up and I looked into his eyes, I remembered the Harvester. I remembered the burning woman. Despite all the reconstructive work my body had undergone, my old wounds ached. Find, and kill. Only then would I know peace.

I knew more about Hirasor than anyone else did, although it was little enough.

He liked absinthe and roses.

He had a perfect memory.

He was fastidious about his appearance. Every hair in place, fingers elegant and manicured, the signature ear-studs small and precisely placed on each ear-lobe. His clothing was made from the silk of sapient-worms.

He had no confidant but for the chief of his guards, a nakalchi female called Suvarna, a walking weapon who was also his lover. He wrote her poetry that was remarkable for its lyrical use of three languages, and equally remarkable for its sadistic imagery.

Later I killed three of his functionaries to learn his unique identity-number. It did me no good, or so I thought, then.

In the years of his decline he lost his Harvester units; his three main hideouts were found and his assets destroyed, his loyal bands of followers dwindled to one, Suvarna—and yet he seemed more slippery and elusive than ever. Although he left trails of blood and shattered lives in his wake, he managed to elude me with trickery and firepower.

He left me messages in blood.

Sometimes it was the name of a planet or a city. I would go there and find, too late, another clue, spelled out in corpses. It was as though we were playing an elaborate game across the inhabited worlds, with him always in the lead. Slowly the universe began to take less and less notice. We were two lone players on a vast stage, and the audience had other, larger scale horrors to occupy them.

I began to think of myself as a modern-day Ram. In the Ramayan epic, Prince Ram's wife Sita is abducted by the ten-headed demon Ravan. Prince Ram, beloved by all, has no difficulty raising an army of animals and people and following Ravan to his kingdom.

I was no prince. But Hirasor had stolen my whole world, as surely as Ravan stole Sita. I could not bring back Ramasthal or my childhood, but I could bring Hirasor down. Unlike Ram, I would have to do it alone.

Alone. Sifting through travel records, bribing petty little mercenaries who may have had dealings with his people, tracking down witnesses at the scene of each orgy of violence, trying to think like him, to stand in his shoes and wonder: what would he do next? I would sleep only when I could no longer stand.

Sleep brought a recurring nightmare: Hirasor standing before me at last. I shoot an arrow into his navel, and as he falls

I leap upon him and put my hands around his throat. I am certain he is dying, but then I see his face change, become familiar, become my own face. I feel his hands on my throat.

I would wake up in a sweat and know that in the end it was going to be only one of us who would prevail: him or me. But first I had to find him. So I worked obsessively, following him around from place to place, always one step behind.

Then, quite suddenly, the trail got cold. I searched, sent my agents from planet to planet. Nothing but silence. I paced up and down my room, brooding for days. What was he waiting for? What was he about to do?

Into this empty, waiting time came something I had not expected. A reason to live that had nothing to do with Hirasor. Her name was Dhanu.

She was an urbanologist for whom I had performed a small service. She was a small, fierce, determined woman with long, black hair turning to grey that she tied in a braid. The job I did for her was shoddily done, and she demanded a reason. "I'm preoccupied with something more important," I snapped, wanting her out of my office and my life. "Tell me," she said, sitting down and waiting with her whole body, her eyes mocking and intrigued. So I did.

We became lovers, Dhanu and I. Somehow she found her way past the armor-plating of my mind and body; she found cracks and interstices, living flesh that remembered loving touch, regions of vulnerability that I hadn't cauterized out of myself. Here is a memory fragment:

We lie in bed in my dingy room, with moonlight coming in through the narrow window, and the sounds outside of voices raised in argument, and the sweaty, chemical scent of the dead river that lies like an outstretched arm across this nameless, foul city. She is a shadow, a ghost limned with silver, turned into a stranger by the near-darkness. I find this suddenly disturbing; I turn her over so that the light falls full on her face. I don't know what I look like to her. I don't know what I am. I've been calling myself Vikram for a few years, but that doesn't tell me anything.

"Tell me a secret," she says. "Something about yourself that nobody knows."

I pull myself together, settle down next to her and stare at the ceiling. I don't know what to tell her, but something escapes my lips unbidden.

"I want to die," I say, surprising myself because lately I haven't been thinking about death. But it's true. And also not true, because I want this moment for ever, the light from the broken moon Jagos silvering her hair, and the way she looks at me when I say that: a long, slow, sad, unsurprised look. She begins to say something but I stop her. "Your turn," I say.

"I'll tell you what I want to know, more than anything," she says after a pause. "I want to know what it is like to be somebody else. I remember, as a very small child, standing with my mother on a balcony, watching the most amazing fireworks display I had ever seen. It made me happy. I looked at my mother to share that joy, and found that she was crying. It was then that I realized that I was a different person from her, that she was in some profound way a stranger. Since then I've sought strangeness. I've wanted to know what it is like to be a tree, a sapient-worm, and most of all, a made-being. Like a nakalchi or a Cognizant-City. Can you imagine what the universe would look like to an entity like that?"

We talk all night. She teaches me what she has learned about nakalchis and Cognizant-Cities, Corporate Entities and mother-machines—in particular, their rituals of death, because that is what interests me. I realize during the conversation that I am no more than a vessel for the death of another, and that is perhaps why I seek my own. Some time during the night she teaches me the song with which nakalchis welcome Nothen, their conception of death. She learned it from a nakalchi priest who was dying, who wanted someone to say the words to him. I cannot pretend to understand the lore and mysticism that the priests have developed around Nothen, which to me is simply irreversible non-functionality, the death that comes to us all. Or the philosophical comparison between Nothen and Shunyath. Dhanu tries to explain:

"If you go into Shunyath, you contemplate what nakalchis call The River, which is inadequately translated as the Cosmic Stream of Being. If you go into Nothen, with the Last Song echoing in your mind, then you *are* the River. You are no longer separate from it—you *become* the River, see?"

No, I don't see. Never mind, she says, laughing at me. She says the words of the Last Song, breathing it out into the moonlit air.

It has a pleasing, sonorous lilt. It is supposed to induce a state of acceptance and peace in a dying nakalchi. I am not sure why, but there are tears in my eyes as I repeat it after her in the gray, hushed light of dawn.

Shantih. Nothen ke aagaman, na dukh na dard . . .

Lying with her, seeing her hair unbound on my pillow like seaweed, I find myself in a still place, as though between breaths. Hirasor does not walk the paths that Dhanu and I tread.

Looking back, I see how the paths branch out of each temporal nexus. For every pivotal event in my life, there was always more than one possible path I could have taken.

This is the path I chose:

I had accompanied Dhanu during one of her urbanology expeditions. We were in the bowels of a dying Cognizant-City on the ruined planet Murra. This was the first time she had had a chance to explore what was probably one of the earliest Cognizant-Cities in the galaxy. She was a few levels below me, attempting to salvage what was left of the City's mind. All its recorded history and culture, its ruminations over the years of its existence, lay spooled in cavernous darkness below. The inhabitants had been evacuated, and even now I could see the last of the ships, a glint or two in a reddening sky over the bleak mountains of Murra's northern continent. I was perched on the highest ramparts, standing by our flyer and looking out for rogue destroyer bots. Every now and then I saw one rise up, a distant speck, and crash into the city-scape in a small fireball. Thin spires of smoke rose all around me, but there was as yet nothing amiss where I was waiting.

Then I lost Dhanu's signal.

I searched the skies, found them clear of bots, and descended quickly into the warren-like passageways that led into the city's heart. Two levels later, my wrist-band beeped. She was in range.

"I'm all right, Vikram," she said to my anxious query. She sounded breathless with excitement. "I had to go down a couple of levels to find the rest of the data-banks. This City is one of the first Cognizant-cities ever made! They still have direct human-to-City interfaces! I am hooking up to talk to it as I record. Go on up! I'll only be a few minutes, I promise."

When I relive that moment, I think of the things I could have done. I could have insisted on going down to where she was, or persuaded her to leave everything and come. Or I could have been more careful going up, so I wouldn't lose my way.

But I did lose my way. It was only one wrong turn, and I was about to retrace my steps (I had the flyer's reassuring signal on my wristband as a guide) but what made me pause was curiosity. Or fate.

I found myself in the doorway of an enormous chamber which smelled faintly of blood and hydrogen peroxide, and was lit by periodic blue flashes, like lightning. I saw the great, monstrous hulk of an old-fashioned mother-machine, her long-abandoned teats spewing an oily broth, her flailing arms beating the air over the shattered remains of her multiple wombs. She was old—it had been a long time since she had brought any nakalchis to life. As I stared at her I realized (from what pictures Dhanu had shown me of ancient made-beings) that she was probably a first-generation mother-machine. A priceless collector's item, salvaged from who-knew-where, abandoned in the evacuation of the City. And now the City's madness was destroying what little functionality she had, taking her to Nothen. Moved by a sudden impulse I went up to her and spoke the words of peace.

Shantih. Nothen ke aagaman, na dukh na dard . . .

Peace. As Nothen comes, there is no sorrow, no pain . . .

I regretted my impulse almost immediately because after I stopped, the mother-machine began to recite the names of her children, the first part of her death-ritual. In her final moments she had mistaken me for a nakalchi priest. I don't know what made me stay—there was something mesmerizing about that old, metallic voice in the darkness, and the proximity of death. Perhaps I was a little annoyed with Dhanu for delaying, for wanting to join with the City in an orgy of mutual understanding. Dhanu's signal flickered with reassuring regularity on my wristband.

Then I heard the mother-machine utter the name that to me meant more than life itself: Hirasor.

I will remember that moment until I die: the grating voice of the mother-machine, the dull booms in the distance, the floor shaking below my feet, and that pungent, smoky darkness, pierced by occasional sparks of blue lightning.

In the midst of it, clear as a bell, the name—or rather, Hirasor's unique numerical identifier. Each of us had our identity numbers, given to us at birth, and I was one of the few people who knew Hirasor's. But I had never suspected he was a nakalchi. Partly because of nakalchi lore and history—there never had been any confirmed master criminals who were nakalchi, conceived as they had once been to gently shepherd the human race toward the stars. Meanwhile the great uprising of the nakalchis in times long before Samarin, the consciousness debates that had preceded them, had all ensured that they were treated on par with human beings, so I had no way of knowing from the number alone. You can't tell from appearance or behavior either, because nakalchis claim access to the full range of human emotion (or, if their priests are to be believed, to more than that). By now even we humans are so augmented and enhanced that the functional difference between nakalchi and human is very small—but important. To me the difference meant—at last—the possibility of vengeance.

Hirasor: a first-generation nakalchi!

That is why I had to wait. That is why I couldn't go down to find Dhanu, why I ignored her frantic signals on my wrist-band. I had to wait for the mother-machine to tell me her name.

At last she said it: Ekadri-samayada-janini, intermingled with a sequence of numbers that made up a prime.

I left her then, to die. I left, repeating her name—what would always be, to me, the Word—so I would not forget. The floor was twisting and bucking beneath my feet, and a lone siren was blaring somewhere above me. I staggered against the rusting metal wall of the passage, and remembered Dhanu.

I got up. I went back. I wish I could say that I went into the bowels of the City, braved everything to find her and rescue her. But I didn't. I went down until I was stopped by the rubble of fallen masonry. Her signal still flickered on my wrist-band but she did not answer my query.

There was a seismic shudder far below me, and a long sigh, a wind that blew through the wrecked passageways, running invisible fingers through my hair. I sensed—or imagined—Dhanu's breath flowing with the breath of the dying City, her consciousness entangled inextricably with that of her host. But as I turned away I knew also that my real reason for abandoning her was that I was the only living being who had the means to bring Hirasor down. For that I couldn't risk my life.

The roof of the passageway began to collapse. I was running, now, veering from one side to another to prevent being hit by debris. I burst into open air, my chest aching, and flung myself into the flyer. As I rose up, three destroyer bots honed into the very spot I had vacated. I had no time to activate the flyer's defenses. A great fireball blossomed below me. I felt its heat as I piloted the rocking craft upward through the tumultuous air. Up, in the cool heights, I saw that there was blood flowing down my right arm. My shoulder hurt. I looked down and saw the myriad fires blooming, forming and dissolving shapes that my imagination brought to life. Monsters. And lastly, a woman, arms outstretched, burning.

In the Ramayan, Ram braves all to recover his consort Sita from the demon Ravan. But near the end of the story he loses her through his own foolishness. He turns her away, exiles her as he himself was once exiled, and buries himself in the task of ruling his kingdom.

All that: the war, the heroes killed—for nothing!

One of the most moving scenes in the epic is at the end of the story, when Ram goes down on his knees before Sita in the forest, begging her forgiveness and asking her to come back to him. She accepts his apology but she does not belong to him; she never has. She calls to her mother, the Earth; a great fissure opens in the ground and Sita goes home.

In the One Thousand Commentaries, there are different views on the significance of Sita. Some interpret her as signifying that which is lost to us. For a long time I had thought of Sita as my world, my childhood. I had seen myself as Ram, raising an army to win back—not those irredeemable things, but a chance for survival. Abandoned by my fellow investigators, hunting for Hirasor alone, I had, after a while, given up on analogies. Certainly I had never thought of Dhanu as Sita.

Dhanu was what I had to sacrifice to reach Hirasor, to rescue Sita. Dhanu had never belonged to me, anyway, I told myself. She could have come up out of the City at any time; it was her obsession with the made-beings that led to her death. Sometimes I was angry with her, at other times, I wept, thinking of the fall of her hair in the moonlight. At odd moments during my renewed pursuit of Hirasor, she would come unbidden into my mind, and I would wonder what her last moments had been like. Had she seen the Universe through the eyes of the dying City? Had she had her epiphany?

But I had little time for regret. My life narrowed down to one thing: find Hirasor. I set various agents sifting through mountains of possible leads; I re-established contact with criminal informers, coaxed or threatened information from scores of witnesses. At night I lay sleepless in my lonely bed, thinking of what I would do when I found Hirasor. My mind ran through scenario after scenario. I had to first put him in a hundred kinds of agony. Then I would say the name of the mother-machine and lock him in Shunyath for ever.

His silence lasted over two years. Then, at last, one of my agents picked up his trail. This time, curiously, it was not marked with blood. No small, artistically arranged orgy of violence betrayed his presence. All I had was proof from a transit shuttle record that he had been headed for the planet Griddha-kuta two months ago.

I went to Griddha-kuta. Apparently he had headed straight for the Buddhist monastery of Leh, without any attempt at covering his tracks. I went to the monastery, suspecting a trap. There, to my angry surprise, I found him gone.

An elderly monk told me that yes, Hirasor had been here. What had he done during his stay? Apparently nothing but walk around in the hill gardens and read in the library. Where was he now?

"He said to tell you that he had gone to Oblivion," the monk said, watching me. "But why don't you stay here awhile, before you go? There is no hurry. Hirasor is not running any more. Why don't you walk the gardens and ease your burdens a little?"

They let me search the grounds and the building, but there was no sign of Hirasor. I wondered if he had really gone to Oblivion, a planet about which I knew little, except that it was as close to hell as you could get among the inhabited worlds. It made no sense that he would go to such an uncomfortable place.

While I was wondering what to do, I walked briefly in the gardens with the monk, Chituri. I told him a little about myself and my quest; in return he confided to me that he had been a world-shell citizen, too, before the fall. His world-shell had been Gilgamesh.

There is no doubt that there was some magic about the place, because I stayed longer than I intended. The gardens in the terraced hills were tranquil, verdant, misty with waterfalls. Amid groves of moss-laden stone trees, pale clusters of flowers hung in the sweet air. Memories of Ramasthal, which had faded with time, returned to me vividly. Meanwhile Chituri tried to persuade me to stay, to give up my quest for justice. As we walked, he would tell me stories from the Indic tradition, even resorting to his knowledge of the Ramayan.

"Don't you see," he would tell me, "it is only when Ram forgets the god in him, forgets he is an avatar of Vishnu, that he acts foolishly? What is evil but ignorance of our true nature?"

"You are forgetting that Ravan is the villain of the story, not Ram," I would say coldly. "If you want to talk about evil, talk about him."

"But, Paren," he said, using the name I had given him, "don't your commentaries say that the entire epic is more than a literal telling of an old heroic tale—that the great battle is really the battle within . . ."

He had a peculiar way of sidling up to me, of speaking as though imparting a great confidence, and yet his manner was ingratiating, tentative. He hardly spoke above a whisper. I guessed he had suffered much before his arrival here, but I took a dislike to him after a while.

For me this period was, like the time I had met Dhanu, only an interstice, a time to catch my breath before resuming my quest. I was not interested in academic discourses on morality. Chituri did not understand that. He had seen Hirasor walk these very gardens—Hirasor, who had brought down his world as well as mine—and he had done nothing.

I finished my researches on the planet Oblivion, and made arrangements to go there. It was a difficult place to get to, since there was only one settlement, if one could call it that, and only a small scientific research craft visited at rather long intervals. The day I left, Chituri again tried to persuade me to give up my pursuit of Hirasor. He did this in his usual oblique way of telling me a story.

This time it was an ancient Buddhist tale about a murderer called Ungli-maal. Ungli-maal had been a bandit in the time of the Buddha, a man so depraved that he wore the fingers of his victims as a garland around his neck. The Buddha was the only man he waylaid who was unafraid of death, who faced him empty-handed, with compassion. Eventually Ungli-maal—despite all he had been—became a Buddhist monk and a great teacher.

"If you are trying to persuade me that Hirasor has become a saint," I said between clenched teeth, "you must think me naïve indeed. He is still the man who butchered millions, destroyed countless worlds. He will not escape justice."

"That was not the point of my story," Chituri said, rather sadly. I was glad not to see his face again.

Oblivion, they say, is another word for hell. A bleak world, barely habitable, it was once known as Dilaasha, and was considered a reasonable candidate for terraforming. Those hopes have long since vanished. The "habitable" zones are deserts, subject to violent dust-storms, and all indigenous life is primitive—bacterial, algal, and inimical to coexisting with humans.

But all this does not explain why the planet Oblivion is hell. Oblivion earns its name because those who stay there long enough slowly lose their minds.

It begins with forgetting and slips of tongue, peculiar speech disorders, waking terrors, and finally, silence. The rescue teams who first observed the early explorers (consisting of both human and nakalchi) could only speculate as to why the subjects walked around without apparent purpose, neglecting the basic needs of their bodies, muttering in unknown languages, reacting to things that nobody else could see. The second stage was one of great distress—the subjects howled or whimpered and ran about the compound as though to escape a terrible, invisible enemy. They could still, at times, respond to their names; they would look up when called, frowning, as though trying to remember who they had been. Sometimes they would weep in the arms of the staff; a terrible, heart-rending weeping it was. The final stage was silence and withdrawal. In this last stage the sufferers seemed to have completely lost any knowledge of who they were—they did not respond to their names or to instructions; they wandered around with dead eyes, tracing out complicated patterns with their feet.

Only three victims had been taken off-planet. When removed in the second stage they would resist with maniacal strength—both such subjects had met violent death at their own hand. The third had been in the final stage and had simply faded away after removal, although he had been in fine shape physically. However an autopsy had revealed a bizarre restructuring of his brain that no scientist had yet explained.

So now all that is left of the original settlement on Oblivion is a study center where the remaining subjects are incarcerated. Regulations decree that nobody can stay on Oblivion for more than a hundred and ten local days. It's after that that most people seem to start losing their minds, although in some rare cases twenty days is enough.

There are theories—volatile compounds containing nano-organisms that are slowly released by the soil, pervading everything, that act like psychotropic drugs, low frequency sound waves that boom through the barren hills, disturbing the inner functioning of the body, peculiar surges in radioactive emissions in the environs—but none of these are adequate explanations. Oblivion remains a mystery.

So I came, at last, to Oblivion, to the final confrontation. It was a fitting place for a last stand. The dome-town was mostly uninhabited, the empty buildings testament to the defeated hopes of the original settlers. The insane were housed in a primitive building built around a dusty compound. The skeleton crew that had managed the place for the last shift was irritable and moody, waiting to be taken off-planet in a week, and the few scientists looked depressed and preoccupied. Nobody seemed interested in talking with me, despite the fact that I was apparently a representative of a rich philanthropist considering a major donation. Everyone seemed curiously lacking in vitality or enthusiasm, as though under the influence of some drug. Within a few hours of my stay there, I, too, felt a distinct mental lethargy, punctuated by spikes of nervousness and paranoia. The medic who examined me, a thin, dark, spidery man, was pessimistic.

"You're one of those who will succumb fast," he said, not without some relish. "This is a terrible place, affects some people much more quickly than others. Get out while you can, or you'll be joining them!"

He waved his long fingers toward the observation window behind him. There was something ghoulish about the way he stood watching the crazies, describing for me in painful detail every stage of the terrible sickness. The afflicted—men, women, most of them half naked, wandered aimlessly around the yard, muttering and drawing patterns in the dust with their feet. Some wailed incessantly, beating their chests, while others tore at their clothes. Still others sat very quietly on the ground, looking straight ahead of them with blank eyes. I felt as though their pain and confusion was somehow connected to me, that theirs was a sorrow that was drawing me in slowly. The dust patterns on the ground (the subject of much debate among the scientists) seemed almost to make sense, as though they were the script of a language I had known and forgotten. I shivered and looked away. The medic was right. I couldn't stay here long.

But when I looked back into the compound, there was Hirasor.

He came into the yard through a door in the wall. A tall man, he now walked with a slight shuffle. He sat down on an unoccupied bench and watched the sufferers. I couldn't see his face clearly, but the gait, and the arrogant set of the shoulders, was unmistakable. My heart started hammering.

"That's the other visitor," the medic said, noting the slight start I gave. "Claims to be interested in our subjects, but he seems to have problems of his own."

He didn't explain. Hirasor sat for a while, then moved his hands upward in a gesture that I didn't recognize, and returned through the door, which shut behind him.

I went into my narrow cell of a room to make my plans.

It was hard to think clearly. Blood, revenge, murder—the sufferings of those who had lost to Hirasor—my own long years of trailing him, giving up love and life for this one obsession—these thoughts reverberated in my mind. When I closed my eyes I saw Hirasor's face, or the Harvester's toothed mouth. When I opened them, I saw the stark, claustrophobic room, and the view from the skylight of a yellow dust-plume over the dome. The air smelled faintly of dust and burning. I knew then that Hirasor had chosen wisely. I didn't know to what extent he, as a nakalchi (and a hardened one at that) would be affected by the place, but he had gambled on it being a disadvantage for me.

The next day there was a message from him, an audio. Giving me the location of his rooms, and telling me that he would let me know when I should come, when Suvarna was not around.

Bring your weapons, he said.

This is the last memory fragment, the one most fresh in my mind.

I had been waiting for days. Hirasor and I would make an appointment, then he would abruptly cancel it because Suvarna had returned unexpectedly to their quarters. He did not want her to be in the way. I could sense that, like me, he wanted our final confrontation to be between us alone. At times I suspected that he was playing with me, that I should be more circumspect, perhaps induce someone to spy on him—but this was not the time to play detective. It was fitting that at the end there should be no tricks and subterfuges, only him and me, face to face at last.

There was no doubt that he was wearing me down, however. I lay restlessly in my room, plagued by headaches and nightmares. I started at every sound, and the dust devils visible from my window became fiery-eyed monsters.

Thus Hirasor and I waited, like illicit lovers, for the final assignation.

Then his summons came.

I will remember that last journey to the end of my days:

My armor-plated body, all weapons systems readied; the dull, booming pain in my head keeping time with my footsteps.

The walk through the complex, through which the other inhabitants seem to float like ghosts. Everything tinged faintly with red, as though the world itself is rusting. The stairs, dusted with Oblivion's fine grit. The door, a white rectangle, that scans me with a round eye and opens in silence.

Inside is a sparsely furnished receiving room. On a low divan sits a woman. Her hair cascades over her shoulders in black waves; her legs are crossed, her long, tapering, steel-tipped fingers folded over one knee. Her eyes are a metallic dark gray, multi-faceted like the eyes of moths; a quick blink in the direction of the door behind me, and it shuts.

"Greetings, Suvarna," I say, as calmly as I can, after the first heart-stopping moment. "Where's Hirasor?"

"Out," she says. "I intercepted some of his messages to you. It was I who sent you the last one."

I am standing before her, outwardly calm, inwardly berating myself for my foolishness. Her nakalchi eyes track every move I might make, every muscle-twitch.

"My business is with Hirasor," I say. I am determined that at the end of it all, she will not stand between Hirasor and I. But she will be hard to kill.

"I don't think you understand," she says, rising. She's an impressive woman, tall, all teeth and muscle, but also beautiful.

"This may be a game for you and him," she says, "but my job is to keep him alive. If it hadn't been for you, he wouldn't have taken to planet-hopping. He wouldn't have found this accursed place. It's time we stopped playing, Vikram, or whatever you are calling yourself now."

I can sense her coming alive, the way a killer weapon comes alive when it finds its target. Through the fog in my brain it occurs to me that Suvarna might be Hirasor's sibling, birthed by the same mother-machine.

I say the Word.

"What?" she says. She laughs. "Are you trying to distract

me with nonsense?"

So it means nothing to her. She raises a finger-tip.

The next moment my alarm system begins to scream coordinates and trajectories; I leap aside just as a spot on the wall behind me blackens with heat.

I remember that she likes to play.

"If only you'd left us alone," she says, watching me. "Hirasor is old and sated now, Vikram. All he wants—I want—is to be left in peace."

"Don't give me this old man nonsense," I say breathlessly. "I know Hirasor is a nakalchi. He could live for hundreds of years."

She stares at me, the perfect mouth hanging slack with surprise. I tongue a mouth-dart, but she recovers quickly, catching it in mid-air with a burst of flame. It falls smoking to the floor.

"How did you find out?"

Before I can answer, a door opens behind her. I see real terror on her face, then, as Hirasor walks into the room.

Except for the slight shuffle, he still walks tall, like Ravan-Ten-Heads.

"Get out!" she tells him, covering the ground between them in long strides, watching me all the time. "I'll deal with him!"

He gives her a glance of pure hatred.

"Let me fight my battles, will you?" A look passes between them, and I see in that instant that what they had once shared has turned bitter; that they are locked in their relationship out of habit and necessity rather than passion, hating each other and yet unable to let go.

I study him as they glare at each other (one of her eyes is still tracking me). Now that I see him at close range, I am shocked by his appearance. How he has fallen! All that is left of his affectations is the silk tunic with the embroidered collar. His hair is ragged and unkempt, and his face, lean and aristocratic as a prize hound's, is covered with scars. His burning dark eyes look out as though from a cage. I remember those eyes; I remember him peering down at me from the Harvester's face. Silently I mouth the Word, waiting until he will be in my power.

He has turned toward me. He holds out his hands to show that they are empty.

"I want to die," he says. "Even here, I can't get rid of . . . I can't go on. I have a perfect memory; I remember everything I have ever done, whether awake or in my dreams. All I want now is death . . . at your hands—"

"No, no," Suvarna says to him. "Don't talk like that. I won't let anyone kill you." She holds his arm, trying to pull him away. Her voice rises in a scream. "Don't let him kill you! I'll be all alone!"

"She thinks it will get better with time," he says to me, ignoring her. "But I want to end it more than anything. I have had not a moment—not one moment of peace. Six times I tried to kill myself, and six times she prevented me."

He turns to her: "Foolish Suvarna, we are all 'all alone.' I can't allow you to interfere this time. Now go away and let me die."

He pushes her suddenly and violently, throwing her across the room. She lies against the far wall in a huddle, staring at him with wide, shocked eyes.

"Death is not what I had in mind," I say, coming closer. "Death would be too good for you, Hirasor." I bring my armored hands up to his throat. He stands in front of me, not resisting, waiting. For a moment I think it is the old dream again, him and me at each other's throats at the world's end, but it is all going wrong. His wild eyes beg me for death. He shudders violently. I dig my claws into his neck, feel the pulse of the machine that he is, prepare myself to rip him half to death, to say the Word that will condemn him to perpetual hell, a hair's-breadth short of death. "Please, please, hurry" he begs, half-choking, not understanding what it is I am giving him.

I cannot do it. This pathetic being—Hirasor, destroyer of worlds! He is no adversary. He sickens me.

Besides, he is in hell already, without my help.

I let my hands fall.

"Live, then," I say angrily, backing toward the door.

His nostrils flare, his eyes widen. He begins a terrible high-pitched keening, clawing with his hands at his face and hair. Suvarna, who seems to have forgotten about me, has stumbled to her feet and is by his side in an instant. She puts her long arms around him.

"You are safe now," she says, crooning, putting her red lips to his hair. "I'll take care of him later. Nobody will take you away from me."

"Let me go, Suvarna," he weeps. "Leave me here on Oblivion. Leave me alone!"

As he thrashes in her arms, she says it, loudly and clearly.

The Word, which I had let slip in one panicked moment.

He becomes limp in her arms, his horrified gaze locked on hers. She lets him down gently on the divan.

She will not be alone now; she will have the perpetually suffering Hirasor to care for all her life.

I shoot him once, in the chest. She falls in a heap by his side, screaming and cursing. Over the wreck of his body, the slow and certain ebbing of his consciousness, I begin to speak the words of passing.

"Shantih. Nothen ke agaman na dukh na dard . . ."

And I walk out of the room.

Hirasor got his freedom, but what of me, the man-woman with a hundred aliases, none of which were Ram after all? There I was, boarding the first shuttle out of Oblivion, cheated of true victory at the end, my life's purpose lost. I had been tempted to stay on, to live with the crazies and let my mind descend into chaos, but the people there wouldn't let me. They seemed to think Suvarna had killed Hirasor; nobody cared to connect me directly with the crime, but his violent death was enough for them to send the stranger packing. I don't know what happened to Suvarna; I never saw her again.

At the first opportunity I switched from the shuttle to a passenger ship that made numerous stops on various inhabited worlds, thinking I might go back to my last residence on the planet Manaus. But when it came time to disembark I couldn't manage to do it. I am still on the ship, waiting until the impulse comes (if it ever will) to step out under the skies of a new world and begin another life. What has passed for my life, my personal Ramayan, comes back to me in tattered little pieces, pages torn from a book, burning, blowing in the wind. Like patterns drawn in the dust, half-familiar, a language once understood, then forgotten.

Here are some things I have discovered about myself:

I have no pleasure in life. I like nothing, definitely not absinthe or roses.

I want to die. But a curious inertia keeps me from it. The things of the world seem heavy, and time slow.

I still have nightmares about the burning woman. Sometimes I dream that Dhanu has a mantram that will bring me peace, and I am looking for her in the tunnels of a dying city, its walls collapsing around me, but she is nowhere to be found. I never dream of Hirasor except as a presence behind my consciousness like a second pair of eyes, a faint ghost, a memory. There are moments when I wonder what led a first-generation nakalchi to become a monster. The Ramayan says that even Ravan was once a good man, before he fell prey to hubris and lost his way. If legend is to be believed, there is a cave on some abandoned planet where copies of the first-generation nakalchis are hidden. Were I to come across it, would I find Hirasor's duplicate in an ice-cold crypt, dreaming, innocent as a child?

Lately I have begun to let myself remember that last climactic moment of my encounter with Hirasor. I shot my Ravan, I tell myself, trying to infuse into my mind a sense of victory despite the loss of the chance for true revenge—but I no longer know what any of those words mean: victory, revenge. Still, there is a solidity about that moment when I shot him, small though it is against the backdrop of all the years I've lived. That moment—it feels as tangible as a key held in the hand. What doors it might open I do not know, although I am certain that Sita does not wait behind any of them. Perhaps it is enough that it tells me there are doors.

CHOOSERS OF THE SLAIN

by John C. Wright

The time was Autumn, and what few beech trees had been spared released gold leaves into the chilly air, to swirl and dance and fall. Defoliants, and poisons, had reduced the greater number of the trees to leafless, sickly hulks, unwholesome to behold; and where the weapons of the enemy had fallen, running walls of fire had consumed them, leaving stands of wood and smoking ash. But here and there within the ruin, defying destruction, a kingly tree raised up a bounty of leaves, shining green-gold in the setting sun. Through the ruins of the forest came a man. He was past his youth, and past the middle of his age, but not yet old. His posture was erect, untiring, unbowed, and strong. His hair was iron-grey with age, his face was lined and careworn. The sternness of his glance showed he had been a leader of men, used to command. The sorrow and cold rage kindled in his eye showed he was no more. The furtive silence of his footstep, the quick grace of his flight, showed that he was hunted.

He wore the uniform of a warrior of his day and age. The

fabric was soft dove-grey, broken into unpatterned lines and shadows. The fabric faded to dull green when he stood near a flowering bush, or darkened to grey-black when he ran across an open space thick with piles of ash.

Across his back he bore a weapon which could fire a dozen missiles no larger than his littlest finger. The missiles could be programmed to seek and dive, circle and evade; or to search out specific individuals, whose signatures of heat, or aurenetic patterns, matched those locked within the little bullets. The little bullets could fly for hundreds of yards, hunting, or, if fired with a booster, reach enemies miles away. On his shoulder, he wore his medical appliance, with needles stabbed into the great veins of his arm, and colored tabs to show what plagues and viruses of the enemy had been found and contradicted in his blood.

Hanging open at his throat, there hung a mask to filter poisoned air. He left it dangling loose now as he walked, for the wind was fresh, and smelled of the salt sea, and blew into the east, toward the patrols he fled. When he came clear of the trees, he saw a rushing mountain stream, but poisoned now, and clogged with stinking fish and blood. He had climbed higher than he knew. Not a dozen paces to his left, the stream fell out into the air, and let a bloody waterfall tumble down high cliffs once green with trees.

He knew these cliffs; he had climbed and played upon them as a boy. Once he had climbed their craggy sides to a high place not far from here, and felt such crowning triumph and such joy as he had not felt again, not even when the many fighting factions of his land had united all beneath his hand to join in common bond to repel the invaders from over the sea.

For many years he had ruled a turbulent people, united them in one cause, and laid down strict laws to govern them, laws he prayed were fair and just. Now, remembering the way, he climbed the rocks again to find, unchanged, that wide and grassy ledge where once he viewed in triumph the green field of his youth.

When he turned and looked out upon the world, he saw the hills and deep-delved valleys fall away into the roads and fields and cottages, now blackened and deserted. By the river in the distance, he could see the city burning which once had been his capital. The bridges leading to the city had been shattered; the tall towers beyond had been thrown down, or tilted on their foundations like senile drunks. The airfield, bare of ships, was cracked and torn. Where once his mansion stood, a crater smoked.

Sirens wailed to no avail. There was no one to answer.

On the far horizon, red with sunset, was the sea. Against the clouds stained red with dying light loomed angular, grim silhouettes; the warships of the enemy were gathered in great force. Midmost, and taller than the others, was the flag-ship, a giant vessel, whose every armored deck and deckhouse held up dark mussel-bores of many cannons.

He took his weapon into his lap and lit its tiny screen. The symbols showed the codes and patterns for the five highest officers of the enemy forces, as well as that for their commander. Only on the last day of the war, now, too late, had his spies discovered what those patterns were; only now, too late, would vengeance be fulfilled. He gently touched the button with his thumb which programmed his ammunition.

The man took out his knife and turned it on, and scratched into the rock these words: OWEN PENTHANE SEPTEMBER THIRD STOOD HERE AND FIRED A FINAL VOLLEY INTO THE FLAGSHIP 'ATLAS'

He paused in thought a while, and watched the setting sun. Already the lowlands were in shadows. The rocks and trees around him gleamed cherry-pink. Now he wrote more words into the stone: THAT ALL WOULD KNOW BY THIS, THAT WE HAVE BEEN DESTROYED, BUT NOT DEFEATED,

AND EVEN TO THE LAST MAN, LAST BULLET, FOUGHT EVER ON.

He stood and raised the weapon to his cheek. The magnified image on the screen before his eye displayed the deckhouse of the mighty warship, and the moving figures bent over their controls. Webs of wire covered all the windows; these would detect incoming shots, and control the massive counter fire.

He wondered if he should step away from the rock which bore his epitaph; were it to crack or melt within the counter-fire, no future generations would read his final words.

And yet again, the circuits woven in the fabric of his suit were designed to bewilder and confuse the electric brains of approaching fire. It was possible he would not be harmed at all.

Nonetheless, he stepped aside for many paces. Now he raised the weapon once again.

A touch of his finger spun tiny gyroscopes within the stock. His weapon was now as firm on target as if it rested on a tripod. The computer built inside adjusted for the minute pitch and roll of the warship's deck, and for the vibration of the intervening air. The image on the aiming screen grew steady, clear, and fixed. A woman's voice spoke gently from behind him: "Lord Owen Penthane. Hold your fire." His thumb twitched on the programming dial. "I can fire behind as easily as ahead." He had programmed the first bullet to circle.

"Fear not," her voice answered softly. "I am unarmed."

He looked behind him. He squinted in astonishment, switched the weapon to stand-by, and studied her closely.

Her hair was yellow as corn-silk, held on top within a web of silver wires set with pearls, but escaping on the sides to fall loose about her shoulders to her waist. Two long red ribbons dangled from the back of her pearly corona, and lifted in the breeze which stirred her hair into a fragrant cloud.

Her face was fair; her eyes were grey-blue as a stormy

sea; her lips were red as sweet roses. Down to her feet white vesture flowed, shimmering like sea-mist, of some fabric he had never seen nor dreamed. Tight around her narrow waist she wore a wide embroidered belt of red; red slippers held slim feet. On her finger was a silver ring, whose stone gleamed with a point of light, burning like a star. It was not electric nor atomic nor any energy he could describe. He knew enough to know she came from places far beyond his knowing.

She watched him watching her, and softly smiled, as if pleased.

"There is rock wall behind you," he said, "And no place to climb except up in front of me. You were not here before I came."

"Not before, but after," she said. "Many ages hence, I shall stand within this place, and use the art we know to travel eons backward in a single step. I am a child of the future many centuries unborn. My name is Sigrune." She smiled, for a moment, at the rock he had inscribed, as if pleased to see the inscription freshly cut.

"Your accent is peculiar."

"I learned your speech from books, in my time, ancient, in yours, not yet composed."

He glanced at the medical apparatus on his shoulder. She laughed; a gay and lovely sound; and said, "No hallucinogen is in your blood. What you see before you is most real."

He laughed. "Flattering to think myself so famous that posterity will fly out of the deeps of time to talk to me! Flattering, but impossible."

"Impossible to the science of this age, perhaps. Be assured: your works shall not be forgotten, but preserved, and what you have said and done and thought shall shine through all the ages with clear light, and, in days to come, young students shall wonder what it would be like to see and to talk with you."

And now Sigrune blushed and faltered. Owen Penthane

was perceptive. He could imagine some young student of time drowsing over her history books, waiting for the opportunity to meet the man whom time has lent the luster of myth and hero-worship. A famous man in his own day, he had seen such blushes, and received such hero-worship, before.

Somehow, her shy look convinced him she was what she claimed.

"All this is most pleasing to me," he said, nodding to her, gravely. "Since all my work, till now, has been futile, and led to nothing more than ruin, I take your presence here as a sign that great things are left for me to accomplish in what few years a man of my age has remaining. Perhaps my scattered folk will rally, or my treacherous allies repent, and combine to drive the invaders from our soil. Now stand away; for with this shot, I hope to signal the return of hope to my oppressed nation. Having seen so fair a child from the future, I now have cause to think that hope shall not be vain."

She looked down, smiling uncertainly. It was a demure gesture, but also betrayed a strange hesitation, a hint of fear and sorrow. He stood, weapon in hand, staring at her for a long moment. Her fingers were twined together before her, and her head was bowed.

Owen Penthane said, "If you are a time traveler, how is it that your ventures do not imperil you? Any smallest change could unravel all the history you know, or thwart the marriage of your ancestors, undo the founding of your nations, and make you fade away like ghosts. What makes you proof from change?" There was a steely edge within his voice.

"There are two precautions that we undertake." she said, still not daring to look up. "The first is this: our grandchildren and their grandchildren have the government of our span of time, warning us of bad results to come, and wiping out mistakes, to make them as if they had never been. If any ill were fated to befall us on any of our journeyings, the Museum of Man at the

End of Time would warn us of the outcome, long before it ever could arise. Their knowledge is perfect, for they cannot ever err."

"And the second?" he said, grimly.

Now she raised her head and met his eye. "We show ourselves only to those who are about to die."

He was silent, frowning, while she looked on. Her gaze was steady, calm, and sad.

"I meant to cause you no pain, Lord Owen," she said. Soft breeze sent ripples through her hair. "Bid your world farewell: a finer world awaits you; a world which lacks no joy."

"You have told me nothing I did not foresee. The soldier is a fool who thinks to live forever. I suppose if I do not fire upon the flagship . . . ?"

"There are enemies lurking in the woods below. The result is much the same."

"Indeed." He turned and put the weapon to his shoulder. "Again I thank you, madam. Now that no hope torments me, my mind is put to rest. I am resolved."

"Wait! I beg you, wait!" She stepped forward suddenly, and put her hands on his weapon. He caught her one wrist with a hard grasp, and stared angrily at her.

"Why now do you interfere?" he asked. Her skin was soft, untouched by any scar or plague. Since the bombardments, he had not seen many women with unblemished skin.

She put her other hand gently on his rough fingers, and gazed at him with wide eyes. "Set your weapon on its timer." she said. "And hold my hand and come with me into my land, beyond all history. At the Museum of Man, the arts and sciences of every age are gathered, the bravest of men, the most beautiful of women, the greatest of philosophers, and the most lucid of all poets. Our medicine can restore your vanished youth to you; it is a country of the young, where aging is unknown, and death by accident is undone before it can occur. In the twilight of all time, sorrow is unknown to us, and all those wise and great and glorious enough to join our company have been called up from out of the abyss of history. You will sit in our feast-hall, to eat whatever meats or breads delight you, or drink our sweet and endless wine. A place has been reserved for you, next to the seats of Brian Boru, Alfred the Great, and Charlemagne. We feast and know no lack, we who can change time to restore drained goblets back to fullness, or resurrect the slaughtered beast to roast again. Only for us, the flame of a blown-out candle can be unblown, and brightly burn again."

He released her wrist. She saw the cold and unmoved expression of his face.

Grief made her voice grow shrill, but no less lovely. She knelt, and clasped her shaking hands around his waist. "Come away with me, I pray you, Owen! I offer what all men have dreamed in vain! Our joys do not pall, cannot grow stale and wearisome like other joys, for we can change unhappy days not ever to have been! All great men, except for those who died in public places, in the witness of many eyes, are gathered there. All these great men, your peers, will cheer your coming to our halls. You shall hear the thousand poems, each grander than the last, which Dante and which Homer have composed in all the many centuries since they have dwelt among us, or sample the deep wisdom Aristotle has deduced in his thousand years of subtlest debate with Gotuma, Lao Tsu, Descartes, and John Locke."

He said sternly, "What chance have I to open fire, and survive? To gather up my scattered people, and lead them once again against a foe, which, if my bullets find their aim, will be, for now, leaderless and demoralized? What chance?"

She rose slowly. "I was told to tell you, you have none."

"But you cannot know for certain. You know only that, in the version of the history you know, I did not fire, but went away with you."

She bowed her head and whispered a half-silent, "Yes." But then she raised her head again. Her eyes now shone with unwept tears, and now she raised her hand to brush her straying hair aside. "But come with me, not because you must, but because I ask. Give up your world: you have lost it. You have failed. I have been promised that, should I return with you, great love would grow between us. We are destined. Is this ruined land so fair that you will not renounce it for eternal youth, and love?"

"Renounce your world instead, and stay with me. Teach me all the secrets of your age, and we will sweep my enemies away with the irresistible weapons of the future. No? If you change the past, you cannot return to find the future that you knew, can you?"

"It is so," she said.

"You will not renounce your world for love? Just so. Nor will I, mine. Now stand away, my dear. Before the sun is set, I mean to fire."

She whirled away from him in a shimmer of pale fabric, and strode to stand where she had been when first he saw her. Now she spoke in anger, "You cannot resist my will in this! I need but step a moment back ago, and play this scene again, till I find right words, or what wiles or arguments I must to bend your stiff neck, and persuade you from your folly. Foolish man! Foolish and vain man! You have done nothing to defy me! I shall make it never to have been, till finally you must change your mind!"

Now he smiled. "Let my other versions worry what they shall do. I am myself; I shall concern myself with me. But I suspect I am not the first of me who has declined your sweet temptation; I deem that you have played this scene before. I cannot think that any words or promises could stay me from my resolve."

She hid her hands behind her face and wept.

He said, "Be comforted. If I were not the man you so admire, then, perhaps, I would depart with you. But if you love me for my bravery, then do not seek to rob me of this last, brave, final, act."

She said from behind her hands, "It may be that you will survive; but the future which will come of that shall not have me in it."

And with these words, she vanished like a dream.

The sun was sinking downward into night. Against the bloody glimmer of its final rays, the warship which held his enemies rose up in gloomy silhouette. Now he raised his weapon to his shoulder, took careful aim, and depressed the trigger. There came a clasp of thunder.

And because he knew not what might come next, his mind was utterly at peace.

AKHILA, DIVIDED

by C.S. MacCath

Akhila fell out of the sky on Yule's Eve, by lunar reckoning, and blazed across the icy twilight like a bright thing thrown by a god. She thought about dying while she fell, gave in to the tug of the moon's mass and plummeted toward its embrace in the peace that precedes a suicide. Who would know, she wondered, that she hadn't lost her way somewhere between thermosphere and troposphere? Who would be able to tell from the scattered fragments of her corpse that she had chosen to challenge gravity in the hope of failure?

It was only when she sensed a gathering of Organics around a bonfire that she questioned the wisdom of her choice. Her flight path would take her too near them; they might be killed when she crashed. So she slowed, turned and dropped, courting the ground and not crushing herself against it, the reflected light of planet rise illuminating her descent.

She was still a rocket when they approached but was struggling toward a different shape. There was a three-dimensional face on the skin of her silvery surface, and the base of her frame had toes. It was snowing, the first flakes of a heavy fall, and the frozen water evaporated as it fell toward her, leaving the hillside wreathed in mist.

They were naked from the waist up and led by a tall, youngish man with black hair that fell to his hips. She watched them climb the hill with part of her consciousness while she sought the weak, reflected light of the rising gas giant with the rest. It would be morning before she could morph completely, she thought. It was too dark to transform now.

The youngish man turned to wait for the others, and then she knew he was a monk, guessed that all of them were monastics. The skin of his spine bore the mark of each path he had traveled; the Valknut, the Pentacle, the Yin and Yang. After the company crested the hill he knelt down in front of her, too close for his safety, and pressed the tips of his fingers into the frozen grass.

"Don't be afraid. I'm human." She used the last of her energy to force breasts from her middle. "A woman."

"I'm certain you're many things, and I'm sorry for all of them. What is your business here, Augment?"

"My name is Akhila. I have a name." I could have already been dead, she thought. "Do you have a name?"

"I do." He didn't offer it to her. "And I asked you a question."

Organics weep when they feel this way, she thought, but I don't have the energy for tears. Her eyes rolled left, then right. One of the monks was shivering; a fine, white dust covered his blond hair and shoulders. She imagined the snow was ash and then willed the vision away. "I'm not here to hurt you. I don't do that anymore."

The youngish man tensed like a predatory cat, or perhaps like its prey. She wasn't sure. The other monks glanced at one another and backed away. Then she heard a roar, faint at first, louder as it approached the hillside.

"It's a bomb!" The roaring man crested the hill and leveled the barrel of a hand weapon in her direction. His iron gray beard and hair whipped in the rising wind. "Vegar, get out of the way!" He gestured down the hillside with his free arm, and the mantle of symbols on his back and shoulders rippled as he turned.

Vegar rose, his hair falling forward as he looked from her to the weapon and back again.

"No, I'm a person." Her desire for life rekindled then.

"Father, wait." Vegar lifted a hand to block the weapon.

"You don't know what it can do, what those things have done."

"She hasn't threatened us."

"I said to get out of the way!"

"Sigurd, I can't let you murder her."

"I take refuge!" Akhila cried. They would take her in. They were obligated by their oaths. "I take refuge in the spiral that leads outward and in the spiral that leads inward. I take refuge in the one road of many paths and in the company of fellow travelers. I beg the sanctuary of this hostel."

"You have no right to sanctuary!" Sigurd shifted his aim to avoid the younger monk and fired at the half bomb, half woman, but Vegar turned in that instant and flung himself over her frame. A stream of energy passed above them as they fell, and the sharp odor of burning flesh rose from their bodies. By the time they separated, several members of the priesthood had blocked the older monk's path.

Sigurd's lips curled downward, and he spat on the ground, but he didn't fire again. Instead, he handed the weapon to one of the monks in front of him. "I'll call the Councilor and let her know we have a problem." His voice was flat. "Somebody treat Vegar's burns and make sure that thing doesn't go anywhere."

Vegar refused to leave the hillside while a gun was pointed at Akhila, so a medic was dispatched to bring him warmer clothes and treat him where he sat. He also refused pain medication, which would have encouraged sleep. For a while, he hoped she might get up from where he left her, but she remained supine for the rest of the night. She didn't speak again either, but her eyes continued to roll left and right, up and down until she had cooled enough that ice gathered on their surfaces. Then she stopped moving altogether. After a time the monk with the weapon relaxed, and Vegar withdrew to a place within where there was no weariness and no pain.

Akhila began to transform again when the sun rose. Her rocket body split into a head, torso and limbs while her silvery skin grew caramel-colored and soft. By mid-morning she looked like the person she claimed she was, a full-hipped, brown-eyed woman with black hair cropped short. "Thank you for saving me," she said to Vegar when she was done.

He stood up from the place where he had kept vigil and began to pace. "I'm not doing this for you."

"I didn't think you were, but thank you, nonetheless." Her voice was low and soft.

Vegar's wounds were still blistering; he could feel the puffy pockets of fluid ballooning against his bandages. His eyelids felt heavy, and his limbs were weak. The muscles in his jaw knotted. "What kind of refuge do you expect us to provide while your people are butchering ours?"

"I don't know what I expected, and it's war, not butchery." She wrapped her arms around her knees and looked up at him. Her eyes were full of ghosts. "Even so, I've done some terrible things."

Vegar stopped pacing, and his lip lifted back from his teeth. "The Valfather counsels us that the path of strength is to atone for our mistakes, not run from them. I won't be your confessor."

"What would you have me do, go back to the worlds I've blighted and make amends with the dead?"

"Is that why you're really here, to 'blight' us?"

"Don't be stupid. I took refuge in good faith. If I had wanted to kill you, you would be dead." She glanced at the other monk, who had lifted Sigurd's weapon, and smirked. "Good luck with that. I'm not so vulnerable in the sunlight."

"I should have let our Godman shoot you when he had the chance."

"Well, I've certainly earned it. Would you like to see how?" Before he could answer, her body began to stretch, thin, and re-shape into a pair of figures; a smaller replica of herself and a small boy dangling in her grip over a rocky outcropping. The stone under the replica's feet melted away, and as it dissolved, it was drawn up through her legs and torso, which pulsed in a slow but steady rhythm. Then her mouth opened wide, and a flood of tiny, transformed particles poured from her nose and lips onto the face of the terrified child.

"Little boys go to school," Akhila said. "Little boys go home. And everywhere this one goes, I go too, forever. Let me show you something else." She morphed again. This time she became the boy, a few years older now. He was half silver and half skin. His wrists and ankles were bound, and his ears trickled blood. "He was a good carrier, and he's still alive somewhere in a small, dark place I can't find. But his people are dead; my nanoparticles bled from his pores and burned their flesh away. I went back and collected them before the bones were buried." She resumed her human shape. "It was easier than making new ones."

"Why?" Vegar's vocal cords constricted as he spoke, and his vision blurred. He thought he might vomit bile out of his empty stomach.

"How can you call yourself a holy man and not know why? Were you born on this moon? Have you never left? How could your Godman identify me by my profession, point a weapon at me, refuse to use gender-specific pronouns when he talked about me and never have told you why?" Her voice was growing mechanical, resonant. It whined like metal on metal.

Then Akhila froze and swung her head to the left. "Three people are coming. They want to take me indoors." She surged upward until her body was tall, thin and bulbous at the top. Her caramel-colored skin melted to silver, and the bulb widened. "For later," some indistinct part of her said, "when I can't see the sun."

Sigurd came over the rise with a pair of armed nuns. As Akhila morphed back, he watched her, a rarified hatred on his face. Two bowls of steaming food smelling of grains and honey shook in his tight grip. "I've been on the line with the Councilor all night," he told Vegar. "She agrees the bomb can't be trusted, but she asked me not to destroy it. Says it might be useful to study. I think she's putting the hospital at risk, but I've told her we'll keep it here until the military arrives from off-moon."

Vegar watched Akhila stare back at him as she was led down the hill. "Can we really hold her with three guns? She didn't seem afraid of the one you gave to Clautho."

"Those weapons are mine, and they *are* sufficient, but the Councilor is sending a militia detachment over with a little more firepower. We'll be all right for a few days." He handed the bowls to Vegar and his companion. "Here, I've brought you something to eat. I can't believe nobody remembered to feed you."

Vegar wondered for a moment how the elder monk could be so certain of his guns, but the bowl in his hands was warm, fragrant and distracting. His mouth watered, and his stomach growled.

"Vegar . . ." Sigurd began, and then sighed.

"You were right. I'm sorry I stood in your way."

"What happened?"

Vegar shook his head. "It's not important."

Sigurd nodded. "You tried to do a good thing. I'm just glad it didn't cost you more than a bad burn."

Vegar began to walk down the hillside while he ate. Sigurd followed. Akhila's back was long, straight and brown in front of them, and her hips swayed back and forth like a copper bell when she walked. She looks human, he thought, and remembered what she had said of his mentor.

"Are you all right?" Sigurd put his hand on Vegar's shoulder.

Vegar blinked and realized he had stopped. "I'm glad too," he said, and started walking again.

They shut Akhila in a root cellar and posted the nuns outside. Vegar slept the rest of the day and most of the night in the monastery's infirmary, where his bandages were changed at regular intervals and ointment was applied to his burns. While he slept, he dreamed Akhila was sitting in the dark, statue-still to conserve energy. He woke wondering what she thought he should know that he didn't.

In the early pre-dawn light, he went to the arboretum and paced the Stages of the Pentacle, pausing at each elemental shrine to remember its place in the natural world, its place in his body. The winterbound trees creaked above him in the wind, and a flock of sleepy birds hooted down at him from their icy perches. He closed his eyes at the southern shrine and listened awhile as the perpetual flame warmed his face and hands.

The sky brightened. Vegar left the flame and approached the crest of the star where an empty stone vessel represented the human spirit. He usually offered a prayer here, of gratitude or charity, but this morning he felt as hollow as the bowl itself. He had prevented his Godman from protecting the people in his care and had saved a torturer of children, a mass murderer. Then Akhila the rocket and Akhila the woman blended together like watercolor paint in his thoughts, and he remembered she'd said she didn't do those things anymore.

Vegar wondered for a moment if Akhila's nanobody made her less human, less worthy of redemption. He'd heard of radical augments, machines with human minds, and believed she could have killed them if she had wanted to in spite of Sigurd's powerful guns. There was something about the tone of her anger that sounded old, deep, and unhealed, some wound that seeped and poisoned. Did she hope to cleanse it here?

There would be no answers to these questions in meditation, he knew, so he strode away from the shrine and made his way to the root cellar. Four men with heavy guns were posted outside the door, who refused to allow him in without an escort. Vegar relented after a brief exchange, and two of the guards accompanied him inside. Akhila was motionless as he dreamed she would be, sitting cross-legged on the cellar's work bench, still naked as she had been the previous day. Her eyes opened, and a faint, blue light shone from them, the only light in the room.

"Hello, Brother Vegar. How are your burns?" Akhila heat-scanned his chest and arms as he closed the door. The flow of blood to his wounds was good. He was probably in pain, but he would heal.

"Why were you so angry with me? What don't I know?"

She smiled. "You're awfully brave to be so naive in mixed company."

"I didn't come here for you to insult me." Vegar turned to go and put his hand on the doorknob.

"I'm sorry," she said, but a hint of humor remained in her voice. "I shouldn't provoke you. It was good of you to ask at all."

His hand remained on the door, but he looked in her direction again. Her scent receptors registered nervous sweat, the medicine on his burns and the stale residue of burned incense. It was a pleasant counterpoint to the gunmetal stink of the guards' weaponry, so she allowed herself a moment to soak it in. While she did, she thought about making conversation, perhaps asking about his faith. But then she remembered what she had shown him and what he had said to her.

"It started with gills," she finally said, "so people could mine in deep water without suits. Prisoners got early parole; people dependent on their governments got bigger stipends, and all they had to do was change a little and learn a new skill . . ."

Vegar   interrupted   her.   "Those   people   were volunteers . . ."

Akhila raised an eyebrow and spoke over him. "Most of them died on the bottom of the ocean and were forgotten by everyone but their families, who were offered new opportunities on new worlds. Why go to the expense of terraforming a planet with skilled workers when you can augment criminals and the poor at a fraction of the cost? So gills became chemicals or genetic alterations for breathing hostile atmospheres. Sometimes skin became scales or even better, self-replicating body armor. It's amazing what you can do to flesh when you don't care whether or not it survives for very long."

"What does any of this have to do with your war?" Vegar's heart rate increased, and she heard his breath grow shallow. Good. She was making him angry. Maybe she could make him think as well.

"Did you know that drowning is a terrible way to die? You can't hold your breath until you pass out; your body will force you to inhale eventually. So you breathe in water knowing it will kill you, but it takes a minute or two for you to lose consciousness. Chemical burns are bad too; they linger on the body, and no amount of medicine can make it easier to look in a mirror."

"I don't support any of that, and I'm sure the little boy you destroyed had no idea it was happening at all."

"Of course you support it. This is a terraformed moon, and you're living on it without any regard to the people who made it habitable."

"But why children?" He was shouting now.

"Yes, Vegar. Why children? Is it because they're easier to augment? Is it because they fit into smaller spaces? Is it because a child's mind is as malleable as her body is?"

"I'm just a monk. I haven't hurt anyone."

"You're a . . ." She paused, chose a word from his argument with Sigurd, ". . . murderer. At least I have the grace to get my hands dirty."

"You've butchered entire worlds full of people!"

"Who refuse to tell the truth when they know it and refuse to listen when they hear it. Who are living on the bones of other people who died to put them there. Who will never have to run out of oxygen or water or food or wonder what kind of abomination they'll turn into if the augmentation fails. Who've never had to sell one daughter's mind to pay for another daughter's medicine. And I will keep on killing them, every one of them, every man, woman and child of them until you stop it, stop it, stop it!"

Akhila heard the guards cock their weapons and realized she was standing on the table. Her body glowed a faint blue in the darkness. She shuddered once and slumped into a seated position again. "Oh, Vegar." She began to rock back and forth, her arms wrapped around her belly. "Help me."

But the guards were already escorting him out.

Some time later, the door opened again and Sigurd entered the cellar alone. He was wearing the same expression he had worn on the hillside and carrying one of the weapons he had brought there. He strode over to her as the door closed behind him and shoved it under her chin. She didn't move to stop him.

"Do not speak to the boy again," he growled, "or I will melt your nanobody slowly, over a period of hours, while you beg me for your life."

"Father Sigurd, where have you seen a radical augment before, and what did it do to you?" She ignored the gun.

He picked her up by the throat and threw her against the dirt wall of the cellar. Gravel and soil crumbled around her. Again, she didn't struggle but rose to her feet in a single, fluid motion as he crammed his fingers into her mouth and gripped her jaw.

"You are not allowed to call me 'Father.' I'll kill you for that, too. I should kill you for that now." He wasn't shouting anymore, but his body was shaking, and his breath hissed in and out over his teeth.

Akhila remained calm. She had come to this moon seeking death and was not afraid to meet it. Her mouth peeled back from his fingers and rematerialized beside them. "For whatever it was, and for whoever did it, I am profoundly sorry. I invite you to do to me whatever you believe is just in order to avenge your loss."

Sigurd's eyes misted then, and he looked away from her. When he spoke, his voice was thick with emotion. "It wasn't a 'who', and neither are you." His barrel chest heaved. "Leave the boy alone," he repeated, leaning on the door and stumbling out into the afternoon sunshine.

Akhila sat in darkness for the next day, a slender nanofilament extending outward from her body, through the micro-cracks at the base of the cellar door and up into the grass. It didn't collect much sun, but if she was still, it was enough. At the end of that time, she had sufficient power to stretch the nanofilament farther, make it longer, and escape the cellar altogether without attracting the attention of the guards.

She spent the rest of the afternoon draped over the metal roof of the monastery like frost on a window, glinting in the early winter sun. After planet rise, when all was quiet, she slid down from the roof and went walking in the arboretum.

Vegar stood at the edge of a sand sculpture of the Yin and Yang. His hands and shoes were gritty; his chest and arms ached. He had been there all evening with a rake, combing the sand into place when he heard the crunch of snow underfoot and spun around, startled.

Akhila reached forward and covered his lips with a flat-handed seal to keep him silent. "I didn't mean what I said before."

She withdrew her hand, and Vegar considered her for a moment. "You really aren't here to kill us, are you?"

"I've made a choice, and I intend to see it through."

"Even though you can't stay here?"

"I don't think I ever believed I could."

"The military will be cruel. You probably won't live long."

"I'll deal with that when the time comes."

Vegar turned back toward the sand sculpture and sat down. "Nobody deserves cruelty, not even someone like you."

Akhila sat beside him. "So I'm a person, then?"

"I think so. I don't want to think so, but I do."

"That will carry me a long way."

Vegar examined her body. Her breasts were round and dark, there were thatches of fine hair in her armpits and her skin looked real on close inspection. He reached out a hesitant hand and touched her arm. It was warm. "How long has it been since you were Organic?"

"Bharati was never my mother, and Dhiren was never my father. They were deep sea miners who sold the right to copy their little girl's mind. It doesn't hurt to have your mind copied; you just go to sleep, and they wire you up and take an imprint. Only their Akhila went home with them, and I stayed in the machine."

Horrific, he thought. She must have been terrified. Then

he remembered something she had told him. "Did your sister get her medicine?"

Akhila nodded. "For the rest of her life. Or at least that's what my parents were promised. It was a long time ago."

Vegar gathered his robe around his body and buried his hands in it for warmth while Akhila brought the tips of her fingers together. Sparks flew between them, and a fine dust began to accumulate on her legs. He watched her for a while. There was a faint smell of hot metal, and he had the sudden urge to hold his hands up to hers the way he had held them up to the fire shrine. After a moment he asked, "What are you doing?"

"My nanoparticles are self-policing. When some of them malfunction, I use others to destroy them." The flame faltered and died. "Vegar, I didn't just decide to come here. I was sent, like you said, to blight the hospital and surrounding community."

He stiffened. "But you haven't."

"No, I haven't."

"Why not?"

"I recently found my granddaughter and made a carrier of her before I realized who she was. Gorgeous girl, about five years old. Her father must have been fair-skinned because her hair was blond, and her eyes were green, but her skin was like . . . was like her mother's. Of course, she wasn't *my* granddaughter, but she might have been." Akhila grew still, and her body began to shine blue in the darkness. "So you see, there isn't anything you or anyone else could do to me that I don't deserve, and I had to land somewhere."

They sat together in silence for a while. Akhila closed her eyes and tilted her head while the barren branches above her creaked in the breeze. Vegar watched his sand sculpture soften.

"Are you familiar with the Tao?" he asked a few moments later.

"I know the data."

"Humph." Vegar's lips lifted in a half-smile. "This isn't a good representation of it." He pointed at the sculpture. "The one on my back is better. Here, I'll show you." He shrugged off his robe and unbuttoned his shirt but sucked in a breath as he tried to pull it from his shoulders.

"Let me help you." She lifted his collar and moved his hair. His torso was still swathed in bandages, but the Yin and Yang was tattooed above them. Akhila leaned down to look.

"Do you see the two halves?"

"Yes."

"The dark half represents the receptive part of nature and the bright half the aggressive part. The opposing spots in each are the seeds of one in the other, the hope for integration."

She raised her head. "You think I can heal."

"I don't know. Your path is a hard one. But I do know there's a place beyond duality where the Tao is eternal, a place we all come from, a place we all return to."

"And what happens when we return?" Her hand rested on his bare shoulder.

"We come to understand why we had two halves to begin with. Help me with my shirt again, would you?"

Akhila slipped the garment over his arms and helped him with his robe.

"It would be better if nobody else saw you out here." He stood and prepared to leave.

"I know. I won't be much longer. I just want to take in a little more light before it gets too dark."

"All right, then. Good night, Akhila."

"Good night, Vegar," he heard her say as he walked toward the monastery kitchen, where a cup of evening tea and other human comforts could be found.

Sigurd was waiting in Vegar's room when he returned there.

"Where have you been?"

"In meditation."

"Ah."

"Is there something I can do for you, Father?"

The older man opened his mouth to speak, fell silent, and then opened his mouth again. "How are you feeling?"

"I'm better than I was."

"Good."

"Are you all right?" Vegar sat on the bed and put his elbows on his knees.

Sigurd shifted in his seat. "Do you believe in fate?"

"Well, I believe our ancestors needed the idea of fate, and I think our thoughts and behaviors create ripple effects we often don't understand, but no, not really, not in the way I think you mean it. Why do you ask?"

"I . . . do you know how I came to be a priest?"

Vegar smiled. "I'm afraid that was before my time."

Sigurd gripped the chair seat between his legs, shifted again, and looked out of the window. "This war with the Augments has been going on a long while."

"Did you lose someone, Father?"

The knuckles on Sigurd's hand whitened. "I've tried to be a good priest."

"And you've succeeded."

Sigurd turned his head and stared at the floor. "Some wounds never heal."

"Priests don't have to be perfect; they have to be present. You taught me that."

"You're a good man, son." Sigurd rose from the chair. "Remember I said so." He left the room and closed the door behind him before Vegar could formulate a reply.

Akhila was still sitting beside the sand sculpture when Sigurd finally found her. She rose and turned to face him in a single, fluid motion. "Good evening."

"How did you get out?" He raised his weapon and aimed at her chest.

"You've never imprisoned a nanobody before, have you? You're a long way from the war, here."

"Not long enough." His hands shook, and the lines of his face were hard.

"I see. Well, you don't need your weapon, Father. I'm here of my own free will."

"Stop calling me Father."

"Of course, Sigurd."

"You look just like a woman." He took two steps toward her.

"I am a. . . ."

"Shut up." He took two more. "You shouldn't look like a woman. You shouldn't look like anything you've killed. It's obscene." His eyes filled with tears, and he ground his teeth together. "Obscene."

"You went to the root cellar to kill me." Akhila looked from the weapon to his face, so red and full of rage. This is it, she thought, and waited for the blast.

"There is no sanctuary for you, no redemption, no peace." He lowered his weapon and closed the space between them. His free hand grazed the skin of her belly and then gripped a breast. "No."

"What are you doing?" She put her hand on his coat and pushed a little, but he lunged forward instead, closing the space between them. Then he buried his nose in her neck and his hand traveled upward, tightening around her throat.

"You don't smell like a woman."

"You don't want to do this, Sigurd. I don't want you to have to live with this. Please, shoot me or go back inside."

"Are you a woman?"

Akhila shuddered. "Yes, I am."

"Didn't you invite me to do whatever I thought was just

to avenge my loss?"

"Yes, I did."

"Then I want to do this." Sigurd lifted her into the air by her neck. "Open your legs, woman," he said, and threw her onto the sand sculpture.

She reached into the place where she carried the imprint of a small, half-metal boy lying in a dark place, of all the children lying in dark places because she had ruined them. She thought about the sun on her nanobody. She remembered the touch of Vegar's hand and the long threads of hair she held aside so that she could put her fingers on his shoulder. She thought of the girl who would have been her granddaughter, who should have been her granddaughter, and of all the things, the human things her body would never be able to do.

She opened her legs.

He shoved his gun inside her, and she opened inside so it would fit. Then he flipped her onto her stomach, grabbing her hair and pushing her face into the sand while he loosened his trousers.

"Can you bleed?" he roared into her ear as he shoved himself into her rectum, which she opened for him as well. "Let's see if you can bleed!" He spat on the right side of her face, and she closed her eyes while his saliva crossed her nose on its way to the ground. "Let's see if you can bleed like my sister bled! Let's see if you can bleed like my son bled! Let's see if you can bleed like my wife bled!" Akhila's body rocked with his thrusts, and the gun rocked loosely in her body, but she didn't resist him, and this only inflamed his rage. He punched her face again and again with his free fist, and when she didn't respond, he reached behind their joined bodies and slammed his gun into her with a repetitive, jerking motion. When he was spent, an anguished howl escaped his throat, and he held her pinned while he wailed. Tears streamed down his cheeks and onto her face, where they cooled on her lips and eyelids.

The crunch of footsteps on frozen ground and the muffled chatter of worried voices moved toward the arboretum from the monastery. A crowd was gathering, looking for him, looking for her.

"Sounds like your guards are coming." Sigurd wiped his face on his coat sleeve and leaned down close to her ear. "Why don't we see if they're interested in any 'justice' before I melt you into scrap metal?" He rose from Akhila's back and reached for the weapon still buried inside her. But half of the barrel was gone, absorbed. He stepped back, trousers around his knees, and watched as she began to glow. A second passed and she was bright, blazing. A face appeared in the back of her head; hands and arms reached out of her back. Then her body halved. The fiery part of her got up out of the dark self still lying in the sand, whipped long fingers around Sigurd's neck and lifted him into the air.

"Thank you Father," she said as she left her other self behind, "for renewing my sense of purpose. You'll make a fine carrier."

Bright Akhila was half the size of her whole body, but she began to remedy her lack by drawing sand up out of the sculpture and processing it. As it was diminished, her darker self stirred and rose, a diminutive shadow to that growing brightness. Vegar found them then. She watched him look from her to Bright Akhila and then to Sigurd's half-naked form struggling against the burning fingers that held him.

He screamed. "Akhila, no!"

Dark Akhila turned to him then and threw out a hand in his direction. "Stay back!"

"What did you do to her?" Vegar turned to Sigurd, but the older man could only roll his eyes in the younger priest's direction and plead with his lips.

"I couldn't stop him. I tried. And I couldn't stop her," Dark Akhila said and then addressed her other self. "Let him go.

Please let him go."

Bright Akhila sneered up at the man choking in her grasp. "What was it you said? No sanctuary, no redemption, no peace."

Then Dark Akhila drew the remaining sand up into her body, processing it, growing with it. "I can't let you make him a carrier. I took refuge among these people."

"For what? So they could lock you in the dark? So they could rape you?"

"For him." Dark Akhila's arm spanned the rest of the distance between her body and Vegar's. She brushed her hand across his chest, and for a moment he held it close until she slipped it out from under his grip and brought it back to her center. "He said that I'm a person, and I will believe it. I have to believe it."

Then Dark Akhila blazed blue-hot, her face full of compassion. Her arms extended, elongated, and stretched forward, inviting her brighter half to step inside the circle of her embrace. Bright Akhila turned, a pivoting motion on legs still pulsing with gathered sand, and the rhythm of her body faltered; the leer on her face softened. Her fingers tightened once and then loosened. Sigurd fell to the ground, dead.

A moment passed, and both bodies stilled. Then Bright Akhila fell forward, a scream filling her throat and filling the air. Dark Akhila caught her, brought her close and wept blue tears that fell from her cheeks and dissolved in the mass of pale hair beneath her chin. They shook together for a time, and the barren trees shook with them.

Then Dark Akhila looked up at Vegar. "Is there redemption? Is there peace?" she asked as her body began to wrap itself around Bright Akhila's seething form.

Vegar's face was grief-stricken. "I hope so." He looked down at his broken mentor and added, "For both of you."

"You need to go now." Her dark, blue body converged

around the raging woman inside her. "This will be hot."

Vegar turned and ran. As he ran, he could smell hot metal, could hear a crackling sound like the spark of a welding torch, could feel a rising heat chasing him out of the arboretum, could see a reflection like daylight in the night sky over his head. When he finally fell to the ground gasping for breath, the world was cool and dark again.

The Councilor arrived with the military an hour later to take custody of Akhila, but there was nothing for them to retrieve but the mingled ashes and bone fragments of tree, bird, monk and nanobody. Vegar was kneeling in prayer just outside the blast radius, where smoke still rose from the earth. When the Councilor asked if he knew where his mentor was, he fell to his face in the snow and sobbed.

In time, his body healed and the bandages came off, but a reddened, stretched place remained on his chest. As the scars softened, they took the shape of Akhila's elongated face in the throes of change, pleading for her life. The day he first recognized her face on his body, he packed his belongings and left the monastery to walk the path that had marked him, gathering broken Augments in Akhila's name, mending broken Organics in Sigurd's. When the time came, he had his scars limned in black and filled with a blue that shone even when he walked in darkness, which he often did.

THE MOON-KEEPER'S FRIEND

by *Joanna Galbraith*

*M*ohammed Muneer's Twenty-Four Hour Tea Service was a rather long name for a roadside teahouse but Mohammed had liked it from the moment he'd conjured it. Painting the words neatly across an old wooden plank, his hand had cramped twice before he'd finished the first coat. He thought the long name would catch the attention of drivers. Make them slow down. Give their stomachs ideas. But the sign was too elongated for those who were weary so they drove straight on past him and stopped further down. Outside the burger joint with the squat name of *Munch*, lit up in pink neon by the side of the road.

On top of the teahouse was a small crescent moon which Mohammed Muneer polished each morning after the Fajr. Humming *Nahna Wil Kamar Jeeraan* in three different octaves, he burnished it vigorously until his fingers shred skin and sweat hung like a necklace across the brow of his forehead. The manager at *Munch* often watched on bemused. Eating jam doughnuts, belching black coffee, shouting between mouthfuls:

"You should go neon, mate. More glow for less grind."

Mohammed Muneer's tea house rarely saw visitors even though he served tea in gold-lipped tulip glasses and offered ruby-inlaid nargiles from which to smoke tumbak. Even though he made sweets as fragrant as spring: churros glazed with rosewater, pistachio baghlava, rice-flour cookies sprinkled with crushed poppy seeds.

Road weary travellers, it seemed, simply weren't interested.

Their tastes were much simpler, their guts far too staid. Cheese-and-bacon fingers. Fat plastic tubs filled with mousse. A *Munch* burger special with extra egg and thick beetroot. Who needed tumbak when you could smoke *Bensons?* Three puffs in the parking lot beside the dry spinifex grass. Butts flicked in the air like butterflies with torched wings.

Alas, for Mohammed Muneer, the townsfolk were no better.

Narrow in mind, if not in their girths, the very idea of something edible even being called a *pashmak* had them crossing the road promptly without checking for traffic. They crossed even faster when Mohammed Muneer was about. Waving them over with his wide, beckoning arms, apron to armpits, smiling so hard the tips of his moustache tickled the lobes of his ears. They'd rather risk their lives on the fast metal of the highway then engage with a man who didn't serve milk in his tea.

It hurt Mohammed Muneer to be so scorned but in some small ways he was actually quite fortunate. The townsfolk were slobbish. They ate with their mouths open. They also had a rather perverse inclination for walking through dog poo instead of around it, so though he felt sad he was actually quite blessed.

There was only one local who ever visited his tea shop and that was Reggie Macklewaite, the town's sort-of handyman.

A softheaded fellow who wore lime velour tracksuit pants; he liked to help Mohammed Muneer wherever he could. Fix cracking pipes, empty clogged cisterns, sweep earwigs from gutters and the treads of the stairs. He used to come round every morning with his tools in a supermarket trolley until Mohammed Muneer told him he could sleep out the back, in a shack he had furnished with a bed and a basin.

Now it was true that poor Reggie Macklewaite hadn't always wanted to be a handyman.

Indeed, he'd dreamed of being a pilot until cruelly advised to aim lower. "Stick to what you're good at," his teacher had said grimly. "And if you're not good at anything then just be damn good at that."

It wasn't, however, that Mohammed Muneer's tea shop *never* had visitors. (Reggie aside; but he was more of a fixture than a bona fide guest.) It was just that his visitors weren't the usual types. Arriving at dawn from far-flung lands, they'd stagger through his bead curtain, eyes stung from no sleep, and collapse at his tea counter, feet shredded and sore. They would speak in strange tongues. Use their hands to make gestures. Tell tales that made no sense except to each other. Like the Argentinean fisherman who had lost his way at sea. Thought he was tracking a Patagonian Toothfish across the Southern Ocean, chasing the whites of its terrified eyes until one night he discovered he was tailing the moon instead. Or the pretty young girl from the Mekong Delta who carried a stash of hairy cherries in the cone of her hat. Said she'd wandered for months with a grain of rice in her eye that wouldn't wash away no matter how much she tried.

Usually when such visitors arrived it was Reggie who would welcome them.

First offering them a seat, as he had been taught, and pouring them a tea: ginger root, lemon rind and honey from hived bees, specially blended by Mohammed Muneer to rejuvenate weary souls. Then he would listen as each of them asked him the very same question that had haunted every one of them separately since their journeys had begun.

Did Mohammed Muneer realise he had the moon on his roof?

Reggie always found the question to be quite absurd.

Of course he did.

Everyone did.

No one, not even Reggie, could miss the sickle-shaped ornament that spun on his roof. Shimmering rose-gold in the dawn rinse of the sky.

But Reggie was a gentle fellow not out to fool others.

So instead of calling them ridiculous or laughing in their face, he would simply lean over the counter (being very careful to tuck in his own personal moon which tended to appear rather regularly on account of his low-slung pants) and say with a wink: "The moon on his roof, eh? Well y' don't say. I've heard that the sun shines out of his arse too."

It was a lonely life for Mohammed Muneer, despite these strange visitors (and Reggie, of course.) A life most men would have despaired at. Grown hairs on their palms. But Mohammed Muneer accepted it without gripe or growl. For Mohammed Muneer believed he was more than a simple tea shop owner and if anyone (other than his stray, passing travellers) had cared to look closely they would have noticed that his spinning rooftop crescent was no ordinary ornament. That what lay cradled in its gold-plated curve was no strange adornment, no waxed pearl or satin button or lost tooth from a baby. It was the very moon itself, come down from the sky to rest on Mohammed Muneer's rooftop during the light hours of each day. Weary from the night spent travelling the skies, casting a light one million times greater than its own actual size.

For the moon was, in truth, no larger than a juniper berry and as delicate to touch as a silkworm's cocoon. Easily worn out by its nightly travail it would sleep through the day until evening came once more. Then it would rise to the sky to shine once again, as a whole or a part or sometimes not at all, depending on how tired it was, how well it had slept.

The fact that the moon rested on his roof top was known by no one else but Mohammed Muneer himself. A secret so small it could fit in the palm of a man's hand as it had in the past and would do so in the future.

Insha'Allah.

He told no one of its existence, not even his strange visitors, for he feared were it to fall into the wrong human hands, it would be its undoing. It would be its very end.

It never bothered him though, the idle banter of his guests; swearing they'd seen the moon sitting on top of his roof. For he knew they might talk until their teeth ground to gum but there was nobody about who would pay them any regard. Apart from Reggie, of course, but Reggie was much better with his hands than his head, so though he always listened he seldom understood.

Now it wasn't as if the moon had always lived on Mohammed Muneer's rooftop.

Since the beginning of time it had worn many guises:

the jewel in a queen's crown;

a polished fountain stone;

the centre piece of a mosaic in an ancient Persian garden.

Every time it changed guises it had changed for one reason; because its keeper had been lost or had moved on in some way.

The queen with the crown, dethroned in a battle.

The gardener from ancient Persia dead amongst the pomegranates.

Whenever such an event happened, which inevitably it did, the moon would be forced to seek out a new keeper; for the moon knew very well that it could only ever have one—a person whose sole responsibility was to shield it from harm.

Now it wasn't as if the moon consciously chose who its keeper should be. It just gravitated towards those folk it could sense had pure hearts. Who would sacrifice themselves and expect nothing back. Who had been born on the nights when the moon had been full and whose souls compelled it to shine brightest when it hung over their heads.

Sometimes, once found, the moon would reveal itself to its new keeper. Other times it did nothing at all. Just slept in their presence with a deep, abiding certainty that should it suddenly require protection this mortal soul would provide it. Indeed the only reason at all why Mohammed Muneer even knew about the moon was because he'd spied it one morning while polishing his gold crescent. He never breathed a word though, just raised his fingers to his lips. For Mohammed Muneer was a wise man. He had a good heart. He knew the moon was precious, too precious for this earth.

As host to the sleeping moon, Mohammed Muneer rarely left his tea service in the hours that it lay resting on his roof. However, once a year at the beginning of summer he would leave for the big city to see the doctors about his arrhythmic heart—a condition he'd inherited along with bowed legs. How he hated leaving his teashop for the choking grind of the city but every year Reggie, bless his own perfectly beating heart, would offer to keep things running until he returned. And every year Mohammed Muneer would thank Reggie with a bowl of sugared almonds, while explaining that he'd really much prefer to keep the teashop closed. Whereupon Reggie would clap his short foreign friend in the small of his back and say "alrighty mate" invariably throwing Mohammed Muneer's capricious heart into even greater chaos.

Mohammed Muneer was only ever gone three days. And every year he was assured by the doctors that his heart seemed fine—as fine as a heart that chose its beat from whim instead of necessity could ever really be. And every year Mohammed Muneer would drive back home feeling restored and confident that he could shelter the moon for another coming year.

But not this time.

Driving west with the remains of the day, Mohammed Muneer could see from the sky that something awful was unraveling around him. Gone was the cobalt blue of summer: the Indian yellow of the sun. Both had been swallowed, or so it seemed, by a blood-orange beast with cindering breath.

Roads had been closed by burly policemen. Fire engines screamed past, their lungs cranked up high. Radios shrieked warnings of firestorms out west, as if the raw, blistering sky wasn't warning enough. But Mohammed Muneer knew the back route, down by the dams, so he drove like a desperate bugger, crouched low in his car. Praying out loud that he would make it in time, though deep in his heart he already sensed he was too late.

Arriving in town, Mohammed Muneer saw that *Munch* was already gone. Nothing remained but a grim twisted melt of gristle and plastic: a super-size imitation of a *Munch* daily special. Some of the local folk had gathered around, licking their chops and rubbing their hands. They could feast on the remains for days before the crows came to town.

Mohammed Muneer left them to scavenge (for it is what they did best) and trailed down the black road in search of his tea house. His head slung low, shoulders defeated, he was afraid to look up though he knew that he must.

In sight of the point where he knew his tea house should be, he peered between his fingers to find his worst fears confirmed.

His teahouse was gone and there in its stead was a fierce, roaring dragon with tangerine-coloured breath. This monster, it seemed, was swallowing his shop whole.

Mohammed Muneer dropped to his knees.

He was too exhausted to holler, too shocked to weep tears.

Praying out to *Allah* to save the sleeping moon, he was surprised when he heard a voice rising out of the flames.

"Bleedin' heck!" it bellowed and then: "Bugger me."

Mohammed Muneer looked up aghast, to see Reggie crouching on top of his roof, moving slowly, defensively, against the copper coloured winds.

"Come down," he shouted. "Come down, my good friend."

But Reggie could not hear him, or perhaps he chose not to, for he had his mind on the gold crescent and nothing else would do.

The crescent was spinning wildly, fanned on by the flames but Reggie was determined to save it for his one friend, Mohammed. He knew how much it meant to him, this glimmering roof top ornament. How every day he would polish it so it gleamed in the sun.

Reggie clamped his hand firmly on the ornament's base so it broke easily away in the palm of his hand. Then, smiling triumphantly, he waved it high above his head.

The smile did not last long however; nor did his jubilant wave.

The crescent moon was hot.

Viciously so.

It seared the big man's hand so he yelled from the pain before flinging it skywards. The ornament spun high, slicing the air as it twirled, but gravity dictated that it must eventually descend. Hitting Reggie once on the head and then the small of his back as it tumbled its way back down to the fire. Reggie lost his balance too and tumbled from the roof. Straight after the crescent moon, straight into the fire.

Mohammed Muneer heard a thud and then heard nothing at all, just the sound of white-hot teeth, roaring as they ravaged.

"Reggie," shouted Mohammed Muneer but he heard no response.

"The moon," he said again mournfully, his voice lost to the air.

Mohammed Muneer turned his head away, he could not watch any longer. He had seen too much already. He could bear the fire no more.

Crouching amongst the dirt, he buried his head in his hands and wailed.

Suddenly the tea house shuddered violently, shaking the grass and the dirt below Mohammed Muneer's feet. He stared at the ground, too afraid to look up.

He noticed a great shadow looming across the earth. Creeping towards him, unable to stop. Soon enough, he feared, it would cross over his skin.

He looked up to face it.

What else could he do?

But instead of confronting a fire monster, as he had thought that he might, he was greeted instead by a sight most peculiar.

A sight most spectacular. A sight worth a song.

It was Reggie slowly rising out of the jaws of the fire beast, cast in silhouette by the fierce light behind him. Lifted, somehow, by the seat of his pants, so he hung like a coat hanger up there in the sky.

Mohammed Muneer gazed on in wonder at this great

floating man as he hovered above the land, a giant balloon in the breeze. Swooping and soaring in the early evening winds, with a broad, beaming smile and wide, gleeful eyes.

"I can fly," shouted Reggie, joyfully waving down at Mohammed Muneer. "They said I never would but look at me now."

Mohammed Muneer said nothing; he just waved back with both arms, wearing an expression both elated and extremely confused.

How could Reggie Macklewaite just have risen from the flames?

The answer soon came to him in the shape of the moon; slowly rising out from behind Reggie—from Reggie's pants to be exact. Wriggling its way free from where it had been hiding since it woke to find itself falling out from the gold crescent. Tumbling from the ornament's nook as it struck Reggie's back, rolling straight into the rear of the man's rather low-slung pants.

Admittedly, it wasn't the most elegant place the moon had ever tried to seek refuge but it was moody and dark and strangely reassuring. Here it could hide safely while it properly woke up before starting its steady climb to the great sky above.

And it was a fortunate thing too it had rolled where it had because when Reggie had fallen he had hit smouldering wood unlike the gold crescent which had landed in blue flame.

"I'm a bird," shouted Reggie again, stretching out his arms, blissfully unaware of the moon in his pants.

Eventually, the moon began to tire. So it could continue its journey into space, it brought Reggie down, dipping him twice more, for it knew how he loved it, and then tenderly depositing him in the fork of a gum tree.

Gliding free, it rose up behind him, drifting higher and higher, a little white pearl against night satin. The moon had saved Reggie as had Reggie the moon, though the big man would never know it.

"Did you see me?" Reggie shouted breathlessly.

"Yes I did," replied Mohammed Muneer and he said nothing more.

He just gazed at the moon until it disappeared into the heavens, leaving nothing behind but the brightest of lights which shone down on Reggie still sitting in the tree, then down further onto Mohammed Muneer, who understood now that the moon never belonged to him—but gave thanks that he had the good fortune to be the moon-keeper's friend.

THE TAILOR OF TIME

by Deborah Biancotti

The Tailor of Time sat at his sewing machine, stitching night to day.

He joined the clear cloth of dawn to a full bright afternoon like a circus top. Then he smoothed on a panel of smoky rouge for dusk and finished it off with a thick purple evening. Brushing his hand over the result, he felt a thin echo of satisfaction.

The Tailor worked with a minimum of noise or fuss. He suffered only the occasional grunt or shrug (to indicate 'this is done' or 'bring me cloth'), aimed at the tyros who also worked in his rooms. The tyros were pale, bald children that could pass as the Tailor's own. They looked like a ramshackle circus, dressed in scraps of cloth that tied at waist or shoulder. They worked at the Tailor's demand, darning or mending or gathering what needed to be darned, or mended, or gathered.

The Tailor ignored them. He existed in a meditative cocoon, his voice so unused it had all but healed over. His mouth sagged like a pocket, his eyes drooped like the shoulders of an old suit and his whole body slumped like a smock on a hanger.

Only his hands remained steady, darting leanly under the light of his sewing machine and out again before they could be caught by the quick, sharp tooth of the needle. In and out, swift as the very machine itself. In and out.

With the day laid out in cloth before him, the Tailor added a hem, threaded a drawstring through both ends and slung it like a cloak over a bare globe to his right.

Thus dressed, the globe was spun onto tracks like train tracks, where it butted against other globes and sloshed with the weight of water in its guts.

The water served to hold it steady.

Dismissed, the globe and its partners creaked and shuddered, working their way along the tracks circumventing the room. They passed the industrious tyros, the bare stone walls and heavy curtains of the room. They passed towards the arched window in one thick-cut wall, and would have passed out, but here they snagged and pushed back, bubbling against each other.

Coming through the window was a man. He shoved his way into the chain of gowned globes and climbed into the Tailor's room.

The tyros saw him first. In a sudden frenzy of panic they fell into a silence even deeper than their usual quietude. One ran towards the Tailor and stopped, confused, unsure how to encroach on her master's concentration. One ran towards the man, the stranger, and halted just as cautiously as her cousin.

The Tailor was unaware of the alterations in the room, sewing night to day, day to night. Until he received a bobbing tap to his elbow from his most recent globe (scuttling back along the tracks), and jumped hard in his seat.

His finger snagged in the great machine, and the Tailor cried out to see the cruel incisor pierce all the way through. Blood beaded into the sworls of his fingertip and spilled on the cloak of time he was making.

"Oh!"

The first clear sound he'd made in a hundred years.

"Ouch!"

The second.

He stepped off the foot-pedal at once and rescued his stricken finger, pulling his bloody hand free. He drew the injured appendage to his lips to taste the unexpected saltiness of his mistake.

On the cloth with the bloodstain, war broke out for a day. It commenced seemingly from nothing and returned there just as quickly. History would refer to it as the War of Hours.

The Tailor, however, was not concerned with this. He looked up to find the cause of the commotion and caught at once the eye of the intruder. The man had completed his expedition through the window and now stood surrounded by tyros up to his waist.

The tyros divided their gazes between the stranger and the Tailor, chewing the blood out of his injury.

The stranger said, "You the Tailor of Time?"

The Tailor, mouth still entertaining his finger, nodded.

"You make the cloak of time that clothes the world, you determine night and day, the colours, the length of hours, the pattern of seasons and years?"

The Tailor nodded and shrugged so that his ear travelled painfully close to his shoulder. He hoped to signify both regret and well-intentioned acceptance.

"Then my name is John Avery, and I have a favour to beg."

The Tailor cleared his throat, but the first sounds to come out were not words. He had to try twice more before he managed to say, "Beg it. John Avery."

Avery drew breath. "Tailor," he said. "You are largely forgotten where I'm from, and many places besides."

Not forgotten enough, it seemed. Though the Tailor was

engaged in the act of polite conversation, it did not escape his attention that Avery had breached walls which had not seen a visitor in hundreds of years.

Avery was not privy to the Tailor's befuddlement. He dragged an empty stool to the Tailor's side, and rested his elbow on the table where the machine sat glowering and grinning.

Up close Avery was older than his spryness belied. Much older than an adventure like this warranted, climbing walls and windows and rooms, vaulting or swimming, surely, the moat which still must hug the base of this fortress. He had a light beard that deepened to faded brown at his ears. His hair was thick but receding, lending him a horned look. And he had long, wiry eyebrows over narrow brown eyes. He looked kind, but sure, and careful.

"I paid witches and bribed fools," he said. "I followed dreams and rumours from elders and madmen, seers and scientists. It took three years."

"And," said the Tailor, voice still thick and unpractised, "what do you want?"

"Time."

Of course.

"I want you to slow down time for a day. No, an afternoon. A set of hours, even. Just some small, very small, amount of time."

The Tailor let out a bark that might've been a cough, might've been, instead, some descendent of laughter.

Avery continued, "You expected me to ask that."

The Tailor nodded.

"You want to know why I ask?"

A grunt, meaning 'naturally'.

Here it came, all sorts of tales of great deeds and discoveries to be made if only time would permit. Of acts of humanity planned and mistakes to be rectified. Of love to be given or taken, of fears that must be faced, of favours to be returned. Particularly to the Tailor, if only he would grant this one wish.

He tried not to roll his eyes as he faced this newest petitioner.

"I intend to waste it," said Avery.

"W—?"

This was new.

The Tailor spread his hands and gestured Avery forward, indicating with the tilt of his ear that he should repeat the request.

"Waste," said Avery, leaning in and enunciating carefully. "I want some time to waste."

"Because . . . ?"

"Because that's exactly what youth is meant to do."

The Tailor paused, even more confused than before. John Avery, he was convinced, was not young. But was he mad?

"I would waste every precious second. I would engage in all the childish pursuits my old-man frame would allow. I would run after dragonflies and kick at puddles in the mud and roll in grass and thread plastic spoke rattles onto my pushbike, I would—"

"Spoke rattles—?"

"Because this girl," said Avery, reaching into a pocket, "deserves that, don't you think?"

"Your . . . ?"

"Daughter, yes."

The Tailor drew breath.

He was trying to clear the constriction that threatened to overwhelm his throat and stomach, and ease the tension that dragged his shoulders backwards like broken wings.

Avery held a photograph of a girl (of—what?—seven, eight years?). Sunlight limned her fair head and lay on the top curl of her grin. She was squinting, standing by a pushbike with one hand gripped to the handlebar, one hand curling the seat.

"This is Bella. Some days she can breathe," said Avery. "Some days she can even ride her bike. Some days she gasps and coughs up the fluid that is drowning her from the inside out."

He let this sink in.

"Unlikely I could repay you, Tailor, understand."

Not even a favour traded.

What was the Tailor to make of this?

He dropped his hands to his lap and sat, looking lopsidedly at his visitor. Then he gazed around at the drapes, the thick stone walls and finally, to the childish tyros who had returned, by degrees, to their work.

He looked at the chain of globes emptying from the room, the spill of blood on the cloth still caught in the machine, the floor and then, his own lap (filled with threads and scraps of cloth). He shook his head slowly like he was waking from a dream.

How had he . . . ?

How did any of this . . . ?

How could . . . ?

"One problem," said the Tailor, voice heavy, "I don't know how."

"You . . . ? Oh," It was Avery's turn to pause. "Is there someone who does?"

The Tailor gestured broadly. "No. Only . . ." He paused.

"Yes?"

"Perhaps the Engineer."

"Okay?"

"She built everything."

"An engineer?"

"*The* Engineer."

"You've met her?"

"No," he grunted at the impossibility of that idea. "Well, once. Saw her, more like. But she was . . . I called out to her, but perhaps she didn't hear. She was busy."

The Tailor couldn't find any other excuses for the way the Engineer had looked at him. Blankly, like he was a swatch of fabric and she was thinking what to do with him.

"Okay." Avery looked like a man trying not to give up. "And she made this strange place?"

"Some suggest she built all of everything that there is."

"Oh? Okay. And what does she do now?"

The Tailor shrugged. "Maintenance?"

Avery nodded, thumbing his beard thoughtfully. "Can she be found?"

The Tailor was uncertain. And even then, he explained, it was unlikely she could be prevailed upon. The Engineer was cold and unyielding, like the stone that made up this place.

Avery leaned back, clenching his hands over his stomach almost in prayer. He stared at the stone ceiling. "Unlikely . . ." he repeated.

They say time heals all wounds, but it wasn't as true as this: time, most often, runs out.

Avery was thinking that then, as he leaned his chin into both hands beside the Tailor's grand, grinning machine. He stayed there, bowed, for a long time. When he spoke, his voice was muffled by his fingers. "Then how . . . ?"

The Tailor had never granted a request. Had, in fact, attempted to make sure he was in no position to hear them.

But now, stalled in his work, he couldn't *not* consider John Avery and that cheerful girl with the sunlit grin who looked directly from the photograph like she might leap from its shallow page.

"Bring her here?" said the Tailor.

But here there were no dragonflies, no spoke rattles, no mud. And could such a small girl travel the whispers and rumours it had taken Avery just to reach here?

No. The only way to do it was to stall the globe. And not just any globe. What they needed was to stall the globe that was in use, the one determining time at that very moment.

The Tailor reached out a hand to Avery, but hesitated, uncertain, and said instead, "I will help you, John Avery. Somehow."

For Bella, with the smile like daylight.

Avery stood to leave, the plan agreed. On a good day, when Bella could breathe without help, he would send word.

"You'll know," said Avery, cutting off the Tailor's next question. "And Tailor—"

"Welcome," nodded the Tailor. "You're welcome."

He left the way he'd arrived.

The Tailor returned to his sewing as best he could. His focus was gone and he was aware of the dull throb of his injured finger, and how the injury made him cautious now, lest he wreck some other part of him in the maul of the machine.

Almost at once the machine hit a snag and ran rough temporarily, and he was forced to reach for the pouch of tools in his pocket, to poke and prod it open and check its gears and screws, discover a loose one and right it, then return to his work. This he did as required while he waited.

Also while he waited, he drew in several of the tyros at a time, their bald heads shining in the light of the machine, and he lead them through what to do and how to clothe the globes.

Just in case there was ever another Tailor needed.

The word from Avery, when it arrived, was a whisper carried on whispers. It breached the room, starting with the tyro nearest the window and working its way around to where the Tailor sat ready.

"This is the best way to tell you that today is a good day for spoke rattles and dragonflies, dear Tailor," whispered the nearest tyro.

"Time," replied the Tailor, "has come."

He rose from his machine and watched as his training took effect. The tyros shuffled into position, two of them dragging the swathes of cloth up to the machine; another two feeding it through.

Unsentimentally he left them to it, straightening his spine with effort and pausing a moment to savour the release of standing upright. He crossed to the tracks where the globes travelled and climbed, unsteadily at first, but with increasing assurance. He pushed out a gap in the line and pulled himself along, nose bumping the sheathed globe in front while the ones behind caught at his toes. He crawled, hands gripping hard to the track, knees pressing painfully.

The window caught him on each shoulder and threatened to dislodge him. He had to back up and remove his cloak and thick shirt, then clamber forward again naked to the waist, skin trembling from the effort, elbows alternatively locking then shaking.

When he breached the other room he took a moment to get his bearings. There was a passage, the track snaking across to exit another window just as small as the first, light glowing messily from the other side. He approached and squeezed through, scraping his upper arms, awkwardly pinning his wrist under him and wrenching it enough that it ached.

After the second window was daylight and a sheer drop over which the tracks meandered in confused circuits.

What a crazed, hellish design he'd found. What singularly unfriendly efforts had been spent constructing this track and the struts that suffered its support. And then affixing the lot to a cliff at angles and heights that sent the senses spinning.

But of course this was exactly the point, he realised. The maker of the machines did not want for interference. The Engineer built monsters so others would think twice about abuse or ownership. She made them unfriendly with all the purpose and intent possible.

He thought again of those blank eyes and the unsmiling fixture of her mouth, and none of it surprised him after that.

He took a shuddering breath and then another. He kept his chin high so he wouldn't be tempted to look down.

The globes here had stalled. To move forward, he would have to climb over the top of them. He clasped each one in turn, pulling it into the shadow of his belly and then pushing it back between his thighs to where it washed against its followers. The soft thud and glub of the waterlogged spheres behind calmed him.

Still, he cursed his newfound friend more than once and then cursed the crazed mind of the Engineer who'd built this thing. But he couldn't go back on his word. If he failed, the memory would nag and fill him up and leave no room for anything else. He had, as he saw it, no choice.

He gripped hard, chin between shoulders, forcing himself to breathe, to squeeze his eyes shut against the inertia that dragged at him. He focused on stilling the tremble in his arms and isolating the ache in his knees, willing both into ignorance.

Only then did he find the focus to look ahead for his quarry, the globe that determined the current day. And there it was—that had to be it—a globe that stood alone on a plinth, lit from above and below, held steady and rotating methodically.

The lights made it look as though it floated. It rotated slowly, already shifting from a pleasant pink dusk to a throaty, overcast day. He didn't remember sewing that one. It hadn't seemed special in his machine, nor had the cloth inspired him as he ran it through his hands. And yet, here it was. The day John Avery had deemed a good day.

He crawled forward, slow but sure, traversing the track in-between. He passed another globe and another, closing in on his prey shining with the bliss of its being.

One final globe and at last he was there. Now all he had

to do was stall it. He needed to wedge something into the mechanism to hold it steady. This way he would give John Avery those hours he'd asked for.

The Tailor stood upright on the tracks with the gaping void on either side of his feet. His ankle shook and nearly gave way, and he had to wave his arms out straight on either side of his body to keep himself right.

He stabilised, and let out a slow breath that was too passionate for a sigh.

The globe, by now, was rotating closer and closer to night. Soon it would slip its mooring and sail off along the track to where the other used-up days sat, their coats faded from the harshness of the spotlights. Soon, soon the day would be done, and the Tailor's promised unaddressed. And he had come so far, climbed so far, was even now perched precariously above the sheer drop that emptied out to nothing but a grey horizon.

In his pockets were all manner of implements and needles and miniature tools to mend the machine. His pockets, however, were all in the coat he'd left on the floor of his room.

He took a moment to curse.

Then he leaned over the globe and found the tiny mechanical catch that kept it isolated, and he wedged his thumb against it—that lean, learned thumb that had been used to pinch and hold and size the demands of thousands of years of sewing.

Almost too late he realised that wasn't the right spot. A latch opened outside his hand and he had to swiftly move to keep it from closing. There was a grinding noise as the globe attempted to dislodge, and the whole world quivered and seemed as though it would topple.

But it held, the clicking latch pressed back on the Tailor's sinewy thumb. It held and the bank of globes behind him waited dutifully, and the globes in front continued to bounce along, oblivious.

For one full rotation he waited. Then he waited another

and another, averting his face from the dull glare of the spotlights (dimmed but not extinguished, signifying night). He held himself in place with one strong hand gripping the appendage that kept the lights and plinth together.

The cloth grew faded.

Slowly at first, then like a day where the sun refuses to rise or set, the cloth faded as if smog covered the world. He should let go. Soon he should let go. One more moment, one more . . .

Brown patches of burn appeared gently, the soft cloth falling to ash. By then his thumb was so stiff with the weight of the latch that he couldn't even be sure he was holding it anymore. And finally with a click, the globe rolled off.

For a moment, no globe took the plinth.

The tailor had to haul himself bodily over the spot, convinced he would fall, his knees so stiff and shoulders so weak he couldn't feel when he was touching the track and when he wasn't. He moved out of the way, willing the next globe into place.

Sure enough, the next globe rolled onto the plinth, latches and catches working perfectly to hold it steady.

The Tailor was too spent to even breathe a sigh of relief. He made to lower himself to the track, reaching out a shaking hand and bending to an awkward squat. He offered a silent acknowledgment for John Avery and his daughter, hoping it had been enough. Surely it had been enough.

He was so wrapped in his thoughts that at first he didn't realise his hand had missed the track. His own hand, on which he relied every day, and now it fell beyond safety with an almost pre-ordained determinism. It dropped in something akin to slow-motion and pulled the rest of him with it.

His inside elbow scraped the track, following his hand. His chin snagged, but it wasn't enough to hold him.

And then he was falling.

Head first, body unfolding behind, swooping with an uncanny grace. Plummeting through grey.

He fell and—

He fell and—

He fell.

Nothing caught or saved him. He plunged into the gap afforded by the precipice. He dropped towards a grey void that could've been anything but ultimately turned out to be stone and earth.

He fell and hit the hard ground.

He died.

The impact shook free the Tailor's soul, which blossomed and ballooned above his crumpled form and then spread thin like a bubble exploding.

When it rose past the windows of the place that used to shelter him, only one witness was there to see it. Not the tyros, still busy at their work in the Tailor's room, bald heads bobbing almost in time to the needle on the great machine.

It was the Engineer who leaned from the window, round-eyed with bemusement, reaching with short, stocky fingers for the suds of the Tailor's soul. She rubbed with finger and thumb at the smooth stickiness it left on her skin. She frowned and gazed and wondered what other force could call her tailor-man away, and to where. What higher force could there be, she thought, than an engineer?

As he drifted from her reach and travelled, uncertain at first, then with increasing urgency into the grey-blank sky, she merely stood, paying heed to the last of her lost man.

The Engineer seemed—seemed, only—more human than her fellow occupants in this strange place. Were it not for the blank, calculating eyes and the permanent downturn of her mouth, she might be mistaken for a child of—what?—seven or eight. But she moved with the steely calculation of an intellect that had observed thousands of years.

One more Tailor, she calculated, had just been lost. The best one yet. One more disappearance, one more example of the only remaining mystery in a world she once believed herself to have built. It frustrated her. But frustration, like all emotions, was barely more than an intellectual effect. What benefits others received from emotions, she had never determined.

The remnants of the Tailor were all but gone, a bare shimmer in the distant air. The Engineer dismissed the sight, turning from the window. She slid to a seated position with her back against the stone wall, and pulled out a strip of plain cloth and a white tailor's pencil. She looked thoughtfully to one corner of the ceiling.

Then, balancing the cloth on her knee, she wrote:

'The Tailor hopes . . .'

In bulky, childish script.

She licked the tip of the pencil and chewed her lip and thought. She drummed her thumbs on the bones of her knee. Then she continued,

'. . . hopes there were dragon flies and mud and spoke rattles for your bike and more—'

And more.

Then she crumpled the note in her fist, since cloth and pen marks cannot travel through whispers and rumours. John Avery and the unmet girl, Bella—if they were to be reached at all—must be sought in the traditional way, through muted words and the spaces in-between the words.

The Engineer leaned back to feel the smoothness of the wall behind her and to wonder idly, idly, what places she might visit. That is, if she could travel whispers and rumours, beg favours and elicit curses, roll across silence, across water-coloured skies. She wondered what more there was and more there could be.

ROOT AND VEIN

by Erin Hoffman

In the time before time, when the world was young and spirits
now ancient walked the earth on their first legs, there lived a
dryad of the green wood. In those days the trees had not yet their
stillness, and roamed on curling roots dexterous as acrobat
hands, searching.

The dryad gave her first heart to an alchemist. She
watched him at his work; his blunt-fingered hands were soft and
clever with herb and glass, and surely he would know how to
care for living wood. With a paring knife she opened her chest,
golden sap blackening as it ran in rivulets to her waist, and cut
away the soft spring green of her first heart.

The two that remained skipped a beat, leaving a lingering
moment of promised silence.

The alchemist accepted the heart as he would a great
treasure, and studied it. "No," he said at last, rueful. "I am afraid
I can find no use for this. What purpose may it serve, needing so
much care? A thing of value would live on its own. Imagine
wood that creates its own light, and feeds upon air! Truly this

one is quite plain."

As the heart withered on the alchemist's shelf, the dryad's roots slowly stiffened. The packed earth of the town's road confounded her footing, and she returned to the soft forest loam, where she found a painter who spoke of the hearts of trees with great reverence. He walked among the shells of the first stilled, spirits of trees whose roots had fled forever into the dark safety of the soil, silent monuments to love that feared and failed. Their branches, crowned with sunset stars in the crisp fall wind, whispered a requiem for their questing.

Under the shade of her brethren the dryad rested, and the painter remained, reciting his legends of arboreal beauty. He spoke of the glory of twilight, of the everlasting merit of shadow.

The dryad's second heart was the color of falling leaves. When she pulled it from her ribs it gave a crack as of an autumn apple bitten at its ripest perfection, and her next breath was shallower than her last.

"How beautiful," the painter said. "It is my greatest treasure, beyond my deserving."

He crafted a pedestal and painted it white, the better to contrast the heart's crimson veins and bronze wood. And there the heart rested in its loveliness, but under the elements, with time, began to fade. "I will travel to the white rivers of the far mountains and bring a font of crystal water," the painter said. But this was a great undertaking and there were many things he must do first.

While he planned the heart began to dwindle, its crimson veins collapsing slowly to rust powder; the painter wept for it, but his tears were of salt that could not quench its thirst, and at last it died. The painter remained captured by the memory of its beauty, and stayed by the pedestal singing songs of its loss. His high voice haunted the whispering forest, and the dryad, with a deep quiet spreading through her, could not remain.

Beyond the borders of the forest thick snows had blanketed the roads, so the dryad did not stumble, and in their stiffness her feet no longer felt the cold. In time it seemed that the brightness of the snow under the dove grey sky was soothing and complete. Why not linger with the ice, succumb to the quietude that filled two thirds of her hollow breast? To her last heart the silent arms of the still forest beckoned.

But it could not be, for nothing mythical can rest, and there remained only the road ahead and the one behind. She was a creature of nature, and hers was not to retreat, though the forest with its dark warmth compelled. With no sun in the sky she followed the road, and with time the shadows of the still forest faded behind her.

Across her path passed a cloaked traveler, and his charcoal steed was an old work horse. They shared the road, and in that companionship the cloaked man told of his travels, and asked the dryad of hers. For the first time she tested a throat that had known no sound, and learned her voice.

"How old is the sky?" she asked him, when the stories of their travels were done. For it seemed as though she had walked the earth for centuries, and the sky had always been there.

The traveler thought on this for many miles. Finally he said that he did not know, and though he had met many wise men on his travels, none had been older than the sky. But he spoke of places where the sky had been the burning scarlet of young flame, or painted with strokes of colors so luminous they had no names. And he spoke of what he did know, of trees that swayed beneath autumn ghost moons, and of the stars that had been his compass.

The dryad's third heart came forth so red that it was almost black, the color of summer grapes in the shade, and of winter pomegranates. The traveler's dark eyes were serious as his weathered hands closed around it. Many more leagues they traveled together, the cloaked man, the dryad, and the grey horse.

"It grows dry," the cloaked man said of the heart one day, and from a skin at his saddle he poured a careful measure of water upon it. Its wood drank deeply and stretched, growing two slender limbs that reached to the sky. Deep in her empty chest the dryad surged with life, cool and heady. This sustained the heart, and something within the dryad began to awaken. But the traveler with this was not satisfied. "It needs the sun," he said, indicating buds that dotted the heart's reaching arms, the color of polished wood, and his eyes. "We will go west, to the summer country."

After three days the clouds broke and branches of sunlight reached down to melt the snow. As it ran away in rivulets that etched the spongy ground the dryad felt startled warmth returning to her feet.

And when the sun touched the dryad's heart, its buds grew palest spring green before exploding into violet flowers. Its blooming arms lengthened, and downward stretched roots that found the ground and grew steady upon it. At last it opened eyes of charcoal grey, eyes that shone with the newness of spring. Within the dryad's chest new life bloomed, a new warmth that carried its own sunlight within, and fed upon the air.

The dryad and her daughter did not have much time, for the younger could not remain still, even in the warmth of the summer country. The older dryad warned of alchemists that would measure a dryad's heart and find it wanting, of painters that lived trapped in an image worshiped greater than life. And she told her of gentle travelers, who knew what it was to seek the sun. The traveler told the new dryad of the ways of the road, and the importance of caring for one's steed. With this advice they were rueful, for they knew as they watched her that her heart was her own, neither spring green nor the violet of winter pomegranates, and it would require its own language, a language of sun and snow and withering.

As they watched the dryad's daughter begin her journey south, the traveler shed his cloak and folded it across the grey horse's saddle. "You dryads are fortunate to have three hearts," he said. "Men have but one, and it can never leave us."

"Then it should be carefully tended," the dryad said, and placed his hand in hers. Beneath the traveler's skin a new life stirred, life that had grown a dryad's heart. "For it must last through all the seasons of the world."

PINIONS

The Authors

Born in the Pacific Northwest in 1979, **Catherynne M. Valente** is the author of the *Orphan's Tales* series, as well as *The Labyrinth*, *Yume no Hon: The Book of Dreams*, *The Grass-Cutting Sword*, and five books of poetry, *Music of a Proto-Suicide*, *Apocrypha*, *The Descent of Inanna*, *Oracles* and *A Guide to Folktales in Fragile Dialects*. She is the winner of the Tiptree Award and the Million Writers Award and has been nominated for the Pushcart Prize, the Rhysling and Spectrum Awards, and the World Fantasy Award. She currently lives in Northeastern Ohio with her partner and two dogs. She says, "I began writing 'The City of Blind Delight' after reading several medieval legends of the land of Cockaigne. I was fascinated by the details, such as the roasted calf and the houses of cakes. How do you live in the land of plenty? What is desire there? Add to this that trains are one of my constant obsessions, and you have Gris and his ticket. I want these places to be real, I want them to have always been real, as real as any other city on the railroad, and as accessible."

David Sandner has published in *Realms of Fantasy*, *Asimov's*, *Weird Tales*, the *Mammoth Book of Sorcerer's Tales*, and *Baseball Fantastic*, among other odd gatherings of words. He is

Associate Professor of English at Cal State Fullerton, where his purview is Romanticism, children's literature and the fantastic. He wrote *The Fantastic Sublime* and edited *Fantastic Literature: A Critical Reader*. He wrote 'Old Foss is the Name of His Cat' in honor of the complete nonsense of Edward Lear who, he hopes, needs no introduction but is, nevertheless, too often in the shadow of that other famous nonsense poet of the Victorian era. Like Mr. Lear, David knows what it is to be friends with a cat, what it means to fear losing someone, and what it is to be unable to stop contemplating the ever-present mystery of impossible things and other such realities.

John Grant is author of some seventy books, of which about twenty-five are fiction, including *The Far-Enough Window*, *The World*, and *The Dragons of Manhattan*. His "book-length fiction" *Dragonhenge*, illustrated by Bob Eggleton, was shortlisted for a Hugo Award in 2003; its successor was *The Stardragons*. His first story collection, *Take No Prisoners*, appeared in 2004. He is editor of the recent anthology *New Writings in the Fantastic*. Among his nonfictions are *The Encyclopedia of Fantasy* (with John Clute), *Masters of Animation*, and *The Encyclopedia of Walt Disney's Animated Characters*, as well as the recent *Discarded Science* and *Corrupted Science*; he is currently working on a companion volume to these two, *Bogus Science*, on a book about *film noir*, and on "a cute book for kids about a velociraptor." His powerful mosaic novel *Leaving Fortusa* is to be published by Norilana in the fall of 2008.

As John Grant he has received two Hugo Awards, the World Fantasy Award and a number of other international literary awards. Under his real name, Paul Barnett, he has earned for his editorial work a Chesley Award and a nomination for the World Fantasy Award. He says that, like many of his stories, "'All the Little Gods We Are' owes its genesis to one of those little fancies that pass through one's head a dozen times a day and are mostly forgotten before they've even come out the other ear, as it were. In this instance, I had an image of dialing a phone number and being answered by myself. Who knows how many times that notion must have been used by fantasy writers? Whatever, the rest of the story just flowed from there."

After growing up in Texas, Santiago, Kansas, Mexico City, and Indiana, **Cat Rambo** wandered through Baltimore, Bloomington, and Brooklyn before beating the B curse to settle in the Pacific Northwest. "I grew up in South Bend, Indiana, which does feature a 'Dew Drop Inn Restaurant Lounge' on Lafayette Street that was once just the Dew Drop Inn. I was always amused by the expansion, and when I was accosted in a Seattle coffee shop by a woman who thought I was her blind date, the two concepts interacted with each other and became 'The Dew Drop Coffee Lounge.'" Other stories have appeared in *Asimov's*, *Weird Tales*, and *Strange Horizons*, among other places. Her collaboration with Jeff VanderMeer, *The Surgeon's Tale and Other Stories*, is available from her website at http://www.kittywumpus.net. Yes, it is her real name.

Leah Bobet lives in Toronto, where she works in Canada's oldest science fiction bookstore and has just completed a degree in linguistics. Her fiction has appeared recently in *Strange Horizons*, *The Mammoth Book of Extreme Fantasy*, and *On Spec*, and her poetry has been nominated for the Rhysling and Pushcart Prizes. She says, "'Bell, Book, and Candle' came from hearing a regular phrase, an ignorable phrase sidewise, and the way the world tilts at an angle when you realize it might have meant something different all along." She is currently writing a novel about a girl with bee wings and a boy who grew up underground.

Michael J. DeLuca has the utmost respect for prophets. Sometimes he wishes he'd been one, but he was never quite crazy enough to make it happen. "I carried the ideas and images that compose this story around in my head for a very long time before anything came of it. When I saw that stark church in the desert, I was just a kid, and a very different person by the time I came across the angel. What finally brought it all together was the riff of a Bob Dylan song called 'Wicked Messenger.' If you'd heard that song with those things in your head, you'd have written this story too. Or so I'd like to think."

Michael asserts that fiction is a compromise. Read more of his compromises in *Interfictions*, or on his blog at michaeljdeluca.com.

Laird Barron's work has appeared in places such as *The Magazine of Fantasy & Science Fiction, SCIFICTION, Inferno: New Tales of Terror and the Supernatural*, and *The Del Rey Book of Science Fiction and Fantasy*. It has also been reprinted in numerous year's best anthologies. His debut collection, *The Imago Sequence*, was recently published by Night Shade. Mr. Barron is an expatriate Alaskan currently at large in Washington State. He confides, "The core horrific conceit of this piece originates from a nightmare as recounted by a relative who served in the Marine Corps and who apparently survived many a hedonistic adventure while abroad. The relative's name is withheld to protect the guilty, of course."

Ekaterina Sedia resides in the Pinelands of New Jersey, and shares these thoughts about the genesis of "There is a Monster Under Helen's Bed": "This story was written as a reaction to an increasing number of foreign adoptions—and the realization that these are often complex and wrenching. I find the conflict between an adopters' need to help and the adoptees' frequent inability to recognize it especially heartbreaking."

Her new novel, *The Secret History of Moscow*, was published by Prime Books in November 2007. Her next one, *The Alchemy of Stone*, was published in June 2008. Her short stories have sold to *Analog*, *Baen's Universe*, *Dark Wisdom* and *Clarkesworld*, as well as the *Japanese Dreams* and *Magic in the Mirrorstone* anthologies. Visit her at www.ekaterinasedia.com.

Cat Sparks is a writer, graphic designer, editor and photographer, with stories and artwork appearing in and on magazines, anthologies and book covers in Australia and abroad. She was born in Sydney, Australia, but relocated to Wollongong eight years ago. She has travelled through parts of Europe, the Middle East, Indonesia, the South Pacific, Mexico and the lower states of North America. Her adventures so far have included: winning a trip to Paris in a Bulletin Magazine photography competition; being appointed official photographer for two NSW Premiers; working as dig photographer on three archaeological expeditions to Jordan, and winning seven DITMAR awards including one for Best New Talent in 2002.

"I can't be sure where 'Palisade' came from," she says, "but I suspect it was influenced by the years I spent working as a government media monitor. Daytime talkback radio presented so much ugliness. At some point it occurred to me that whatever horrible things I could imagine, somewhere out there in the world were people doing them to each other. When I combined this thought with the promising advancements of science . . ."

In 2004, she was both a prize winner in Writers of the Future and received the Aurealis Peter McNamara Conveners Award. In 2007 she won the Aurealis Award for best SF short story and the Golden Aurealis Award for best Australian speculative fiction story of the year. In 2008 she won the Ditmar award for best novella.

Check her newest happening at www.catsparks.net or http://catsparx.livejournal.com.

Born in 1947 in London, England, **Tanith Lee** is one of the leading fantasy authors working today. After working various jobs she became a full-time professional writer in 1975 and has written nearly 90 novels and collections, among them the best-selling Flat Earth Series and *The Secret Books of Paradys,* over 260 short stories, four radio plays broadcast by the BBC, and two episodes of the cult TV programme *Blake's 7.* She has won the World Fantasy Award numerous times as well as the August Derleth Award.

Tanith's most recent books include the adult fantasy trilogy: *Lionwolf, Cast A Bright Shadow, Here In Cold Hell* and *No Flame But Mine*; the 3 YA novels: *Piratica, Piratica 2* and *Piratica 3;* and *Metallic Love,* (the sequel to her adult SF novel *The Silver Metal Lover.*) And coming soon, two volumes of collected short stories, *Tempting the Gods* and *Hunting the Shadows.* She lives near the sea with writer, artist, husband John Kaiine and two black and white cats.

Lee described the inspiration for "The Woman" thusly:

"The spur to this story was the news that in modern China, and also in some areas of India, young men, particularly the less well-off, are having one heck of a time trying to locate wives—even girlfriends, due to various policies to restrict family sizes to one child only—and the general wish to bear/keep only males.

"It occurs to me too certain feminists may quibble over the ethic of the story, (not that I care, everyone should have their own opinion). I'd just say on that, simply reverse all the gender roles. It works just the same, and the point stays constant."

Marie Brennan is an anthropologist and folklorist who shamelessly pillages her academic fields for material—as she did for "A Mask of Flesh," her contribution to this volume. "I once flexed my archaeologist muscles and did a silly amount of research into Mesoamerican history and culture for a role-playing game. If you ask me when I'm feeling noble, I'll say that I think fantasy could and should explore a broader range of models than it does at present—but the truth is also that I wanted something to show for all that effort." Her short stories have sold to more than a dozen venues. Her most recent novel, *Midnight Never Come*, is an Elizabethan faerie spy story that taught her why more people don't write historical fantasy. So, being a sucker for punishment, she's turning it into a whole series. Next up is the Great Fire of 1666, for the sequel *And Ashes Lie*.

Jennifer Crow lives near a waterfall in western New York, and listens to the stories the water tells. Her work has appeared in a number of print and electronic venues, most recently in the *Desolate Places* anthology from Hadley-Rille books. She tells us that "'Seven Scenes' grew out of a fascination with the ways in which different cultures handle death, change, and the sacred. It interests me how certain places or objects can become symbols for a person's life, or even for an entire society. I'd like to go back to Harrai's world someday, and find out what happened to the sacred mountain and its people."

Vandana Singh is an Indian writer currently living near Boston, where she also teaches college physics. Her science fiction and fantasy have been published in numerous venues, including magazines like *Strange Horizons* and anthologies like *Interfictions*, and have also made a couple of appearances in Year's Best collections. Her children's fiction includes the ALA Notable book, *Younguncle Comes to Town* (Viking, 2006). She says "Oblivion: A Journey" came about because she wrote a random sentence, and followed it by another and another, not knowing where it was going, until it led her to some strange places in the far future. The story owes a great deal to both the epic Ramayan and the wonderful, lurid Indian comic books she read as a child. Somewhere in the blend are also memories of summer-time wanderings among Buddhist ruins in her home state of Bihar. For more about Vandana, see her website at http://users.rcn.com/singhvan.

John C. Wright is a philosopher, a retired attorney, newspaperman and newspaper editor, who was only once hunted by the police. In 1984 he graduated from St. John's College in Annapolis, home of the "Great Books" program. In 1987 he graduated from the College of William and Mary's Law School (going from the third oldest to the second oldest school in continuous use in the United States), and was admitted to the practice of law in three jurisdictions (New York, May 1989; Maryland, December 1990; DC, January 1994). His law practice was unsuccessful enough to drive him into bankruptcy almost immediately. His stint as a newspaperman for the St. Mary's Today was more rewarding spiritually, but, alas, also a failure financially. He presently works (more successfully) as a writer in Virginia, where he lives in fairy-tale-like happiness with his wife, the authoress L. Jagi Lamplighter and their three children: Orville, Wilbur and Just Wright.

When his first novel *The Golden Age* was published, it was greeted by the comment from *Publishers Weekly* that Wright was "This fledgling Millennium's most important new SF talent." Since that comment was made only in the first month of 2001, it actually meant Wright was the most important new SF talent of the month. He has written fantasy novels, *Last Guardian of Everness* and *Orphans of Chaos*, and was greatly honored to pen the authorized sequel to Science Fiction grandmaster A.E. van Vogt's *World of Null-A*, entitled *Null-A Continuum*. He has also written nonfiction articles for BenBella books, appearing in *Star Wars on Trial*, *King Kong is Back*, *Finding Serenity*, and *Batman Unauthorized*. He calls "Choosers of the Slain," his contribution to this book, "a meditation on what it means to be selected by a futuristic version of a Valkyrie to receive the honors and plaudits of history. It is also a comment on the wish-fulfillment psychology that underpins all time-travel stories."

C.S. MacCath's fiction and poetry have appeared or are forthcoming in *The Pagan Anthology of Short Fiction*, *PanGaia*, *newWitch*, *Murky Depths*, *Mythic Delirium* and *Goblin Fruit*, among others. She says, "For me, 'Akhila, Divided' speaks to the idea that injustice and suffering often have far-reaching consequences and that some of these are the perpetuation of injustice and suffering. It also speaks to the idea that despite our best efforts, some wounds don't heal, so we are well-advised to be careful with one another." You can find her on the Internet at www.csmaccath.com.

Joanna Galbraith was born in Australia in 1972. She now lives in Switzerland with her partner, Damien, where she spends her time writing stories, teaching English and eating cheese fondue. Her stories have been published in *The Writers Post Journal*, *Wanderings* and on www.writelink.co.uk. She says the idea for "The Moon-Keeper's Friend" first came to her while sitting on a broken-down bus in Ghana, West Africa. Unable to get off (as this would have involved climbing over an entire bus load of goats, chickens and women in spectacular Sunday garb) she passed the countless hours watching "Mohammed Topkapi's Twenty-Four Hour Tea Service" through the cracks of the bus window. Housed in an adobe mud hut with a beautiful domed roof, painted ultramarine blue and adorned in small, yellow stars, it struck her as the sort of place that someone as foreign as herself (and perhaps even the moon) might feel at home in. She dedicates this story to Ambrose.

Deborah Biancotti lives and works in Sydney, Australia. Her first published story won the Aurealis Award for Best Horror

Short Story. More recently, her work has appeared in the *Years Best Australian SF & Fantasy* and the *Australian Dark Fantasy & Horror* anthologies. She confesses, "'The Tailor of Time' came when I was post-operative, healing at home, and suddenly unable to tell night from day. It occurred to me then how hard I'd been working lately—working day to night, as the saying goes. I felt lonely, and a long way from my childhood, and so the idea of a Tailor who could stitch time together became attractive to my feverish imagination." Keep an eye out for her upcoming work with Twelfth Planet and Gilgamesh Press. Deborah can be found online at http://deborahb.livejournal.com and http://deborahbiancotti.net.

Erin Hoffman is a writer, game designer, and wandering philomath. It is her solemn duty to protect the world from the machinations of two cantankerous parrots while paying the bills as a video game consultant and freelance essayist. Her nonfiction can be found primarily at *The Escapist*, and links to her fiction can be found at philomathgames.com and on the shared weblog *Homeless Moon* (homelessmoon.com).

Erin tells us, "I'm very fascinated with the idea of taking modern trials—things we talk about now that would have been anathema or poorly understood in 'romance' eras frequently emulated by fantasy—in allegorical terms. 'Root and Vein' is about staying pliant, staying alive, after heartbreak, and how we learn from it, even when our every instinct is to shut down against pain; it's kind of an anti-happily-ever-after, being about walking away from something that hurts you. It is also a reflection of my fascination with trees as living records of their experiences—abundant summers, harsh winters—as are we all, but trees display this on their very skins."

Mike Allen writes, "As editor, I enjoy stories that experiment, that push the envelope, that dazzle with their daring, but I'm often personally frustrated when such stories end without feeling complete, without leaving any emotional crater for me to remember them by. At the same time, I find myself increasingly bored with the traditional competently-assembled Good Story Well Told. For better or for worse, I conceived of *Clockwork Phoenix* as a place where the two schools can mingle and achieve Happy Medium; where there is significance to both the tale that's told and the style of the telling.

"My previous anthology projects, *Mythic* and *Mythic 2* (Mythic Delirium Books, 2006) contained some of this same strangeness, but those projects had constrictions on subject matter that I found somewhat limiting. Despite the whimsical introduction I've written just to go about things a little differently *Clockwork Phoenix* is not meant to signify a literal clockpunk mythology, but rather a place where unexpected things juxtapose."

He is also the long-time editor of the poetry journal *Mythic Delirium* and the co-editor of *The Alchemy of Stars: Rhysling Award Winners Showcase* (SFPA, 2005). Mike is himself a three-time winner of the Rhysling Award for speculative poetry, and his newest poetry collection, *The Journey to Kailash*, has just come out in hardcover and trade paperback from Norilana Books. His website is www.descentintolight.com.

Printed in the United States
131809LV00002B/118/P